CAN YOU TRUST
YOUR BANK?

Can You Trust Your Bank?

by ROBERT HELLER
and NORRIS WILLATT

CHARLES SCRIBNER'S SONS · NEW YORK

Copyright © 1977 Robert Heller and Norris Willatt

Library of Congress Cataloging in Publication Data
Heller, Robert, 1932–
  Can you trust your bank?
  Includes index.
  1. Banks and banking. 2. Banks and banking, International. I. Willatt, Norris,
joint author. II. Title.
HG1572.H44   332.1   77–9101
ISBN 0–684–15176–6

ACKNOWLEDGMENTS

    Neither the title of this book nor the views expressed in its pages are intended to
reflect in any way on the bankers of our own acquaintance—gentlemen whom we would
trust with our last penny, cent, centime, or whatever. Our book is about the system: or
rather about the system at a particularly unattractive stage in its history. We are both
grateful to all those who have helped us to understand and document that history. Among
others who have been of great help, we would like especially to thank Tom Lester, for
reading the proofs, and Felicity Krish, for her exemplary assistance in preparing the
manuscript.

ROBERT HELLER

    In addition to echoing Bob's words, I would like to express my own special apprecia-
tion to Bob Bleiberg, editor of *Barron's* magazine, and my own old colleagues there
(among whom I would especially mention Armon Glenn) for the use of a desk and
practical help in research; the staff of the Long Beach, California, public library for their
unfailing courtesy in helping me locate references; and my cousin, Alys Barrett, whose
generous hospitality over a long period to my wife, Marjorie, and myself helped create
an atmosphere highly conducive to drafting the American chapters of our book.

NORRIS WILLATT

CONTENTS

PROLOGUE

1. The Greatest Crash

WALTER J. DRESSLER, of 1453 Elm Street, Plainsville, Long Island, was an assiduous reader of newspapers. He read them folding the pages longitudinally, and he missed nothing. Thus one ordinary morning, he noticed (and was one of the very few people on Long Island, or even in the entire United States, to notice) that a German private bank, whose name he had never heard before, had been forced to close because of foreign exchange losses. The losses were stupendous in size; but since the bank meant nothing to Mr. Dressler, he went on comfortably reading his paper until it was time to leave for work in a nearby aircraft plant.

The bankers of America, including those who ran the bank where Dressler kept his savings and his current account, had received the news many hours earlier. All of them had reacted with concern, some with unusual ferocity. The collapse of the bank had left several American banks, and many more European ones, stranded with uncompleted foreign exchange deals. They now stood to lose hundreds of millions, unless the same German banking authorities that had closed the bank's doors would now allow the uncompleted deals to go through. Burning up the telephone wires between New York, San Francisco, Los Angeles, and Chicago on one side of the Atlantic, and Frankfurt and Düsseldorf on the other, the bankers were not a bit reassured to learn that bungling by the official Bundesbank had been central to the collapse.

By the time Walter J. Dressler next picked up *The New York Times,* the story had reached the front page—but still without arousing Mr. Dressler's interest. Europe was rife with rumors about one of Britain's Big Four banks, about one of the large provincial banks in Germany itself, and banks on both sides of the Atlantic controlled by the same Italian financier. All were supposed to be heavily involved in huge foreign exchange losses, either linked with the collapsed private German bank or else all the other banks' own work. Denials by the authorities carried the usual almost complete conviction; but before the ru-

mors had time to die down, a Swiss bank crashed, and its fall generated the first burst of panic.

Its title sounded unfortunately close to that of one of Switzerland's Big Three banks. Actually, the offending outfit was the Swiss subsidiary of a large California institution. But in an atmosphere thick with rumor and counter-rumor, the coincidence of the names was enough to precipitate some unusually heavy withdrawals from the Big Three bank. Its directors put out a statement, with the full backing of the Swiss authorities. The bank had no connection, said the statement, with the crash victim: it was true, however, that the giant bank had sustained substantial losses in foreign exchange dealings on behalf of a private client; the amount, some $40 million, could, of course, be readily absorbed.

Far from reassuring the financial world, the statement caused a furor. How many other large banks were nursing big losses in secret? The immediate pressure was felt on secondary banks everywhere, especially in Switzerland. The Italian financier's bank was the first to fall. Nervousness turned into fear when the news leaked out that the authorities in both Italy and Switzerland had seized documents and sealed doors, that the tycoon himself had skipped off to the United States, and that the foreign exchange losses were only the beginning of a tangled tale of banking vice and avarice run wild.

The Italian's bank in the United States was the one where Walter J. Dressler banked. It should have been closed at once by the Federal Reserve Board, especially since, as it later transpired, the authorities had received (and largely ignored) adverse reports on the conduct (or misconduct) of the bank for several years past. Like the German and Swiss authorities earlier in the crisis, the Americans showed a fatal insensitivity. At a hastily convened meeting in Washington, they cobbled together a club of big banks; the latter agreed to join the regulatory authorities in shoring up the tottering edifice—which, the statement to the press declared, was solvent.

This time Walter J. Dressler caught the news on his transistor radio at the plant. He had meant to withdraw all his money; now, he thought, it was safe to wait. Other depositors didn't share Dressler's faith. A mild run on the bank developed. That in itself could have been contained. But the chief operating officer installed by the bankers' club produced a new, sickening flash report on its condition, which made closure inevitable. A high proportion of the bank's loans, the officer discovered, were not merely of high risk but had already gone bad. They couldn't be collected, and any further millions poured out by the club would merely go into a bottomless pit.

The closure was a tremendous shock—not least to Walter J. Dressler, who had $31,000 at stake, a great deal of money to him. The authorities promised that ordinary depositors would get their money,

which reassured Dressler more than it comforted officials in the Federal Reserve and the Federal Deposit Insurance Corporation. They had begun to fear that other large banks would need similar assistance. Many of these were stuck with debts owed by the collapsed bank; others were still nursing foreign exchange losses through the German crash, and a hasty check revealed that in many cases the exposure to high-risk debt—in loans to shaky property investment funds, to deficit-ridden countries in Latin America and Africa, to weak-kneed corporations and wobbling municipalities—accounted for a terrifyingly large proportion of loan portfolios.

The authorities again kept their anxieties to themselves. But the number of banks on the "problem list" maintained in Washington had swollen as a result of the checks—and the story broke in the *Washington Post*. This time the denials inevitably rang less true (apart from anything else, they were downright lies). In any event, they were overtaken by savage events on both sides of the Atlantic. The banking troubles had caused an inevitable contraction of credit as the banks tried to adopt conservative positions, and as frightened depositors took their money away, especially from lesser banks, which in London in particular had attracted massive deposits from industrial corporations. As credit tightened, so interest rates began to soar.

Overborrowed corporations (of which at that time there were all too many) suddenly found themselves paying gigantic interest costs. Many were forced to borrow to pay the interest—the classic route to perdition. The property companies were the first to crack. Their only hope was to sell the completed and uncompleted buildings on which they had borrowed; but the property market, already weakened by the atmosphere of financial distress, broke completely under the threat of forced sales. Suddenly the market disappeared, and with it went the collateral for the bulk of the banks' secured lending.

Most of the remaining collateral was in the form of stocks and shares, and here the drying up of credit and soaring of interest rates had wreaked even worse havoc. The sickening realization dawned on bankers, regulators, and politicians right across the West that the banks had no hope of realizing the security on which they had lent. They now depended entirely on two hopes: first, that their borrowers would stay or be kept solvent, so that it would not be necessary to call in the loans; and second, that the depositors would keep their money in the banks.

The first prop was the first to give. In Britain, a number of property companies, smaller banks that had specialized in property loans, one merchant bank, and a major multi-national company went to the wall. The Bank of England organized hasty rescue operations in all cases, but in so doing dangerously stretched the safety margin of the banking system as a whole. The system was now in no condition to withstand the next shock from the United States when, in rapid succession, a major defense contractor, a giant store chain, a transportation company, and New York City announced that they could not pay their debts.

Originally the major American banks, with enormous amounts owed by the four delinquents, had hoped to go on carrying the burden. But it became painfully clear that all four had again become bottomless pits; and that the banks, with panic withdrawals and loan defaults mounting all the time, had enough trouble on their hands at home. Like New York City and the other giant defaulters, the banks looked to the White House for salvation. But the president, who had taken over in mid-term, was woefully inexperienced and unable to resist the advice of conservatives who urged him not to heed the voices of panic.

It was easier to do nothing, in any case, because neither the president nor his advisers had any definite idea of what to do—or where to do it. By now the economic crisis had begun to subdivide, and each element was as desperately worrying as the others. The wave of bankruptcies, led by the four giant collapses, had produced a sharp rise in unemployment, to which the credit shortage and high interest rates added powerfully. Even the majority of citizens who did not hide their savings under the mattress in fear now began to draw heavily on bank balances, simply to cushion the impact of sharply reduced earnings and to buy goods.

The panic buying affected everything from gold bars to canned goods. The price of gold doubled in a flash, until it was standing at four times the official level. The rush to the stores to stock up with supplies soon exhausted the shelves when manufacturers, unable to obtain new credit and under heavy pressure from their banks to cut down their borrowings, could not finance the necessary production. The more terror-stricken citizens began to stock remote country lairs with rifles, ammunition, gold coins, and cans of food, so that they at least could survive the holocaust.

The effect of the bankruptcies started to snowball. Out on Long Island, Walter J. Dressler's employer, which had large subcontracts from the crashed defense contractor, started massive layoffs. Walter was among the first to go. His situation was pitiful—a proud man, who had saved all his life, he was unable to find work, forced to live off his unemployment pay, and unable to get hold of his savings. The authorities had hoped to protect the depositors by merging the collapsed bank with a bigger institution; but the latter, too, was now high on the problem list, and nothing else had been worked out. Only a loan from a brother in New Jersey, a car dealer whose bank still had its doors open, saved the Dresslers from an even more critical situation.

The mounting distress in America was repeated and reflected in

Europe. In every country, savings were decimated, unemployment soared, major and minor firms went out of business. In Britain one firm of accountants alone, acting as receivers in bankruptcy, found itself the largest property owner in Europe, possibly the world. The most embarrassing contretemps was provided by the Bank of England. It carried a heavy burden of guilt for deliberately creating the mushroom growth of the secondary banks in the first place. Casting around for a solution as these smaller banks folded on all sides, the Bank demonstrated its lack of comprehension by choosing the largest of the secondary empires for the task. Very shortly, the elected bank collapsed too, revealing a mess hardly cleaner than the condition of the banks it was supposed to save.

The British government was in no position to upbraid the Bank, because one of the Crown's own institutions, charged with looking after the funds of overseas countries, had poured money into investments so unwise that only an unprecedented subvention of tax money saved the day. Throughout the West, government deficits were being swollen by the demands of collapsed or collapsing banks and other companies. The outpouring of public money had so far preserved the money of most small depositors; but large depositors, mainly corporations, were now suffering severely from the drain of funds as their accounts were frozen or written off.

In this situation, the last thing that the authorities in any country wanted was a scandal. But the investigations of bank failures were now uncovering almost daily evidence of fraud and misconduct on a global scale. A California bank had been used by its controlling genius to finance his own business activities, with no regard whatsoever for depositors' interests, and altogether too much regard for the millions he could siphon off into his own pocket. A major investment group collapsed, and in the wake of its collapse the investigators discovered that its funds had been spirited away through the medium of convenient banks, while the perpetrator had escaped to a cozy exile.

In Europe, a Swiss bank crashed with heavy losses—its Italian owner was found to have diverted millions from the bank through an account opened in the name of a horse. Another Swiss bank, this time owned by an Israeli, had been used to channel funds from an Israeli corporation through Liechtenstein to a suspicious Italian investment. This bank was owned in part by one of the German state banks; its subsequent crisis brought down the state government, and that fall cracked the ruling coalition in Bonn. With the federal government in political crisis, no firm action could be taken to stem the financial panic which had gripped Germany in the wake of the state bank's mess. Memories of the Weimar inflation and the Great Depression were still too strong for Germans to bear money shocks. Before a frightened

Bundesbank closed them down, Germany's banks had suffered a debilitating drain of currency.

Major banks outside Germany had been striving, aided by the national authorities, to limit the amounts of the writeoffs in their balance sheets. A true reflection of their losses would have forced many banks into massive curtailment of loans. Unemployment was already so high, especially in the United States and Germany, that the politicians and the central bankers were terrified of any further contraction. But the total German bank closure made the situation impossible. The large American, French, and British banks were heavily involved in many consortia and other combined operations with the Germans, and a hasty study of the condition of these joint ventures showed that many of them were hopelessly insolvent.

With a stand-in president in Washington, no government in either Bonn or Rome, and new administrations fighting desperately to regain control over events in London and Paris, there was now no hope of the leadership which alone could save the free world banking system from complete collapse. An emergency meeting of the International Monetary Fund—long shorn of its powers and neutered by the unilateral actions of the United States—was hastily convened, to no avail. The currency markets had been in total turmoil for months, so much so that ordinary commercial transactions had become impossible to finance. Now the markets were closed; so were the banks; so were the devastated stock exchanges.

On Wall Street, the first apple-sellers had appeared. In Italy and France, the Communist parties were moving rapidly toward power. With West Germany paralyzed, there were ominous troop movements along the Eastern frontier. In Britain, the trade unions had called a national strike against the retrenchment policies announced by a Labour government. In the United States, black violence had begun to erupt on the streets. The end of capitalism, long trumpeted by its enemies, had at last arrived, engineered by the incompetence of its friends. On Long Island, Walter J. Dressler—jobless, penniless, and hopeless—shot himself with his Saturday night special.

All the events described above either did happen or could very easily have happened as the result of the cumulative crisis that struck the financial world in the seventies. This book is about the banks, not because the bankers were the only or even the chief villains of the piece, but because it is through the bank down the street that the ordinary citizen makes his contact with the secret money government. On the whole, the banks were not corrupt. Just as bad loans were a tiny fraction of the portfolios of most banks, so bad behavior was in a small minority. But betrayal of the image of banks—and the image in the last resort is what the customer buys— was far more general; it was almost, as the above scenario depicts, generally fatal.

Mr. Dressler's story is entirely fictitious. It is vital for the future of the West that it should remain so.

2. Can You?

BANKS are supposed above all other virtues to be trustworthy—a notion which bankers have sought to foster since the first American promoter hung up his shingle with a title like the First National Security Fidelity Bank and Trust Company. The currency of these grandiose names has not been debased with time and repetition, and even those banks with uncommunicative European proper names would subscribe to the same sentiments. They lead, they embody the national ethos, they are secure, they are faithful, they can be trusted; they are, above all and all in all, banks.

For the most part, in most circumstances, the postures have reflected genuine virtues, the image has rung true. People all over the world have been able to entrust their savings to banks with no fear for the money's safety. They have been able to withdraw as much as they want, whenever they please. Their money, if left in an interest-bearing account, has earned a yield which, while never generous, is at least secure. The foundation of the modern economy is the banking system; and the cornerstone of any bank is its security—even banks which get robbed (a more and more frequent mishap) are covered by insurance.

These giant moneyboxes create wealth as well as store it. Without their lending to individuals, businessmen, and public authorities (especially the government itself), economic society would creak and groan to a halt. The banks can circulate the money that their depositors provide, because at any given time withdrawals will only account for a given (and small) proportion of total deposits; thus a bank can safely lend and so create more deposits. The banker knows, too, that old loans will be paid off as new ones are made, and this revolving door also guarantees security. Only if too many depositors suddenly demanded the withdrawal of all their funds at one and the same time—the dreaded run on the bank—or too many borrowers defaulted at once would that security be broken down.

Nor, in the ordinary way, can a bank fail to make money itself. It charges customers substantially more for loans than it pays out to depositors; this is none too difficult to do with demand deposits, which earn no interest at all. The difference, less the bank's expenses, is the legitimate profit which has traditionally made banks safe, reliable, but never speedy vehicles for investment. Their bonds and shares have found a home in the more conservative portfolios, whose owners are content with steady rather than spectacular growth. The growth, like the profits, is guaranteed; so long as the economy grows, so does the supply of money, and every increase in the money supply means a rise in the turnover and profits of the banks, be they ever so unadventurous and conservatively managed.

The falls from grace, with or without fraud, have usually been so exceptional as to be sensational in modern times. But the times can get out of joint; the smooth, perpetual cycle of taking in and giving out money stammers and stutters, the facade of unwavering reliability cracks. During the Great Depression of the thirties, the failure of the Creditanstalt Bank of Vienna knocked over one domino after another, as its creditor banks in other countries collapsed. Disaster and panic on a worldwide scale spread as depositors, borrowers, creditors, shareholders—anybody having business of any kind with banks—tried to protect themselves, and in so doing inflicted even greater self-injury. The bank failures undermined business and helped to throw the millions of the masses out of work.

The domino failure of first one and then many banks was the symptom, not the cause, of the world's economic malaise. But banks and bankers became prime targets for the wrath of a disillusioned society. It took the banks a whole generation of prudence, painstaking image-building, and operation under new and more relevant laws to restore the pristine confidence. The laws sought, among other crucial safeguards, to limit the use of bank credit for greedy, unrestrained speculation. Foolish lending had financed the desire for more than the borrowers could afford: when elevator operators and shoeshine boys borrowed to buy stocks on margin in a wild Wall Street, sober citizens could not sleep secure in their beds, nor could their money rest secure in the banks. The specific mania of the thirties would never recur. But there was always the risk of another pathological illness if society and its lenders forgot the lessons of what had gone before.

The risk proved too great. At the end of the sixties, and into the early seventies, another trauma began to run its devastating course. The sensational series of bank failures and near-failures of the early seventies, accompanied in many cases by shocking scandals, once more severely shook public confidence; not fatally, as things turned out, nor as badly as confidence should have been shaken—whether because people had grown more trusting, or had merely come to lower their expectations of the banks over the distance of a generation.

This book documents the strange and stricken interlude of the early seventies, their similarities to the early thirties. It explains what went wrong with banking this second time around, and why; it identifies the malign influences at work, and investigates how they were able to proliferate for so long without check. In particular, it describes the often crucial role in creating chaos of greedy individuals who exploited the borrowing and lending of money for their own exclusive gain.

Some scrupulous and orthodox banks helped the crisis along by throwing away their normal discretion and balance: more and more unwise loans to unqualified clients; an increasingly hectic chase after deposits from any source, however transitory and unreliable; overexpansion, even of sound loans, beyond the healthy limits of reserves and assets. Even long-established, highly regarded banking establishments succumbed to the fevers of bad banking practice.

In the mood of the sixties, the steady growth of the past ceased to appeal. The new breed of bankers sought to maximize their revenues and profits, to boost their share prices, to enhance their prestige. In the process, the banks came to resemble their worst customers, such as the conglomerates which manufactured evanescent profits by mergers, debatable accounting, and sometimes downright deceit. The atmosphere of go-go mutual funds which whizzed up like rockets, and then fizzled out, leaving only the spent stick to fall to earth, and of real estate investment trusts which lured modest investors with the bait of owning a segment of a skyscraper that then (metaphorically) collapsed into dust, seemed to infect all bank dealings. Governments, provinces, municipalities, whose citizens systematically lived beyond their means and accumulated pyramids of debt, became solicited customers. Bankers competed, too, to lend to stretched Third World governments whose absolute rulers spent much of their borrowed kings' ransoms on armaments, and wasted much else in corruption, while their illiterate populations continued to starve.

The banks which participated in these and other excesses included the biggest in the world. The giants did not go bankrupt in the wake of their more profligate clients; they were saved not by their own caution or acumen, however, but by the sometimes desperate action of the government authorities. Yet the crews which manned the financial lifeboats can claim little enough credit. They had, by negligence and undue delay, allowed the banks to founder. Often the degree of risk which banks were taking was not realized until the damage was finally and irrevocably done. The authorities responsible for supervising and examining the banks, the officials who were supposed to spend every working day ensuring that banks lived up to the fidelity, security, and trustworthiness in their fine-sounding titles, fell down on their own jobs. Worse, some supervisors had actually connived in and covered up crimes against the people's savings and financial safety.

In the United States—the dominant land in world banking—the regulatory agencies, such as the comptroller of the currency and the Federal Reserve Board, conducted housecleanings while themselves under investigation by the supreme housekeeper of the U.S. Congress, the General Accounting Office, to check if they had in fact exercised adequate supervision over banking institutions. As it was, the forty-year-old New Deal came to the rescue of the 1970s. The Federal Reserve Board and the Federal Deposit Insurance Corporation (FDIC), a government agency set up in the light of the thirties disaster to guarantee bank deposits up to a certain maximum, played crucial roles. But the ghost of Franklin Delano Roosevelt could not help the creditors and shareholders of several banks, who lost all or much of their money in those supposedly soundest of all investments.

The shame for banks and bankers can be measured by the cost to those that remained live and whole of rehabilitating their ailing brethren, or quietly interring those who were beyond cure. In Britain, the central bank and the major clearing banks had to cough up some £2 billion to prevent the crash of the so-called secondary banks from bringing down the primary ones—and the whole British economy. In the United States, the Federal Reserve Board had to throw some $1.7 billion into the breach to avoid a national panic in the case of just one bank —the Franklin National Bank, which was known to be on the verge of failure. The bankruptcy of the Penn Central, the procession of real estate investment trusts to the wall en masse, New York City's trembling on the brink of bankruptcy—in all these cases, with huge sums owing to the banks, it took the solemn pledge of the Fed that, in the final analysis, it would pour money into the banking system to support the structure, to prevent cumulative disaster.

In countries like West Germany and Italy, the story was the same: the governments had to mobilize the aid of the leading banks to stop up gaping holes in their banking systems. The guarantee that the state itself will be the backer of last resort in any banking crisis, if necessary, is the last ditch of defense. Fortunately, the defenses held. Governments had to become involved because the financial and economic stability of the country (not to mention their own prestige and survival) was menaced. Nor could a runaway banking crisis have been contained within national boundaries. It was this threat, not the rise in unemployment and inflation, which posed the real crisis of capitalism and the greatest menace to the ordinary people who have most to lose if a bank fails and a banking system crumbles.

Bankers as a community had failed to adjust to—sometimes even to recognize—the changes in the world around them, which had often created totally new sets of dangerous circumstances. The changes outran the limits of their own business experience and competence, but had a decisive impact upon their operations: for example, rampant worldwide inflation, floating currencies, the rise of a giant market in dollars in Europe beyond the control of the U.S. authorities. In a newly hostile environment, banks abandoned the old wisdom of their trade. The history of world banking in the early seventies is of bankers trapped by themselves into forgetting that the fundamental commodity in which they deal is not money but confidence; and loss of confidence, unlike loss of money, cannot be dealt with simply by a writeoff in the balance sheet. This is the story of how the banks came too near to writing off postwar Western prosperity.

PART I

THE U.S. EXTRAVAGANZA

3. The American Aberration

EVEN an American citizen numbed by the trauma of the Vietnam War, and jaded by the sensations of the Watergate scandal, must have jerked to sharp attention when in the closing days of 1974 the comptroller of the currency reported that he was keeping 150 of the nation's banking institutions under "close scrutiny." The comptroller heads a branch of the U.S. Treasury Department which is responsible for supervising and examining the aforesaid banks. Since no names were named, his report set off an alarmed guessing game, as those citizens who heard the evil word speculated whether the suspects included the bank whose friendly neighborhood branch was supposed to be looking after their savings.

True, having administered the shock treatment, the regulators sought to reassure the afflicted. Justin Watson, first deputy comptroller, declared: "We put banks on the warning list when they get the sniffles, and we think they are getting a cold, and we keep them on that list until they have been released from the hospital." And Dr. Arthur Burns, the powerful chairman of the Federal Reserve Board, which also has supervisory responsibility for many of the nation's banks, affirmed authoritatively: "Only a very small number of banks can be described as being in trouble."

That calmed the situation down—until the next time, which came soon enough. A little over a year later, at the beginning of 1976, the banks again were collectively in the headlines when the two most prestigious (and probing) newspapers in the United States broke stories insinuating that the American banking business was beset with problems, including troubles at the very top—Citibank and Chase Manhattan, second and third, respectively, in the country, and the biggest pair in the East bar none.

The New York Times referred to thirty banks which, according to the Federal Reserve, had been having problems during the preceding year; among them were a dozen out of the fifty biggest bank holding companies. The small consolation was that none of this dirty dozen was

17

included among the eleven banks said to be plagued with "most serious problems." That list nevertheless took in such well-known names as Marine Midland Bank, of Buffalo; Union Bancorp, of Los Angeles; North Carolina National Bank, of Charlotte, North Carolina; and First Wisconsin National Bank of Milwaukee.

To a depositor, it's no great joy to learn that your bank has "less serious problems"—and among this group were numbered (still according to the *Times*), Security Pacific National Bank, of Los Angeles; Bank of California and Wells Fargo Bank, both of San Francisco; Republic National Bank of Dallas; Citizens and Southern National Bank, of Atlanta; First National Bank of Boston; and the giant Chase, which was also given star billing, no doubt much to its distaste, by the *Washington Post*.

According to the *Post*'s more sensational inside information, both Chase Manhattan and Citibank had appeared, at any rate for a time, on a super-secret list tagged with the incongruous code name of "Victor" and compiled by the comptroller of the currency's office. This hush-hush listing followed examinations which uncovered evidence, in the case of both great banks, of inadequate capital structure, together with an increase in assets of dubious value since the previous examination.

Neither of the Big Two was described as being in danger of financial collapse. On the contrary, the government agency had described Citibank's prospects as "excellent, barring a worldwide catastrophe," and those of Chase Manhattan as "fair." The latter's inferior rating was merited, it was alleged, by "poor" management, shown by its possession of insufficient staff and inexperienced personnel in vital positions; its poor internal controls and audit procedures; and a "large volume of clerical errors" in certain accounts.

The main problem at both banks was no super-secret in banking: the high ratio of "classified" assets. That means, in plain language, bum loans—loans on which a loss has already been suffered, or where there is a real risk of this happening. A bank examiner's memo written at the time of the 1974 probe identified $109 million of the Chase Manhattan's outstanding loans as showing a loss; $345 million whose recovery was doubtful; $1,600 million as substandard; and some $2,000 million as deserving "special mention," which meant they required particular vigilance. The controlling agency confirmed the *Post* story, in substance, while playing down its significance.

There was thus no denying that both banks had problems; but what got them listed as "problems" was the ratio of their classified assets to gross capital funds, including stockholders' equity and loan loss reserves. This exceeded the currency comptroller's rule-of-thumb safety ceiling of 80 percent. Chase Manhattan's vital statistic was said to be 97 percent, and Citibank's 114 percent. This kind of figure puts a bank in the category of "approaching insolvency" and implies the need for "drastic action, such as changes in control, ownership or management" —none of which, of course, was about to happen at either of these Establishment banks.

Even in the face of such compromising testimony from his own agency, Currency Comptroller James Smith assured the press that both Citibank and Chase were "strong, well-managed banks"; if that was strong and good management, heaven help any bank which is weak and ill-run—a point taken up with great rapidity by a Democratic Congress, which promptly used this stick to wallop the Republican opposition in a presidential election year. The politicos set going no fewer than three probes of the banking business. The agencies (also no fewer than three) responsible for supervising the banks had to testify under oath about the conditions at the institutions under scrutiny and elsewhere—and a sorry figure they proceeded to cut.

The superfluous existence of three distinct agencies results from the special structure of banking in the United States. The nation rejoices in the possession of 14,500 or so banks, with aggregate assets of close to $1,000,000 million. About 4,700 of the blessed have received their charters from the federal government, and so are known as "national" banks (ye shall know them by the fact that the word appears in their titles); the rest have been chartered by the various states. Fewer than half of the 14,500 (5,800, to be precise) belong to the Federal Reserve System, which lays upon them certain obligations, such as the maintenance of minimum reserves; and also confers certain advantages, such as the insurance of deposits (up to $40,000 per individual account in 1977) by the Federal Deposit Insurance Corporation, another federal agency. The same insurance also extends to nonmember banks.

The 4,700 nationally chartered banks are supervised and examined by the comptroller of the currency. The Federal Reserve Board does likewise for over 1,000 state-chartered banks which have elected to join the Federal Reserve System. The Federal Deposit Insurance Corporation is responsible for all the rest. It is scarcely a tidy system; but the constant attempts to change it are invariably opposed by the powerful banking lobby.

The appearance of high officials of this regulatory trio to testify before the congressional committees in Washington touched off an appalling numbers game—as when Currency Comptroller Smith took the stand. (In June 1976, Smith submitted his resignation to President Ford for "personal reasons"—he was considered to have bowed to mounting criticism of his permissive approach to bank regulation.) To Congress, Smith announced that his agency had twenty-eight nationally chartered banks on its "problem" list, of which seven were in "critical" shape (that is, in immediate danger of insolvency), and another twenty-one were "serious" (showing problems which could ultimately lead to a crisis). However, they were mostly smaller institutions; their combined assets amounted to only (some "only"!) $11,500 million, and their deposits to an apparently mere $7,600 million.

The Federal Reserve, not to be outdone, told a tale of sixty-five banks which were under "special surveillance," not far short of twice as many as a year earlier; of these, sixty-three were bank holding companies. The chief bank regulator at the Fed, Brenton Leavitt, also made the significant boast that if his agency had not stepped in with "go slow" warnings to the banking industry on its credit and loan policies from 1973 onward, the situation would have been far worse.

As for the Federal Deposit Insurance Corporation, it testified to keeping its eagle eye on some 350 banks, of which about half had serious problems. The FDIC divided these "culprits" into three groups, according to the degree of anxiety they aroused in its bosom. About twenty had "advanced" problems requiring immediate intervention; the second group might eventually need help; while the third was less vulnerable, though the banks concerned still required close supervision.

The publication of these three sets of figures, though they applied to only a relatively small minority of the country's banks, could not help but be scarifying news. Bankers no doubt felt justified in protesting that the situation had been greatly exaggerated; the regulatory agencies no doubt were right in stressing that a sick bank did not necessarily imply a dead bank; the officials no doubt justly argued that the identification of problems was an essential first step in the direction of solving them. All the same, the facts demonstrated that in the mid-seventies, the whole U.S. banking business went through its worst trauma since the Depression years of the thirties. That last time, everything fell apart. Failed banks fell like autumn leaves; President Franklin D. Roosevelt had to proclaim the famous Bank Holiday, to give everybody a respite in which to pick up the pieces; then those pieces proved all too meager for a whole generation of depositors and shareholders. That much the seventies were spared; but by how narrow a margin?

The mood of the preceding sixties in the United States was in many respects strikingly similar to that of the late twenties, especially in its general euphoria, from which supposedly staid bankers were not at all immune. The myopic preoccupation with growth for its own sake, and the naïve conviction that this was self-perpetuating, were common to bankers and their greedier clients, only to be punctured by the busting of the boom. That the early seventies did not become a rerun of the early thirties owed much to the lessons learned from that earlier experience, and subsequently applied—for instance, the creation of the FDIC to insure deposits.

In addition, the banking system itself could be mobilized, though sometimes with difficulty, to aid the weaker brethren; where that rallying round was not enough, or not forthcoming, the regulatory agencies (for which read the government) could provide often massive aid. Luck played a part, too. The public, on whose deposits the banks ultimately depend, seemed to have grown more sophisticated, or lulled into a false sense of security; or, maybe, more philosophical in the face of adversity. At any rate, the depositors kept their nerve, which was the saving grace for some understandably nervy bankers. At the end of a long and bruising ordeal, the latter emerged severely mauled and somewhat chastened.

Dr. Arthur Burns, worried lest the public be alarmed into less dependability, warned that the "harsh language" of bank examiners' reports was not intended for the ears of the public; better to be fooled and ignorant, in other words, than informed and alarmed. He added the caution that "when you cast doubt on the solvency of individual banks you take grave risks with the welfare of the banks and their communities and with a large part of the financial system." Yet clearly his and other regulatory agencies were partly to blame for the extent to which U.S. banks as a group had overextended themselves, courting risks that were in all cases undesirable and in many cases totally unnecessary.

You didn't have to be privy to bank examiners' reports to have real cause for concern. The bald, regular, official Federal Reserve statistics told a sorry story. Between 1966 and 1974, the typical bank's ratio of equity capital and reserves to loans had fallen from over 7 percent to around 4.85 percent; the ratio of loans to deposits had advanced from 65 to 75 percent; and the percentage of long-term assets covered by short-term borrowing had been unforgivably allowed to zoom from 2 percent to over 13 percent. A *Business Week* survey claimed that some banks had a menacing 20–30 percent of their assets covered by short-term funding.

How had so much gone so wrong? The short answer is that the wheel, as it usually does, had turned full circle. After a lengthy era of banking restrained by the sobering influence of memories of the thirties, the earlier euphoria had insidiously returned, as a new younger generation moved into the upper echelons of bank management. Their enthusiasm had been further encouraged by the boom of the sixties, during which, under the impetus of an overgenerously expanding money supply, the banks' own business had mushroomed.

Bankers, too, are children of their time. The pressure to expand came initially from the economy; the lust for expansion was self-generated. They began to embrace growth as a philosophy, along with everybody else. In part, but only in part, this move was defensive. In an era of conglomerate synergy and go-go mutual funds, something as sober and stolid as an orthodox bank would tend to be overlooked as an investment vehicle. Bankers retaliated: they shopped on Madison Avenue and anywhere else where they could buy, or borrow, techniques that would attract attention to their performance and ideally enhance it.

Performance became a captivating end in itself; and earnings per share were the criterion of performance. To boost the magic figures loans were often granted, and even solicited, which in more normal times would have been rejected with contumely as too risky. Some banks, including First National in the fine old conservative city of Boston, even devised elaborate management incentive schemes based on improvements in year-to-year results, and on their comparison with the performance of rival banks—or, in many cases, bank holding companies. For the banks themselves had become conglomerates. The 1970 revision of the Bank Holding Company Act of 1956 was designed to compensate for the invasion of traditional commercial banking territory by pension funds, insurance and finance companies. But the revision opened a Pandora's box of commercial nonsenses. Holding companies with only one banking subsidiary were allowed to diversify into fields like mortgage banking and servicing, the personal loan business, factoring, real estate, computer leasing, the operation of data-processing centers, even the running of armored car services.

The changes overnight released banks from a straitjacket—not just that of being confined to a single state, or region of a state, but that of being forced to concentrate on banking. It had an electrifying impact. All the major banks, followed by many others less large, restructured themselves into holding companies. The bank became only one of a number of subsidiaries, although (a fact which should have exposed the basic nonsense) far and away the most important source of revenues and profits.

By the end of 1975 a zero total had mushroomed to some 1,700 such holding operations. The nonbanking subsidiaries aggregated some $567 million in capital, not including the $4,000 million pumped in by their parent concerns. The ten largest bank holding companies had combined assets of over $10,000 million. But while this diversification seemed irresistibly appealing as a means of boosting revenues and profits, there were corresponding dangers. The new activities were ones where conventional bankers lacked experience and expertise; where the traditional banking virtues of prudence and restraint could even be a handicap; and which involved higher than average banking risks.

The egregious emphasis on growth, and the slaphappy risk-taking it inspired, brought no retribution so long as the economy continued to boom. But when world and national recession set in, the chickens (and the turkeys) came home to roost. The loans that had once seemed so dynamic were now, for one reason or another, revealed as grossly inept when the debtors had difficulty in repaying, or couldn't repay at all. The backlash of recessionary blows suffered by the corporate customers was one inevitable factor. Big name companies with exceptional problems were major headaches, such as Lockheed Aircraft, Pan American, W. T. Grant, and Britain's Burmah Oil, which had borrowed heavily in the U.S. market.

The whole banking business was shaken by the collapse of the real estate trusts, to which it had made massive commitments. At the peak, the total of these bank loans was some $11,000 million, of which nearly one-half had been blithely handed over by the country's leading money center banks. They and the other culprits were forced to make large-scale writedowns of assets to reflect loan losses, and to set aside equally large reserves to cover other such possible losses in the future.

Another problem area for a banking business which surely had enough unpalatable dishes on its plate was the utility industry. As power consumption leveled off following the 1973–74 energy crisis, and regulatory authorities failed to grant rate increases, the utilities began to run short of financial power. In the spring of 1974, the greatest electric utility in the country, Consolidated Edison of New York, passed its dividend and thus touched off a flight of investors. Utility share prices plummeted so low that it became next to impossible to market new equity.

By early 1975, the Federal Power Commission, too, had a nasty little list of twenty utility companies which were in danger of bankruptcy. Most of the strain was taken by the banks and other institutions which accounted for about 55 percent of the industry's total capitalization. In the early seventies, Chase Manhattan was the leading creditor of forty-two utilities; Morgan Guaranty of forty-one; and Manufacturers Hanover of thirty-one.

Nemesis, not content with the utilities and the real estate mess, also visited the major American cities which had been living beyond their budgets—Boston, Philadelphia, Cleveland, and, above all, New York. And it caught up with the banks which held city obligations on a vast scale. The six largest New York banks had in their portfolios an aggregate $1,700 million in city debt; these obligations, in some cases, represented a precariously large proportion of the total loans of the other 100 or so banks with New York City paper on their books.

Nor was that all. By the mid-seventies, the foreign loans that had been lavishly extended by U.S. banks—both to industrialized countries, such as Italy, which were teetering on the verge of bankruptcy, and to developing countries, whose ability to meet their commitments was highly questionable—looked like another massive millstone round the banking neck. At the end of 1975, developing countries as a group owed commercial banks the world over a total of some $250,000 million, of which almost $100,000 million was the debatable property of banks in the United States and their branches abroad.

The managing director of the world's nearest thing to an international central bank, the International Monetary Fund, Johannes Witteveen, felt obliged to criticize the big banks for lending so generously to developing lands. In its 1975 annual report, the conservative central bank of West Germany, the Bundesbank, used even stronger language, accusing the banks of recklessly lending to high-risk, already heavily indebted countries. Nearer home, Paul Volcker, president of the Federal Reserve Bank of New York, stated that the Fed was tightening its surveillance of the international loans made by New York banks.

How much more could go wrong? In the face of all these adverse developments, the banks stoutly kept their upper lips stiff, insisting that their losses, however horrendous, were sustainable; that, in most cases, the dud loans represented only a comparatively small proportion of their total commitments. But their suffering could not be denied—not when the published results were so horrifying.

In the first quarter of 1976, the operating earnings of most of the biggest U.S. banks read like a falling thermometer. The freeze took in Manufacturers Hanover (down 15 percent); Chemical Bank (down 23 percent); Charter New York (down 24 percent); Bankers Trust (down 38 percent). First-quarter earnings of Chase Manhattan slumped by a grisly 57 percent.

This kind of performance—or, rather, nonperformance—had not been witnessed for a generation, during which the earnings trend had been for the most part consistently upward. The extent and damage of the aberration were self-evident. The hope was that it would prove just an aberration, a sudden nervous twitch or rush of blood to the head, after which the banking business would revert to more normal, steadier behavior. But a deviation so deep and widespread could not be written off as a mere temporary malaise. Nor could its effects be only short-term. The rending and tearing which the banks of America had undergone, mostly through their own errors, could not have escaped the eyes of an anxious public. Among people who had been encouraged and conditioned to trust their banks, the seeds of distrust had been sown.

4. A Hole in the Ground

ANDREW CARNEGIE supposedly said it—and he should have known: The only way to get rich, really rich, is to invest in real estate. Land, and the buildings erected thereon, unlike stocks and bonds, have tended over the long term to move in one direction only, up and up. Those who could just lay their hands on enough real property, and could then alternate further acquisitions with judicious selling at a profit, could not fail to make fortunes which, if somewhat less resplendent than those of Carnegie (who actually did his bit mainly in steel) or the Astors (who bought up so much of Manhattan that the Rockefellers took their leftovers), would still do nicely.

True enough, especially at the time of the wise Carnegie pronouncement. But at that time, and for several decades afterward, the revealed wisdom was of precious little use to the man in the street. Typically, he was hard-pressed to pay his rent (perhaps to one of the propertied rich), or to keep up the monthly payments on the formidable mortgage on his own modest dwelling.

But with the beginning of the sixties, a remarkable, sudden, and sensational change came over the scene. The U.S. Congress, in an effort to stimulate a sluggish real estate market, embraced a novel concept which enabled the property business to tap, not the rich alone but the savings of the small investor. The Real Estate Investment Act of 1960 made it possible for real property, instead of being marketed only in large parcels to the well-heeled, to be merchandised brick by brick, as it were, to all and sundry. In the process, a new twist was given to the ancient adage about the merit, for both the nation and its citizens, of everybody owning a piece of America.

The chosen instrument to achieve this all-American dream was the Real Estate Investment Trust, or REIT for short, an ingenious adaptation of the principle behind the mutual fund, or investment trust. The difference was that the units offered for sale were backed, not by bonds and shares of industrial corporations, but by participations in plants and office buildings, as well as other types of property asset such as apart-

25

ment houses, shopping centers, and recreational facilities.

Many were the small (and larger) investors who responded to the apparently choice opportunity, and for a while it did seem as if everybody might end up at least decently rich. But the whole edifice, it transpired, was a castle built in the air. A scant fifteen years after the first REIT began laying the foundations of the business, the whole development had ground to a standstill; and the value to investors of what had been completed was little more than that of a hole in the ground. Their fate, sad though it was, at least followed an act of free choice. But down that hole, too, went million after million belonging to the innocents: depositors in the great banks of America.

The shares of REITs to which the little people had subscribed ended up well below the surface price paid for them; many investors were completely wiped out, or in imminent danger of total loss. Already in 1974, a disaster year for the stock market as a whole, eighteen of the nineteen worst losers on the New York Stock Exchange were real estate trusts, including the five largest in the business, Chase Manhattan Mortgage and Realty (with assets at the time of around $1,000 million); Continental Mortgage Investors ($883 million); First Mortgage Investors ($670 million); Guardian Mortgage Investors ($501 million); and General American Mortgage Investors ($493 million).

At the end of 1975, the National Association of Real Estate Investment Trusts, the trade association, reported that its composite REIT share index stood at 18.01, compared with a base of 100 at the beginning of 1972, when the whole business was booming. On average, therefore, shareholders had lost over four-fifths of their investment. At that stage, only 48 out of 146 publicly traded trusts (from a total of slightly over 200) were making any money at all, and their dividends had been pared right down.

Ironically, the pitiable plight of the owners of shares got scarcely more than perfunctory mention in the plethora of inquests on the subject. Most of the abundant comment centered on the problems of the banks, the REITs' all-too-willing partners in the grand design to endow everyone with his own miniature Empire State Building.

The banks had managed to excavate for themselves a cavity of truly appalling dimensions, which was swallowing up massive loads of their earnings, and in the few worst cases, threatened to swallow up the very institutions themselves. REITs were set up to derive their assets from two principal sources—shares sold to the public, and loans raised from banks. The enormous funds so realized were employed either to purchase real property directly; or to acquire mortgages on it; or to lend to developers who would create a property asset from the ground up. Some REITs did all three.

To encourage investors to participate, the legislators extended to the real estate trusts the same kind of privileges enjoyed by investors in mutual funds. Unit holders were entitled to receive 90 percent of the profits, on which the REITs were not taxed. As for the banks (and other institutions, such as insurance companies), the new instrument opened up a whole range of lucrative opportunities. Not only were they the main source of loans, but the banks could sell their expertise in the field, in the role of advisers and managers, to the REITs.

Some of the larger banks actually sponsored their own REITs; the Chase Manhattan is an outstanding and pathetic example. At the end of 1975, in fact, there were nearly 40 such bank-sponsored trusts. But all the 200 or so leaned heavily on the institutions for financing. Thus when, in the spring of 1975, some of the biggest concerns in the business turned to the banking community for an aggregate $2,500 million in emergency aid, 41 banks rallied around the drooping flag at the Chase Manhattan Mortgage and Realty Trust; 83 at Continental Mortgage Investors; 100 at First Mortgage Investors; and so on.

The crisis to which they responded resulted from the collapse of an overvalued property market in 1974. The crash caught the REITs with obligations secured by billions of dollars in nominal worth of real property in a depressed market; some of the buildings were only half-completed, and others were still on the drawing board, which many others should never have left. By the end of 1975, at least 50 percent of all such properties were returning not one cent to the trusts which had loaned them money. This left the REITs strapped for funds with which to repay their own loans from institutions.

At that point, when their total assets amounted to some $20 billion, the creditors were being begged to renegotiate some $7–8 billion from a total of around $11 billion of debt on terms less onerous to the borrowers (and so less profitable to the lenders), just to help tide the trusts over the crisis; and about half of all the loans to REITs were paying no interest, and showed little prospect of doing so. Finally, nearly half of the total of $11 billion in REIT obligations was held by only nine large money center banks, specifically, Citibank, Chase Manhattan, Chemical Bank, First National Bank of Chicago, Bankers Trust, Continental Illinois National Bank, Bank of America, Manufacturers Hanover, and Morgan Guaranty (their individual commitments ranging from $500 million to not far short of $1 billion).

For getting landed in this almighty mess, these and other puissant banks could only blame themselves and the exuberance with which they had tossed money into the laps of the REITs. In fact, the banks had been the main architects of the boom—and a phenomenal boom it turned out to be, once the party got truly under way. The REITs were slow starters. They aroused a comparative modicum of investor interest during the first decade, between 1960 and 1970, and in 1966 their combined assets came to only $5.8 billion.

Not that investors were then a cannier breed—quite the contrary. The investment community was too busy with frenzied chasing of conglomerates and the go-go mutual funds (actually, as it turned out, investors were also chasing their own tails here) to spare time or money for property. But after the stock market collapsed at the end of the sixties, the REITs moved into the vacuum. Wall Street, ever resilient, concluded that the wrong pieces of America had been on public sale. Bits of printed paper, such as stock and bond certificates, had no intrinsic value; but bricks and mortar were tangible assets, whose purchase could always realize cash and, preferably, a profit when the investor chose to sell. The small investor, disillusioned by his recent mauling in the stock market and eager to recoup, was all too ready to go along for the new ride.

At the beginning of the seventies, the industry took off. In four short years between 1969 and 1972, more than $6 billion in REIT securities were marketed, or off-loaded. The performance of the more aggressive trusts was spectacular enough to whet any appetite; annual rates of return on equity of 20 percent, plus 100 percent capital gains, were quite standard fare at the peak of the boom. At the more vulnerable end of the business, the days of glory were brief. But certain REITs were never in deep trouble, and right down the line performed at least adequately.

These were the so-called equity and mortgage trusts. The former invested only in completed properties, and the latter in long-term mortgages of intrinsic worth. In the second category were a number of REITs sponsored by leading insurance companies, such as Connecticut General, Equitable Life, and Mutual of New York. Examples of fairly stable equity trusts included Continental Illinois Properties, Bank-America Realty Investors, General Growth Properties, and Property Capital Trust. By early 1976, according to *Barron's* magazine, some of the last-named were even reporting an improvement in their fortunes.

On the other hand, no joy or even lasting relief seemed in prospect for the "short-term" REITs, those which had foolishly concentrated on lending to builders and developers, and which in 1975 accounted for about 60 percent of all REITs. These jerry-built creations were also the trusts whose insupportable debts to the big banks caused such alarm once the boom turned into a bust. The first warning light in this respect was flashed at the end of 1973 when the Kassuba Development Corporation, one of the largest apartment developers in the country, filed for bankruptcy. A score or so REITs were left, along with their numerous back-up banks, to hold the empty Kassuba bag. (One of them, First

Mortgage Investors, the oldest "short-term" concern in the business, was out $46 million, or 8 percent of its total assets.)

Another highly publicized sensation arose at the Cabot, Cabot and Forbes Land Trust, a Boston REIT with a reputation for sound management whose conservatism was redolent in the first two names. Early in 1975, for the first time in its history, the trust was obliged to set up a reserve of some $18 million for "problem" loans, thereby sliding into red ink. Larger headlines were to follow, when the biggest REIT of them all, Chase Manhattan Mortgage and Realty, revealed the same dire necessity. Soon, such announcements became an everyday calamity.

This inevitably had ominous repercussions on the institutions upon which the REITs themselves relied for funds. The big lenders, such as Citibank, Chase Manhattan, Bankers Trust, Chemical Bank, and so on, now faced big losses. As the problems of the real estate trusts multiplied, so did the number of "problem" loans on the bank books in the country's giant money centers. Under pressure from their auditors and the regulatory agencies, the banks began to write down their once-loved property loans on a massive scale, and to build up equally massive reserves against the further disasters which plainly lurked just around the corner.

Ironically, there was no *legal* obligation to decimate the loan values. The general conviction (not yet shown to be devastatingly erroneous) was that the value of real estate could still move in only one direction—upward. Making provision for losses that could never occur seemed gratuitous, until it became painfully clear that the losses had already occurred. The bankers bowed to fact; savage writedowns were made; the protective reserves were set up; the bank profits, and so bank share prices, were clobbered. In retrospect, the banks acted strangely in waiting until their noses were rubbed into the dirt before taking defensive action. Their clients had engaged in practices that bankers would (or should) never condone for an instant in their own businesses. Why, for instance, did bank real estate analysts fail to spot the prevalence of REIT loans on certain types of property, such as condominiums in areas of the country like Florida, where overbuilding was notorious?

What about the bizarre habit of some REITs in providing some developers with not only 100 percent of the capital required for a project, but also the funds to make interest payments to the lender, right up to the day when both the principal and the entire interest fell due? The REITs were legally obliged to distribute 90 percent of their earnings; so those lending 100 percent plus in this way regularly distributed profits which they hadn't even earned. As for the developers, they didn't seek permanent financing, in the hope of getting better mortgage terms on the completed property.

Then, why was the banks' attitude toward certain REITs' lending practices so lax? For the most part, the majority of trusts started out conservatively enough, relying upon mortgage loans and conventional bank loans for their financing. But later, many turned increasingly to short-term borrowing, such as demand notes (which the banks could call at any time) and commercial paper (running for as little as a few days). This money was cheaper, but it involved a correspondingly greater risk; the brilliant REIT managers proceeded to compound that risk by committing the banker's cardinal sin, borrowing short and lending long; they lent the proceeds, in some suicidal cases, for up to two and three years.

The sin came home to the banks because the borrowings were backed by lines of bank credit. So when the REIT profits and the short-term money market alike dried up, the bank credits became not just the last line of defense but the only one. The equity market was as dead as any dodo; the REITs could not have sold additional securities when share prices were plummeting—not even a sound REIT.

When the banks came to count the cost, another oversight emerged to haunt them; they found their burden immeasurably increased by the REITs' widespread use of so-called leverage—the practice of piling up debt in relation to equity. At the end of 1973, when the boom was already beginning to look a trifle winded, a typical ratio was $2.50 of debt to every $1.00 of equity. Later, when the situation grew desperate, some REITs (the prestigious Chase Manhattan Mortgage and Realty reportedly among them) boosted the ratio as high as 7 to 1. This, too, the banks apparently condoned. Publicly, at any rate, they betrayed no signs of concern until a large slice of the REIT business was staring insolvency in the ugly face. What galvanized the banks at that stage was contemplation of the unpalatable consequences of large-scale bankruptcy—massive losses, the certain prospect of lengthy and unsavory litigation, probably irreparable damage to the image of the REITs, and so (through guilt by association) of their financial backers.

If bankruptcy were avoided, the real estate market might—nay, would—come back, and the banks would be able to recoup at least part of their investment. Meanwhile, provided the REITs could continue to operate, they were obligated to pay interest on their loans—some interest, anyhow. Alternatives to bankruptcy were strenuously pursued by desperate men: they studied taking over problem properties, granting a moratorium on interest payments, allowing the REITs to renegotiate loans on more accommodating terms. Groups of banks with claims against the same REIT even pledged themselves not to seek individual advantage, but to unite in guaranteeing a revolving credit for a fixed period, say, one year or two.

But the terrific strain involved had by early 1976, at least in some quarters, become intolerable. In March that year, Continental Mortgage Investors, the second largest REIT of all, filed for bankruptcy; some of the banks to which it owed an aggregate $500 million or so had not agreed to renew a revolving credit arrangement when it fell due. Among the named dissidents, Bank of America, Morgan Guaranty Trust, and Crocker National had combined claims amounting to around $40 million. The evidence that great banks did not recoil from pulling the plug from under the second largest force in the real estate racket represented a complete *volte-face* in policy, the possible beginning of the end for short-term trusts. Some bankers had apparently resigned themselves to inevitable bankruptcy. If so, the bitter medicine they were prescribing would taste no better in their own mouths.

At the very least, the banks were wide open to criticism of the careless way in which their managements had approached doing business in a new and untried field, where ordinary prudence called for special vigilance. But, alas, there was more to the complaints than carelessness. Many critics suspected that the bankers had fallen victims to sheer greed in circumstances which seemed designed to tempt them. Not only were REITs, in case after case, managed by representatives of the banking institutions on which they relied for loans, but the banks also acted as advisers, earning fees based on the volume of such loans (typically 1–1½ percent of asset value), which were to some extent also linked to performance as measured by profits.

Didn't that amount to an open invitation to be self-serving? Many of the stockholders in the REITs apparently thought so, and translated their suspicions into suits. The most conspicuous target was Chase Manhattan Mortgage and Realty, which in one typical action was accused of paying excessive fees to its investment adviser, the Chase Manhattan Bank. The latter reacted by reducing its charges forthwith (some bank advisers waived fees altogether for the duration of the emergency). Another stockholder suit, which specified $20 million in damages, alleged that the Chase had deliberately failed to make adequate provision for loan losses and writedowns because that would have lowered the advisory fees paid, and that the advisers had been running the REIT for their own interest and not that of the owners of its shares.

The banks' own shareholders were thus sucked into the vacuum cleaner. Failure to make provision for loan writedowns and loan losses had overstated (misstated, argued some critics) earnings until the necessary corrections were enforced by forces beyond the bankers' control. The damage, moreover, took no account of the potential profit that the banks had passed up by loaning such huge sums to REITs instead of to more established, reliable clients.

For everybody concerned—banks, trusts, regulators, depositors, shareholders, and especially the trust investors—the story was a dismal account of failure in which the smaller people suffered the larger damage. Worse still, it showed again that the expertise of bankers is strictly and narrowly confined to running banks. Outside that limited zone, the bankers not only proved as gullible and gawky as the rankest amateur but showed a degree of cupidity and inconsequence so marked that even the basic rules of banking itself were cast aside. If such men were the guardians of the people's money, who was guarding the guardians?

5. Mr. Giannini's Goliath

In the summer of 1974, travelers to sunny California returned to Europe with a curious tale. The natives of the rich and fabled state were behaving most uncharacteristically; they were drawing their money out of the local banks—including some of the world's biggest and most successful examples—and stashing the loot in hiding places in their homes, under the mattress, beneath the potted plant, inside the cookie jar, and so on. The next thing the natives knew, so the stories ran, their houses were broken into, and the money neatly removed. Suspicion fell on bank tellers who, it was said, had tipped off outside accomplices about the withdrawals and subsequently shared in the haul.

On the face of it the exported story was fantastic, but many Californians were ready to swear to its truth. Beyond a doubt some people in the heavily banked Golden State had become jittery about entrusting their all to the banks; and, unlikely as it sounded, these nervous Californians preferred to keep a bundle at home, "just in case." Their eccentricity never touched off even a mini-run on the banks, but all the same the behavior was extraordinary; even more remarkable, it had a certain basis in logic.

A couple of rather unexpected and naturally well-publicized bank failures had occurred in the area. First fell the banking subsidiary of the Beverly Hills Bancorp, "Bank of the Stars"; its depositors, starry or not, pulled out some $30 million in a few days on the disconcerting news that the parent holding company had a builder client who couldn't pay off his commercial paper debts. The bank itself was basically sound, and by winding up as part of the Wells Fargo Bank, of San Francisco, it protected its depositors—small enough consolation to the stockholders, who lost most of their shirts.

The second case, far more sensational, was the collapse of the U.S. National Bank of San Diego, virtually a one-man bank ruled over by C. Arnholt Smith, the close friend and financial backer of Richard M. Nixon. With its over- and undertones of conspiracy and fraud, this failure had resounding repercussions throughout the state. Again, the depositors got home safe through a merger of U.S. National with the Crocker National Bank, also of San Francisco; again, the stockholders were left almost threadbare (they battled on valiantly through the courts to try to salvage some vestige of their vanished assets).

Neither collapse was calculated to strengthen the traditional faith in banks and bankers on which we are all weaned. Not only Californians but many other citizens who regularly channeled funds to institutions in the fastest growing, most splendiferous state had understandable cause for apprehension. But if California banks suddenly seemed a less desirable place to deposit savings and then forget about them, and if this triggered the subsequent unaccustomed rate of withdrawals, it was less the fault of the two delinquent banks than of the psychological reaction to certain failings of no less an institution than the Bank of America—the largest bank in California, indeed, in the whole United States, and in the entire world.

This giant among giants has more than 1,000 branches in California, holds close to $60 billion in assets, earned $3,100 million in operating income (in 1974), maintains 104 branches and 114 subsidiaries in 90 foreign countries, and has recorded phenomenal growth down the years. But something very unusual and unpleasingly significant had indeed happened to BofA, as it is known for short. It was perfectly solvent and, in the long term, stable—but the bank of banks was not behaving itself in the way to which big banks (and small ones, for that matter) should have been accustomed—or so it seemed.

The high and mighty executives of the parent holding company, BankAmerica Corporation, had won a severe reprimand from the Federal Reserve Board's regulators for certain goings-on at the bank and its subsidiary, the Bank of America National Trust and Savings Association. Somewhat out of character for bankers, who seldom like to admit they are wrong, or anything but supremely right, the BofA bosses meekly promised to behave themselves better in the future.

The first shock for the bankers (and their shareholders and depositors) came when the Fed turned thumbs down on a plan to establish a Swiss insurance subsidiary, in partnership with Allstate Insurance. Adding insult to injury, the Fed then warned the management to pay more attention to the situation back home, in particular to their overexposed loan position and their capital level, which was lower than the Fed considered appropriate. Californians are not used to seeing their favorite bank, indeed any bank, rapped over the head in this fashion; and the bank's own reaction lent support to the watchdog's growls.

As a follow-up to their report on the results for the third quarter of 1974, BofA shareholders got a humble-pie letter from the president, Alden Winship "Tom" Clausen, in which he signaled a slowdown in growth. In the future, he declared, BofA would limit the expansion of its real estate portfolio (at the time valued at some $5 billion); would decline to make loans for nonproductive purposes; would take smaller positions in big multi-bank credit lines; and would scan new customers more carefully.

An interview with Mitchell Gordon in *Barron's* magazine made observers wonder still more what BofA had been up to while everybody else was assuming that it knew how to bank. Clausen outlined in greater detail the virtuous policy which his management had now decided to pursue. He sounded rather like a junkie promising to go straight. "We're putting greater emphasis on loan quality and cutting back certain types of loans we consider non-productive. . . . We're always rationing credit. That's our business. But it's usually done on the economics of the individual loan. Lately, we've also been rationing on the basis of a certain sensitivity to the marketplace, to the way the public perceives things. We're not worried about a financial collapse, but we are concerned about liquidity and the nation's own economic strength. We think this requires us to be even more conservative in making loans." In other words, the bank was trying to make a virtue of necessity. It had grown too fast, partly by taking too much business at which it should never have looked in the first place.

The country's largest, most liquid, and, in some respects, most diversified bank, by deliberately slowing down its pace, thus blazoned the end of an epoch for U.S. banking, the go-go era. Up to that moment, BofA itself had really gone. For two consecutive years, its assets had expanded by more than 25 percent per year; now the fuddy-duddies of the Federal Reserve Board considered a 10 percent rate more "appropriate." The bank had been pushing no less aggressively abroad, where the aggregate weekly deposits at its 100-plus branches averaged some $17 billion, while overseas business had come to generate about half the profits.

BankAmerica Corporation had plunged into computer servicing, mortgage banking, and consumer finance. It had crossed state lines (a feat prohibited for the banking subsidiary) to do business in other parts of the country. It had established so-called Edge Act subsidiaries (which supply only international banking services out of state) in New York, Chicago, Houston, and Miami. Loan production offices, to solicit wholesale business, were opened in New York and Chicago. This overgrown emphasis on expansion and size—the constant reminders that Bank of America is the biggest in the world are a peculiarly boring piece of public relations—was completely out of character with the spirit in which the bank was founded early in the present century by Amadeo Peter Giannini, an immigrant from Italy. At first he called his venture the Bank of Italy, which wouldn't have got him very far. The inspired change of name followed the takeover of a New York bank already known as the Bank of America.

Giannini paradoxically built his success on his dislike of big banks, with their emphasis on the business of wealthy individuals and large corporations, their distaste for the custom of the *hoi polloi*. His bank, in contrast, would serve the little people—the farmers, small business-men, homeowners, housewives, whom at that point the banks scarcely deigned to serve. A former produce merchant himself, Giannini opened his first branch in the Italian section of San Francisco, with such success that soon he was expanding rapidly and widely, helping people of limited means to borrow money for worthwhile purposes, and help-ing himself to a volume of business which began to rival that of the traditional banks. Giannini left his stamp on banking in other ways: he initiated the American system of "open banking," with open-plan offices, visibly accessible executives, and an environment of informal, friendly contact with customers. When BofA went overseas, these same techniques had even more impact (followed by efforts at imitation) than at home.

The founder retired in the 1920s. He returned in the Depression of the thirties, in time to save his creation from bankruptcy. On his death in 1949, his son Mario took the chair; he died within a few years, and BofA then fell into the hands of professional management. The style of the pros in recent years has shifted markedly toward decentrali-zation. Under Clausen, the bank has been run by a committee—rather, by a series of committees—and this is the system which has changed the character of the bank in ways so little beloved by the Federal Reserve.

In the Giannini period, and for some time afterward, growth was confined mainly to the state of California, which was enough for any-body as the population mushroomed under the effects of the sunshine and the new opportunities provided by the wartime establishment of industry. By this natural process of expansion, BofA in 1945 passed the then Chase Bank to become top banking dog in the United States. Its strongly retail orientation persisted. The deposits, loans, and mortgages were chiefly arranged with individual clients. No great effort was made to go after corporate business outside California; the emphasis was more on luring out-of-state corporations (and their deposits) into BofA's home territory. The recipe guaranteed exceptional prosperity: A. P. Gian-nini's original premise that there were many more smaller clients than big ones, and that in the aggregate the small men's business was poten-tially far bigger, worked as well after 1945 as after 1918.

By the middle seventies, BofA had become incredibly powerful in California. Its 1,050 branches span the whole state, providing bank services for many modest communities, as well as the main urban and suburban centers. The branches are so numerous that, so legend has it, at least one branch is ripped off every week; and the employees are under orders to offer no resistance to the bandits, since insurance coverage is routine. Be that as it may, it is a fact that the bank controls around 44 percent of all bank branches in the state. Its real estate loans regularly exceed $1 billion a year, and in the mid-seventies it had over a million retail consumer loans outstanding. Of the $5 billion in mortgage loans on the books in 1974–75, about three-quarters were on single-family homes and residential units in California. As in the early days of its founder, BofA still does a vast agricultural loan business.

The Bank of America's innovations have changed the face of American and world banking—it invented the bank credit card in the early fifties, extending its application brilliantly by licensing the card to some 5,600 other U.S. banks. By the mid-seventies, there were some 40 million BankAmericard holders, and maybe this brilliant success at home helped to inspire the bank to embark on a wholly new era of international expansion. Until this burst of exuberance, BofA had mainly confined its foreign presence to the Pacific Basin—the countries of the Far East and Australasia with time-honored trading relationships with the Pacific Coast. Branches have operated in Japan, the Philippines, and Thailand for three decades or so. The big change was the invasion of Europe; apart from a London office, opened in 1931, the West Coast bank had no toehold in the Old World.

During the go-go decade of the sixties, all this changed. BofA emerged from nowhere to become one of the leading international banks, both in its own right and through multi-bank operations and consortia; it also became a major force in the burgeoning Eurodollar market. To strengthen its ties with other banks, the bank hired Pierre-Paul Schweizer, who, as former head of the International Monetary Fund, was about as prestigious a figure as a bank could hire when on the hunt for world business—and BofA was hunting everywhere. It was swift to grab for the new wealth flowing into the Arab oil states after the energy crisis. Luxembourg, Lebanon, Kuwait; wherever the money was, there the Bank of America seemed to follow.

This busy thrust abroad naturally raises the question of who was minding Mr. Giannini's store back home—and whether or not the minding was being neglected. In fact, BofA's business in California did suffer some deterioration, if its critics spoke the truth—like loss of ground to competitors, like corporate customers complaining of poor coordination across the world, like individuals grumbling that service at the branches is not what it was, like (above all) the Federal Reserve rebuke of the loan policy and the capital structure.

The almost unthinkable accumulations of wealth in a mighty bank rest on relatively tiny bases of capital, rather like a wooden box supporting an inverted pyramid of circus elephants. BofA traditionally had a smaller box than most—a ratio of capital to assets of 4.4 percent, compared to 5.5 percent for the rest. BofA defends this especially tiny vital statistic by pointing to the ratio of debt in the supporting capital base —just 29 percent, compared with a more typical 40 percent. Its high proportion of consumer loans (20 percent, about twice the figure for some big New York banks) is also stressed as an asset, giving faster returns, more turnover, and greater flexibility.

This still did not spare BofA from being faced, like all banks, with exceptional and execrable "problem" loans when recession struck. Net loan losses in 1975 of $135.7 million were up from $69.5 million in 1974; by the year's end such losses were running at about three times the rate of a year earlier. During 1975, the bank had to provide for possible future loan losses in the thumping amount of nearly $175 million, up from about $106 million the year before. That cost BofA (or rather its shareholders) 21 cents a share in 1975 profit.

One of the problems deserves closer study. The loan customer was not one of BofA's highly prized individuals. It was Memorex, a large company whose basic, once high-flying computer sales and service operation nosedived when the computer boom, as all booms do, came to an end. That Memorex got into financial difficulty is not surprising. That BofA had a liability of some $120 million in loans outstanding to Memorex, plus $30 million in preferred stock which had been exchanged for debt, is more than surprising. How could the nation's biggest bank (to repeat its boast yet again) make so large and gratuitous a mistake—a $150 million exposure to one weak customer? Officials blamed their error, lamely enough, on excessive confidence in the Memorex management, based on its earlier impressive performance. (And, to be sure, subsequently Memorex did stage a comeback.)

When the Fed blocked the Swiss insurance company deal, and in the same breath warned management to improve its domestic housekeeping, anybody could be forgiven for fearing that the Memorex mish-mash was not a single aberration but fitted into a general pattern of mounting loss of competence. This did not mean that the millions of Californians who had made deposits and contracted loans with the bank were in financial jeopardy. Sure, the loan losses were rising; but the amounts set aside for 1975, for example, came to only a minuscule 0.45 percent of the total average loans outstanding—and the more conservative lending policies adopted since should force the figure down further in future years.

In some respects, BofA had been sounder than its contemporaries. It would not lend more than two-thirds of the appraised value of real property, so its losses on the $5 billion of real estate loans were virtually zero. Its own mortgage loans were so vast and important a source of income, too, that the bank had managed to avoid the indefensible risks taken in the field of real estate investment trusts. BofA did sponsor one of these outfits, BankAmerica Realty Investors; but this, too, was conservative, concentrating on equity investments in property, and avoiding interim loans and construction lending. There was no significant commitment here in a $28,000 million aggregate loan pouch, nor did BofA have to anticipate any huge losses on loans to the battered property trust business in general.

The California champions can point to many other strengths, such as the fact that, although they deal in federal funds to a tune as loud as $100,000 million in a single year, they make sparing use of the latter to bolster their own capital structure—unlike some other banks; the same is true of such instruments as letters of credit and certificates of deposit, which have also led others far astray. The customer base, too, is exceptionally broad; what with all those branches, BofA holds about one-third of the total savings deposits in the state. Abroad, the bank is not involved in tricky areas like commodities trading; and it claims to monitor carefully its foreign exchange trading (all the same, when Bankhaus I. D. Herstatt collapsed in West Germany, BofA had some $5 million at stake in currency dealings). So how did what could claim to be a sound, conservatively run bank manage to alarm some of the clientele and worry the Federal Reserve into delivering a rebuke—one, moreover, which the management felt obliged to accept?

The answer is that the distrust and suspicion which swept over depositors in California banks in the summer of 1974 were not based on the available banking data, which people with deposits at the Bank of America or any other bank neither knew nor understood. The relatively trivial (statistically speaking) departures from best banking practices were no more important, perhaps, than the lingering glance or too loving words that Caesar's wife directs toward a young legionary: the banks, like her, must be above suspicion.

With banks, more than with any kind of enterprise, viability rests on the money ratios, but *trust* depends on the invisible confidence of the public. To retain that confidence, a bank must not only be safe statistically, it must be felt to be safe. The lessons of the strange interlude in the mid-seventies, which had some Californians stuffing their savings under the mattress like uneducated French peasants, had been well known to A. P. Giannini, and should not have had to be taught again to his business heirs. At any rate, they reacted in the proper spirit by deciding on a policy of exemplary openness and disclosure, in which admirable departure BofA can claim, yet again, to be leading America's banks. It's an ill wind that blows nobody into being good.

6. The Franklin Fiasco

UNTIL May 1974, the Franklin National Bank, of Long Island—the twentieth biggest in the United States, with over 100 branches and assets of some $5 billion—was, so far as most people knew, one of the minor ornaments of American banking. That month, however, the Franklin board confessed that it would not (indeed, could not) pay a second-quarter dividend, thanks to losses of about $40 million in foreign exchange dealing. Any Americans a little more deeply in the know about the Franklin's affairs might have reckoned that the calamity was what comes of getting involved with foreigners—and one Italian foreigner in particular.

Shortly afterward the bank fell apart completely; and its fall had an obvious explanation. Michele Sindona, the Italian interloper, it might seem, had wrecked a good, sound American bank, frightened its depositors, ruined the shareholders, and given the banking regulators their worst single alarm since the disastrous thirties. It is true that Sindona's brief sojourn in control of the bank manifestly did it no good. But the critical failings were not his. The wrecking process was initiated and perpetuated by some 100 percent Americans, including American bank supervisors. The more the fall of the Franklin is studied, the more questions arise that have to be answered not just by the Franklin's officials, but by officialdom itself.

Why, in view of Sindona's known past and present activities, did the American authorities allow him to gain control of the bank in the first place? Why, in the light of the Franklin National's sorry history under previous direction, was more attention not paid to its current behavior? And why, when there was no hope of averting final disaster, was the death agony so long drawn-out? How could there be any excuse for the postmortem confession of Comptroller of the Currency James Smith? He admitted to a congressional subcommittee that bank regulators had identified problems at the Franklin National several years before the bank failed; and that the watchdogs, though they could have forced reforms by denying applications to open branch offices, failed to act.

Sindona was no stranger to the local scene. In 1967 he had sold a minority interest in the ailing food firm Libby, McNeill and Libby to Nestlé, of Switzerland, and at one time also held a stake in the paper manufacturer Brown Company. When his eyes lighted on Franklin National, however, Sindona had nothing but an economically insignificant stake in two American photographic companies. His summer 1972 buy, for some $40 million, of 21.6 percent of the Franklin New York Corporation, the bank's parent holding company, promoted Sindona into a much higher league. (The vendor, Laurence A. Tisch, president of Loew's, Inc., was significantly thrilled to sell.)

Nine months later, Sindona spent another $27 million on 53 percent of Talcott National Corporation, whose subsidiary, James Talcott, Inc., a big commercial financing outfit and one of the biggest factoring firms, specialized in the purchase and administration of debts receivable by its clients. Sindona's master plan was to sell Talcott to Franklin National and to apply the bank's sizable tax loss carry-forward against the profits of the factoring concern; the deal would also allow him to rip off a large chunk of strictly personal cash. No doubt this explains Sindona's lack of evident concern about the Franklin National's weak performance over a period of several years and his indifference to its poor reputation in banking circles—a combination of adverse factors that, of course, had helped his initial entry.

The bank was the creature of its autocratic, hard-driving founder, Arthur Roth, who between 1950 and 1962 boosted the assets from $78 million to a round $1 billion, while annual earnings averaged 15 to 20 percent of stockholders' equity. The bank's Long Island location became a vital asset as the commuter belt expanded and as fast-developing new communities grew up farther afield. Success was also enhanced, even guaranteed, by the fact that the big New York City banks were banned from opening up branches in the same area.

Roth's one-man band, like most of its kind, was not noted for any great professional quality among his subordinates. The man himself was an enthusiastic risk-taker, willing to accept loan losses double those of the average bank, if that was the price of earning on his loan portfolio 1 percent or more above the average interest for banks in general. Real estate loans based on verbal commitments, and often unsecured, along with other affronts to orthodox banking, were techniques that worked (or seemed to) in conditions like the postwar boom on Long Island. But the early sixties, when construction tailed off and Wall Street wobbled badly—especially in 1962—were a wholly different matter.

Then, borrowers defaulted right and left. There were no more fast-expanding assets or high-level profits; so Roth turned to municipal loans. Showing much the same disregard for conservative convention, he overloaded his bank's portfolio on such disadvantageous terms that eventually the Franklin National had to withdraw from that market. This naturally annoyed the municipalities, some of which took all their business, including their deposits, elsewhere.

But Roth's moment of final truth came in the later sixties, when changes in the banking laws allowed the Manhattan banks to open branches in the surrounding regions of the state. This was a thrust at the jugular of a suburban bank like the Franklin; Roth riposted by taking his rashest risk of all. He decided to meet the mighty head-on by invading New York City in retaliation. In 1967 he merged with another bank in the city, Federation Bank and Trust, and was off and running —to nowhere.

In 1968, Roth was neatly supplanted as chief executive by his smooth-talking former public relations director and alter ego, Harold Gleason. The ex-flack pulled off the palace revolution in table-turning style with the aid of the new directors from the Federation Bank. Where Roth had been too autocratic, Gleason was too easygoing; it is a toss-up which vice proved more dangerous. The new, plush headquarters on Park Avenue were underutilized and helped to send costs spiraling out of control—between 1968 and 1970, salary expenses alone increased by half. An interloper from the suburbs like Franklin could not afford such a burden, not when faced by the toughest competition that the powerful and entrenched money center banks, which were not about to yield anything, could muster.

Often enough, the suburbanites had to be content with the short end of a multiple underwriting, or with handling business their bigger competitors considered too small or too risky. This inferior quality of business was simply handled worse: the bank's expenses per dollar of commercial loan volume were as much as 50 percent higher than those for banks of comparable size. Earnings were hurt badly; and at the end of the sixties another change in the regulations did even more injury. Up to that point U.S. banks were obligingly not compelled to report loan losses on their income statements; instead, these were treated (i.e., hidden) as a reduction of reserves. The new rule, after 1969, demanded that at least a portion of these losses had to be charged against current income.

Under all these varied and accumulating pressures, the Franklin National in 1971 reported a loss of some $7.2 million. Here Michele Sindona came sailing piratically over the horizon. His interest in acquiring a stake in a palpably limping enterprise became plain from the arithmetic of the Talcott National deal. Sindona's unsubtle scheme was to have Franklin National buy the factoring concern's shares; his own holding was to be bought for $27 million (the price which he had paid) plus $3 million in expenses—$30 million in all. The catch was that the market value of the shares had meanwhile dropped to only about $7.6 million; it was yet another of Sindona's spectacularly rotten investments.

But the Italian financier had bigger things in mind than getting out from under a financial failure. He wanted to use this large and still passably convincing American bank to consolidate his financial empire on two continents, and at the same time to strengthen his own position at the summit. Both Franklin and Talcott were held through the medium of Fasco International, SA, a Luxembourg entity which in turn was a subsidiary of Fasco, AG, through which, in turn again, Sindona controlled his European enterprises; and Fasco, AG, was his very own property. Sindona held out seductive prospects of enhancing the potential of both the West and East wings of the house by interaction between the two. According to a *Fortune* magazine study, Sindona was undeterred by associates who warned that Franklin National might prove to be the whitest of elephants. "Don't worry," he is supposed to have said, "I'm going to make most of my money in foreign exchange. That's the way I do it in my Italian banks."

Suiting the action to the word, one of Sindona's first moves on taking over in the summer of 1972 was to appoint as new head of the international department one Peter Shaddick, from the Bank of Montreal. Shaddick hired as foreign exchange specialist Donald Emerich, in spite of (some said, because of) the fact that the latter had been fired by Continental Illinois Bank for unauthorized foreign exchange dealing. Shaddick presumably knew Emerich's background, including the fact that he had also parted company with the Marine Midland Trust for some other irregularities—the two men had been colleagues at Continental Illinois.

With this unpromising human material, Sindona hoped to fortify the international department, and to use its foreign exchange section in particular to revive the low-tide fortunes of the Franklin National in the domestic market. However, events failed to obey Sindona's scenario. At home, the tide continued to ebb, despite the struggles of a new president recruited from Bankers Trust, Paul Luftig. He tried to promote recovery through leverage, that is, by increasing the ratio of the bank's assets to its capital. He did boost loan volume by a good quarter, but profitability was resistant to the therapy. Dragging the bank inexorably down was a vast portfolio of loans at fixed rates of interest (representing about half of all domestic assets), which were now having to be financed with progressively more costly money. Even the unfixed portion of the portfolio was earning interest at below the prevailing market rates.

The bank, already lacking profits, was drifting into a far more serious shortage—that of liquidity; on some days it had to borrow as much as $1 billion in federal funds (that is, reserves kept by the banks which are lent to one another to maintain balances). In the winter of 1973–74, Franklin National's homegrown geniuses took a gambler's throw worthy of the founding Roth: they bought about $200 million in U.S. government and federal agency bonds, yielding 7–8 percent, or some 3 percent less than the bank paid to borrow the money required. The hard-pressed bankers were betting that interest rates would fall. Instead—such was the quality of the bank's foresight—rates rose.

By April 1974, the bank's operating deficit was running at about $3 million a month. At that point the major banks, such as Morgan Guaranty and Bank of America, either refused access to their federal funds or greatly reduced their commitments. It was now crystal-clear that the Franklin would fall from this cause alone, unless some desperate remedy for its liquidity could be found. No help would come from the designated savior, the international department, though not for want of trying. In his very first year, 1973, Shaddick *doubled* the bank's foreign assets, to around $1 billion; but expenses rose accordingly, and the apparent prosperity was largely profitless. Moreover, Emerich's efforts to coin bullion in foreign exchange dealings had predictably backfired, resulting in an eventual deficit of some $40 million.

Nor was the foreign exchange department's activity free from hanky-panky. The Franklin would have been forced to pass the third-quarter dividend in 1973, thus bringing forward the final catastrophe by six months, but for one handy fact: suddenly, a $2 million profit in foreign exchange transactions was thrust into the breach. Subsequent investigation found that the profit never existed. The figures had been created by a currency transaction with a Sindona-controlled Swiss bank, Amincor; the Franklin bought four or five currencies from the latter, and then sold them back at a $2 million profit, the rates of exchange being rigged in both directions.

The same trick was repeated in March 1974, but by then a few paper millions were not enough to save the bank. The omission of the dividend in May, coupled with the news of the foreign exchange deficit, should have been followed by an early, brusque funeral. But the inevitable end was delayed for another five unnecessary months while the supervisory authorities frenetically cast around for a solution. The intent, according to them, was to find the answer that would save the greatest number of people from the most danger.

Their solution was for a consortium of powerful European banks to take over the Franklin National's branches and its $1,620 million of deposits, plus other assets valued at $1,490 million. While that step prevented any loss to depositors, it left undisposed of, to be picked up by somebody else, over $2 billion, mainly in loans and receivables. The Federal Deposit Insurance Corporation took up this heavy load, along with an emergency loan of $1,720 million with which the Federal Reserve Bank of New York had kept the Franklin afloat during the final days. The FDIC forecast that from nine to fourteen years would be needed to clear up the entire estate, by which time the creditors might get something back. As for the 19,000 common shareholders, including Michele Sindona, their dreams were done.

The earlier the bank had failed, the less the damage would have been—if, for instance, it had collapsed at the first sign of serious difficulty in 1973, when the end was delayed by the foreign exchange finagling with Amincor. A death at that time would have destroyed Sindona's plans to merge the bank with Talcott National. The postponement had another advantage if (as some suspicious souls believe) the $40 million foreign exchange loss revealed the following spring covered, in whole or in part, the siphoning of bank money into private pockets. The delay, however, helped neither the bank nor Sindona's essential merger with Talcott, which the Federal Reserve Board refused to sanction. Not surprisingly, it did not fancy Sindona's self-serving arithmetic: a $30 million purchase of shares in the factoring concern, when they were actually worth only a quarter of the sum, stuck in the official craw.

At least on this occasion decisive intervention by the Fed was forthcoming. But what had the Federals and the other supervisory agencies been doing with their eyes up to then? Even if they could not (as they claimed) stop Sindona's gaining control of so important an asset as the country's twentieth largest bank, why were they not alerted into extreme watchfulness by their knowledge of his background in Europe, of his controversial relations with the authorities in his native Italy, of his record at other American corporations he controlled—even at Talcott National? Under Sindona, following his typical pattern, Talcott had diversified into such faraway fields as casualty insurance, fire-fighting equipment, and truck parts, with Sindona's typical unimpressive results.

Furthermore, Sindona had been involved in an embarrassing 1972 squabble with the American Stock Exchange over proxy statements affecting his photographic companies. Exchange officials, concerned about interlocking directorates and possible conflicts of interest, demanded more details and suspended trading in the respective shares for a few days before the dispute was eventually resolved. But the questions of Sindona's past were less puzzling and disturbing than the behavior of his official supervisors at the very end. They allowed the financier to block a merger of the Franklin National with Manufacturers Hanover, which had foolishly lent the Long Island bank $30 million in April 1974. The deal, which could have meant a swift and relatively easy solution to the Franklin problems, was all worked out, up to and including a promise from the Fed that the shotgun marriage would be free from antitrust investigation.

At the last minute, Sindona mustered all his resources for a final, fatal coup. He persuaded representatives of the Federal Reserve Bank of New York, the Securities and Exchange Commission, and the comptroller of the currency to join him and some of his henchmen at a meeting in Washington. The conclave mysteriously passed a project to salvage Franklin National by raising an additional $50 million from the shareholders. Astonishingly, the Fed lent its name to a press release issued after the meeting, which gave the erroneous impression that the $40 million foreign exchange loss was a temporary aberration, confined to a brief spell in the second quarter of 1974; and that the bank, anyway, had been insured "for a substantial portion of the loss." The release also indicated, on the authority of the comptroller of the currency, that the Franklin National was still solvent.

Quick as lightning, the bank's revamped management, which had not been invited to the Washington conference, pulled out the rug from under Sindona and the three government agencies. A press release declared that the foreign exchange loss actually amounted to $46 million, of which $27 million had been sustained during the first quarter (not the second), and stated that the losses came about through "unauthorized and falsified dealings." At the same time, the representative of the currency comptroller's office who was actually investigating the Franklin National's alarming records confirmed that the bank was not solvent, and had no hope of ever seeing solvency again.

Thoroughly alarmed by these disclosures, Manufacturers Hanover backed away swiftly. Several more months went by before the European consortium rescue was organized—months during which the quagmire deepened considerably for the bank's creditors and shareholders. The regulators thus showed themselves inept and inadequate in the period when a crash could have been averted; and again at the time when it was already inevitable; and again when the bank was dead but not gone. The guilty officials, of course, escaped unscathed. Sindona was arrested but was soon free on bail, while his chief lieutenants—including international boss Shaddick and foreign exchange dealer Emerich—were tried and convicted of various offenses connected with the foreign exchange loss. Their misdeeds included failing to record contracts for the sale of foreign currencies; entering into fictitious contracts with foreign banks; and submitting false reports to management and to the federal regulators.

The Franklin National officers pleaded guilty, which simplified and expedited matters (a curious feature was that Shaddick changed his plea from innocent to guilty, and that part of his trial was heard in closed court). Even if their Italian boss was ruined financially, as he claimed—he had lost his stake in the Franklin New York Corporation, and had disposed of his other American holdings—he could still consider himself fortunate. So could the rest of us. The Franklin National fiasco might have been the trigger setting off an explosive chain of events among other banks which, while less incompetently run than the Franklin, were dangerously exposed by their own imprudence and could never have withstood a run on their deposits. Nor could the national and international economy have resisted a chain reaction.

The danger was averted by the ample use of public resources, not following some coherent, planned strategy, but by belated hit-or-miss reactions. And after it was all over, Dr. Arthur Burns, chairman of the Federal Reserve Board, was quoted as saying that the Franklin National had been saved "by luck." If he said it, and meant it, it was a damning admission.

PART II

THE BRITISH
HORROR SHOW

7. The Billion-Pound Bamboozle

A billion-pound bank has a fine ring to it. So when Jim Slater, an ambitious British financier with an impressive string of capital gains behind him, announced to the world (as he frequently did) that his ambition was to preside over a financial empire with a market capitalization of that splendid size, the words themselves enhanced his prestige. To advance as far as Slater had already managed—from obscurity to household name—was an amazing achievement in itself. Compared to the glories of the past, the further progress toward the magic billion seemed but a matter of a few more giant strides.

But Slater Walker Securities, the master company of a convoluted empire, never got further than a third of the way toward Slater's goal. Even at that level, it transpired, far too high a price was being placed on the group's expertise, on the quality of its business, and on the presumed genius of its young master. The truth burst upon the world on September 14, 1976, when investigating accountants, appointed after Slater's dethronement the year before, crowned eleven months of probing with facts that blew sky-high both Slater's reputation and the whole official history of his invasion of the City of London.

Banking was an afterthought in Slater's sensational rise, which one commentator compared to that of Icarus. But the wax wings began to melt not in 1973, when the fires in the stock and property markets scorched the master company's finances beyond repair, but in 1968. Up to then, Slater had made his advance along the conglomerate route: he started by the time-honored City method of the shell game (in which assets are injected into an insignificant public company) and proceeded in direct imitation of the successful techniques of a Litton Industries and a Ling-Temco-Vought.

The catch phrase of "synergy" (allegedly making two merged units outperform jointly their separate selves) became wedded to a peculiarly British notion—that of energizing the private sector of industry by "liberating capital." The latter phrase was Slater's own invention; it became translated into the far more pejorative expression "assetstripping." The process described was the purchase of an industrial company through a takeover bid, followed by the sale of unwanted assets (mostly property) and the closure of unwanted businesses. The immediate effect of Capitalist's Lib was to generate extra millions for the capitalist concerned; but it was justified as the demonstration in microcosm of what the suffering British economy needed in macrocosm.

The idea was so plausible that few people paused to consider the reality of its application. This was an essential truth of the whole revolution of the whiz-kids—those bright lights that almost universally failed. The promise was always so beguiling and so convincing that the results were taken for granted; the medium truly became the message. Thus, when Slater took over the unexciting metal window manufacturer Crittall-Hope, most observers took it for granted that under his management the company had not only been stripped, but simultaneously revitalized. Yet long into Slater's post-conglomerate era the unstripped rump of Crittall-Hope was still cluttering up his premises, still no more visibly dynamic or progressive than it had been under his dispossessed predecessors.

In any event, the turn of the tide against conglomerates on both sides of the Atlantic consigned such exercises to the scrapheap of Slater's history. In the course of a 1969 study of Slater Walker, the magazine *Management Today* observed that it was time for the company to "de-conglomerate." Before the ink was dry on the page, Slater had adopted the word for his own. Now he needed a new game. The opportunity had been provided by a legendary wheeler-dealer, Sir Isaac Wolfson, who long tantalized the City with the mysterious operations of his financial interests, gathered under the aegis of an uncommunicative company called Drages.

Stepping in where angels would have feared to dip their toes, Slater bought the Wolfson interests for a price so pretty that when the Slater Walker share price was still languishing a fifth below the 1968 peak, the excessive cost of the Wolfson interests purchased four years previously was still commonly cited as the explanation. Rubbing salt into the wounds was the knowledge that Slater had been deftly outmaneuvered in the stock market at the same time. The double blow should at least have raised queries about the financial acumen of Slater himself. But the young financier (still only forty-two when he was forced to quit the company's chair) was not the first nor the last clever man to be outwitted by the still wilier maestro. To be outdone by Sir Isaac was less a disgrace than a badge of honorable experience.

Whatever its drawbacks per se, the Drages deal solved the problem of where Slater Walker should head next, now that its industrial career had been cut short—almost before it had properly begun. The timing was immaculate. The City was beginning to bubble with the new ferment created by small, young banks and allied financial operations, whose masterminds regarded the Establishment with the same degree of contempt that Slater and his minions had applied to old-fashioned industrial operators. In the new slang, the latter were "thing-makers": Neanderthal types to be despised in comparison to the "money-makers" who represented the new wave of history.

Jim Slater became the guru of gurus for this new religion, not only because of his considerable powers of articulation and manipulation, but also because of the stream of young disciples he sent forth into an eager and waiting world. Each new company sought to exploit much the same formula as the master, accompanied by suitable obeisance to his teachings. The gratitude was in most cases tangible as well as spiritual: Slater financed his protégés, seeking a piece of their action as well as his own—and that, too, seemed a master stroke for so long as speculative stock markets gave the offspring both opportunity and apparent success.

When excitement turned to disillusion, and bright young things like Christopher Selmes and John Bentley, both mini-conglomerateurs, fell out of their financial beds, their sins were visited on their heads, not Slater's. In the case of his chief disciple, Malcolm Horsman, the latter's fortunes were quite otherwise; the firm was taken over by the paper group, Bowater Corporation. He had turned his talents to a commodity trading company renamed Ralli International and spent three years as chairman and joint managing director before departing to devote more time to his other activities.

Never one to miss a chance, Slater tried passionately to win a favorable result for himself. The multi-millionaire Lord Cowdray, a possibly still richer Arab financier, the Lonrho trading empire, S. G. Warburg, and above all the Hill Samuel merchant bank were involved in the search for a saving partner. The nearest Slater came to salvation was the Hill Samuel deal, which fell through after the details had been announced to an agog world. At the press conference, Slater had acted with uncharacteristic bluntness, making it clear that he, and not his opposite number, Sir Kenneth Keith, would run the merged shop. He noted that Sir Kenneth would now have more time for farming—implying that this was about all the older financier was fit for.

Whether or not the rudeness played a part in Hill Samuel's withdrawal from the deal (an escape in the nick of time), the risky insult looks in hindsight almost like a case of the death wish. It was the second public blow to Slater's prestige. The first came in January 1972, when

Slater launched the Dual Investment Trust. Even his City admirers spotted that the portfolio consisted largely of deadbeat investments transferred from other parts of Slater Walker. The whole unhappy collection was promptly christened "the Dustbin Trust." The portfolio did not fare as badly in the market as the critics had supposed, mainly because Slater Walker bought the shares itself in a curiously misplaced attempt to prove Slater right and the critics wrong.

The episode showed a certain insensitivity on the matter of inside deals—using the different parts of a financial empire to boost the performance of another part. In fact, the complexities of Slater's planetary system, with its various suns and satellites, were such that outsiders had the greatest difficulty in spotting who was dealing with whom. One thing was clear: the importance of dealing profits in maintaining the earnings of the group. From 1968 to 1973, profits before tax and after interest rose from £4.87 million to £23.4 million—as gratifying a demonstration of how a dealing bank could outperform a nondealer as the world could hope to see.

Yet the world was strangely unimpressed by what it saw, as the failure of the shares to budge bore witness. Either the market (in the sense of the investment community as a whole) had doubts over the quality of Slater's earnings, or insider selling, by those with even better reason to doubt the quality, was continually dragging at the shares. The market has never actually shown much love for dealing profits, maybe because market professionals know only too well how the profits can turn into losses. Observers also spotted that Slater was seeking his profits further and further from home—especially in the red-hot Far East markets.

Not only did Slater's Asian wheels and deals (mostly through a Singapore company called Haw Par, originally famous for its Tiger Balm aphrodisiac) complicate his affairs still more mystifyingly; the operations led Slater and his henchmen into some deep Pacific waters. The accusations against them by the Singapore authorities were obviously damaging in themselves, and led eventually to efforts to extradite Slater to Singapore to face criminal charges. But the financial damage when the Far East investments collapsed was a fatal blow to the whole empire.

Expert camouflage made this far from apparent at the time. The received (and encouraged) view was that by deciding to pull out of the Far East in 1973, Slater had shown his habitual excellence of timing, limiting the losses and keeping the rest of the empire free from contamination. The revealed truth was of a very different order. In order to sell its 46 percent stake in Haw Par, the Slater master company advanced a short-term loan to the purchasers. This was ultimately converted into a five-year loan of $16.5 million, plus a standby credit of only $3 million less.

Jim Slater's successors counted themselves lucky to get out from under this crushing load for writeoffs totaling $8.5 million. The costly retreat from the Far East was only part of a pell-mell process of disentanglement, which kindly outsiders credited to Slater's early reading of the warning signs in the world economy, but which hindsight shows to have arisen from the deepening crisis of the economy inside Slater Walker itself. In the first few months of 1974 alone, the group sold over £40 million of assets. The view that this showed commendable prudence, as opposed to dire necessity, was encouraged by the circumspect behavior of the Slater investment management operation, which went into cash to the tune of 35 percent of its funds before most other experts had spotted that golden markets had turned to dross.

The master, again showing the opportunism that was his trademark, seized the occasion to lecture the world on the virtues of cash. "In today's difficult financial conditions and in spite of the present rate of inflation," Jim Slater intoned in May 1974, "cash remains the optimum investment for the major part of your company's available resources. Many people in recent months have found that you cannot always turn property into cash, you cannot always turn large lines of shares into cash, you cannot always turn pictures into cash. Cash you can always turn into other things."

The breathtaking reality of the matter was that Slater had been among the most pained discoverers of this truth. The hoard of nineteenth-century English art of which he often used to boast remained unsold and worth only half its book value (a loss of £350,000) when the crash came. At the same time, £14 million had to be written off the £75 million of properties in which Slater Walker had invested. As for liquidity and the sovereign virtues of cash, the banking business was so desperately short of the ready that only a £70 million loan from the Bank of England, coupled with a £40 million guarantee of debts owing to the Bank, prevented its total disappearance.

In the absence of the Bank's guarantee, noted the investigating accountants, "the bad debt losses which they considered Slater Walker —the banking company—had incurred would have made it insolvent at that time." History records several examples, far too many, in fact, of banks going bust; but none of a banker who, while heading rapidly toward bankruptcy himself, lectures the world on the virtue of avoiding the very vices that are destroying his business. As the accountants' report revealed, Slater's bank could not have become liquid or solvent if it had tried.

They described its lending policy as "inherently weak": a just phrase, considering that four loans accounted for half the total £91 million out on loan at October 31, 1975. Throw in just sixteen more debts, and over four-fifths of the entire portfolio is accounted for. Still worse, the borrowers did not even have to pay interest on two-fifths of the debts—the interest was simply "rolled up," added to the amount outstanding. This unusual generosity can be better understood from the fact that three-quarters of the millions had been lent to companies within the Slater camp.

It was, as the accountants again correctly observed, an "in-house" operation. It was also one that bore no relation to the prudence which Jim Slater had enjoined on his confrères. Two-thirds of the portfolio, even if the clients had been able or disposed to repay, did not fall due for more than two years ahead—and that was well over a year after Slater delivered his prose poem in favor of cash. Small wonder that, when the accountants' report reached an astonished world, the £51 million left on loan was bad to the tune of £40 million—covered, fortunately, by the Bank of England's guarantee, which transferred the pain to the taxpayer. It did not, however, remove the pain from the shareholders, since the Bank's repayment terms meant that something like £50 million would flow into the official coffers before anybody else got a whiff of anything resembling a dividend.

Few City people expected Slater Walker to be alive even in name by that time. The banking and property disasters were not alone by any means. The insurance side, in contrast to its banking bedmates, had apparently followed the master's advice about liquidity; unfortunately, cash is a totally inappropriate policy for a life assurance business. The aggrieved accountants called the long-term fund "over-liquid, badly matched and vulnerable to a drop in interest rates." The 16 percent property content in the portfolio, they thought, was too high. And the stock market investments (dominated by Jim Slater in person) were called "questionable," as well they might be, since £19 million had been lost on a £57 million fund.

The policyholders were saved from the worst possible fate by a quixotic piece of Slaterism. Some of the most grisly investments carried a guarantee: the insurance company could transfer the offending articles back to Slater Walker at the price at which they had been suspended by the Stock Exchange. The results are scarily illustrated by the case of Charles Spreckley, a sound shop-fitting firm in which Slater acquired a one-third interest in 1972. It was used as a vehicle for acquiring property interests, the most important being a now-bust concern called Town and Commercial. The equity stake plus associated loans generated total losses of £15.5 million—the full brunt of which, since the insurance side was protected by its guarantee, had to be carried by the Bank.

The Bank also lost £5 million on yet another of Slater's brainchildren, Equity Enterprises, an entertainment company originally launched in association with the TV personality David Frost. The collapse of this ragbag of a concern, which numbered a crashed bank of its own among the assorted fiascos, involved a provision of £5.6 million —the largest single blow suffered by a "general investments" side that had remained far more important to Slater Walker than most shareholders would have supposed. Even though the days of easy dealing profits were long gone, a quarter of the group's capital employed, when the accountants came to anatomize the body, was found to fit into this "general" category.

The "associated companies" in the shambles were yielding Slater Walker a mere 2.3 percent. Nor was the company reaping the fat capital gains that equity experts like Slater had sold as the concomitants of low yields; a quarter of the portfolio had to be written off when the day of judgment came. At that point, only two sides of the business came in for even the mildest praise. The investment managers, who looked after private clients and various trusts and funds, were considered to run their affairs well and in an orthodox manner. And the property division was said to have been "run professionally."

That said a mouthful for the profession. In addition to the £14 million of writeoffs, the property managers had contrived to build up an income of only £1.5 million (on the £75 million of property) against interest charges which must have comfortably exceeded £6 million a year. The prestigious City board—including Sir James Goldsmith, Lord Rothschild, and Sir Charles Hambro—which had been installed at the time of Slater's departure in October 1975, could find little comfort no matter where they looked.

Nor could Slater's friends—except in the fact that the first post-Slater year had revealed little in the way of skulduggery apart from the allegations in Singapore. At home the only horrors to emerge from the accountants' report lay in the news that Slater Walker had apparently broken the statutory provision that forbids a British company from purchasing its own shares, and in the amazing size of the loans granted to directors of Slater Walker by the friendliest bank they could ever hope to find.

Slater himself had been almost modest in his borrowings, that is, by contrast with his former right-hand man, Tony Buckley. The latter owed the mind-boggling total of three-quarters of a million; half a million had actually been advanced on his leaving the company. The big idea, apparently, was to enable Buckley to generate enough profits to repay his earlier debts—a procedure so bizarre as to defy any logical explanation. Together, Buckley and Slater were indebted to the company to the tune of £1.2 million; half as much again had been lent to other directors in this remarkably cozy fashion.

Yet in June 1975 the shareholders in this appallingly mismanaged institution were comforted by an audited and apparently respectable set of accounts and promised that "survival is now assured." Even a couple of months later, when the interim statement (which did not have to be audited) came out, no inkling of the disaster appeared. The secrecy was maintained to the last. For reasons known only to itself, the Bank of England told nobody about its £70 million loan and its £40 million guarantee. Thus Jim Slater was able to leave office as chairman, if not exactly full of either years or honor, at least with his reputation as a man of high ability more or less intact.

In its lesser way, this was a demonstration of the pervasive effect of the Big Lie. The impact of a public relations triumph can outlive even a cruel reality. Jim Slater had created the image of a new and powerful banking force in the City of London. Although his actual activities were as old as the hills on which the City is built, and although his power was always trivial compared to the established merchant banks, let alone the joint stock giants, Slater became a symbol. The Bank of England presumably felt either awed by the symbol or frightened of appearing to pull the idol down. Either way, judgment could not be indefinitely postponed. The idol crashed from its pedestal; and those peering into the rubble were amazed to discover how little there had been inside.

8. The Hollow Crown

ALL banks make some bad loans. But nobody ever supposed that one day some bank could make only bad loans—not, that is, until the full and grisly truth about Britain's Crown Agents and its ventures in property and secondary banking became known. The title does not, as might be supposed, conceal the masterminds who tend the private or public fortunes of the British monarchy. The royal affairs are looked after by (among many august bodies) the Crown Commissioners, who, so far as anybody knows, have managed their affairs with the utmost propriety.

The governments who put their trust in the Crown Agents come not from home but from abroad, mostly from lands once embraced in the ample reach of the far-flung British Empire. The funds are invested by the Agents on behalf of these prestigious clients; and what the Agents got up to during Britain's speculative go-go era surpasses any other tale of ineptitude in the crises of the banks.

The Crown Agents, true, are not strictly speaking bankers, since they do not take deposits from the public at large. But they certainly did invest in banks—indeed, they seemed to have an unerring instinct for picking secondary banks that were headed straight for perdition. Obviously the civil servants at the Agents had missed their vocation. Had they worked instead at the Bank of England, given their infallible sense of impending failure, maybe the incipient disasters would have been nipped in the bud.

The strangest aspect of all was that nobody (including presumably the government, which had the ultimate responsibility for the Crown Agents' carryings on) had any idea that matters were getting so terrifyingly out of hand. Nobody even guessed that the civil servants had in any way ceased to follow the prudent, cautious policies that such fellows would be expected to learn at their mothers' knees. All that anybody with his eyes open did know was that the Agents were clearly diversifying into territory where they hardly seemed to belong by nature, and where they were rubbing up against some strange bedfellows.

A wandering financial journalist might thus be invited into the

59

parlor of a bank of which he had never heard, established in some elegance in the heart of St. James's; and there he might discover that the bank, whose *raison d'être* seemed flimsy and management nondescript, had won the backing of the Crown Agents. Further inquiry would have been needed to elicit how far the Agents had plunged into this investment, or to unearth the fact that it was not one occasional flutter, but part of a whole policy of searching out high-risk investment.

If that was the object of the exercise, the Agents certainly succeeded. The results were so shocking that in December 1974 the government, although its responsibility for the Crown Agents was moral rather than legal, had to put up £85 million of public money to avert what would have been the most embarrassing bankruptcy in British history. In two years, after writing off dubious loan after dubious loan, the Agents succeeded in losing £185.4 million. Even for an institution which had £634 million of money in its care by the end of 1975, the amount is staggering—equal to almost a third of the entrusted funds.

So heavy a loss would certainly have destroyed any ordinary bank. The customers would have run for cover as soon as the evil tidings became known. But the 100 or so overseas governments and official bodies served by the Agents actually increased their deposits in 1976. The total rose to over £850 million, thanks to the government's demonstration that, in the last analysis, it stood behind the Agents, as (presumably) the customers had always supposed.

Another confidence-boosting factor was that the Agents were now under new management, appointed when the previous debacle first became known. The losses made inevitable by the writeoffs on dud and dead loans (totaling £177 million) were the work of the previous administration, or lack of it. In September 1976, John Cuckney, the man chiefly responsible for clearing up the mess, was at last able to express the hope that "all the horrors have been uncovered." Cuckney, a banker of wide private experience, replaced a man who had come from Her Majesty's august treasury. It cannot be said that any aspect of the Crown Agents' story, or the banking disasters of which it formed part, reflects much credit on the business acumen of the men whose business is the government of Britain.

The business in which the Crown Agents demonstrated their acumen, or failed to do so, was semi-banking. The "semi" produced one far from humorous aside to the institution's near-crash. One liquidator of bankrupt companies against which the Agents had claims (and there were all too many of those) spotted that the Agents were not a bank, and could not claim to be licensed moneylenders either. So he publicly questioned whether the debts could legally be collected by the Agents, much to the chagrin of all those trying to pick up the pieces.

The bankrupt group concerned was the Stern assemblage of dead and dying firms. Among the richer follies of the inspired investors at the Crown Agents was to pour £40 million into this single group—headed, to make matters worse, by a single entrepreneur. William Stern proceeded to create a total shambles simultaneously in both property and insurance. An American, possessed of altogether more dynamism than was good for him, Stern came into British property as son-in-law of Osiah Freshwater, an Orthodox Jew of strict religion and enormous wealth. Stern set out to instill some transatlantic zest into his father-in-law's huge interests, based largely on residential property, where Stern pioneered some highly profitable techniques.

The fateful turning point came when Stern broke away from the Freshwater Group in a bid (and a hurry) to prove that he could do much more much faster on his own. At a time when a total of £60 million had been provided against property loans that had gone sour on the Agents, Stern alone accounted for £36 million. It was a feat of a sort. But Stern's amazing success in cornering (and losing) so rich a chunk of the Crown Agents' money (or rather the money entrusted to their care) implied a remarkable ability in establishing personal relationships with the gray men who ran this quasi-governmental organization (and who, in addition to the botched financial duties, also placed orders for developing countries for everything from postage stamps to technical assistance). So warm were Stern's associations that they even continued after the retirement of the officials. One of the latter, for instance, took up the chairmanship of Stern's Nation Life insurance business before its spectacular crash.

But Stern was not the only entrepreneur who apparently formed a lastingly high opinion of officials who lent money so readily. The former finance director of the Agents, for instance, became a deputy chairman of First National Finance Corporation on his retirement. FNFC turned into a disaster area second in extent only to the Crown Agents themselves, who (of course) held a 10 percent stake in this largest of the secondary banks. Uncharitable souls felt it far from satisfactory that officials should move on so sweetly and smoothly in this way. First lending money entrusted to their care to such companies, and then working for the lucky borrowers at lavish salaries, is a process that smacks too much of jobs for the boys—and the taste left in the mouth was disagreeable for the fastidious.

At the very least, the moves were not in the best traditions of an organization whose history had lasted over 140 years when the chickens came home to roost. An accounting in the autumn of 1975 showed just how imprudent the Agents had been in lending to friends, future employers, and the rest. Out of the £388 million in loans, roughly half (£194 million) had been very properly invested with the leading banks and the discount houses (the latter being somewhat esoteric institutions whose operations create the London money market). Not one penny of these millions, as of that date, had been lost or was likely to be lost.

The £55 million lent to the secondary banks and financial institutions had not fared so well: to the extent of £23.7 million of provisions against losses, or half the total. As for property companies, they had run through the Crown Agents' millions still more rapidly, taking in £106 million, of which £60 million was set fair to vanish without trace. "Other loans" of £33 million had managed to run up £12 million of losses, and a general provision of £5 million was also made, apparently just for luck. Obviously, the Agents needed it. A note accompanying the bad news had no good news attached: "The present provisions," it said delicately, "could be subject to a wide margin of error." Even that wasn't all the damage; a further provision of £27 million had to be made against losses on investments, like the 10 percent stake in FNFC.

How had so appalling a calamity been achieved, and why? The disease that infected the Agents was basically an acute form of the fever that swept over the entire banking world in the late sixties and early seventies. In those 140 years of venerable history, the Agents had gone quietly about their business, placing orders for uniforms and engineering goods here and investing millions every year there, in deposits that were as safe as houses. They sought not to show their cleverness, and as an institution the Agents built up no reserve of funds on their own account.

In these respects the Agents were true to the form of similar sound men who for years after the war went on investing clients' funds in investments like gilt-edged British government stock, which were as safe as those same houses—"were" being the operative word. In the radically changed postwar conditions, these stocks became a license to lose money. The men who were once praised for handling their clients' cash conservatively had their behavior deplored and excoriated by the year 1970. The race was clearly going to the swift, and the Crown Agents saw no reason why they shouldn't try a little speedy footwork on their own behalf.

Like the other excesses of British banking's foulest hour, the Crown Agents' euphoria was encouraged by the fabulously easy money which the government of Edward Heath made available so generously. With money pouring off the printing presses in an uncontrolled flood, the problem was to lend it, not to borrow it. The more money went into the property market, of course, the more property prices soared; so the property developers, and the secondary banks that lent mainly to them, inevitably seemed in their brief day to be the most wonderful investment action ever invented. The Crown Agents decided that they were entitled to a part of that action.

Unfortunately, however excellent they were at procuring postage stamps for new African nations, the Agents lacked any reasonable expertise on the premises when it came to evaluating property deals or financial propositions—still less for judging property tycoons and financial wizards. As one observer, the *Guardian*'s Alex Brummer, noted later, "Their lack of expertise was used by a series of notorious financiers to engage in speculative property and banking projects." Against one success—the profitable sale of a property company (naturally, to another public corporation, the Post Office)—the Agents mostly recorded only abject failures.

Their amazing instincts for future collapse took the Agents into bed not only with London & County Securities, whose demise set the whole downward slide of the fringe banks going, but also with the financial interests dominated by John Stonehouse, the one-time Labour minister whose bungled efforts to fake his own death by drowning in Miami landed him in the Old Bailey and thence in jail. The individual amounts lent to some of these banks were small only in comparison to the £40 million fortune advanced to William Stern; the Burston Group got over £9 million, while Sterling Industrial Securities, another outfit now all but lost to memory, received £10 million.

The loans to Sterling came on top of an equity interest, roughly a quarter, which the Agents had also acquired in an institution which, without their backing, would doubtless never have emerged from obscurity in the first place. The visions of sugar plums that danced in their heads had originally been inspired by some shrewd killings made by other institutional investors in safer times. The Courtaulds textile group's pension fund, in a move much criticized in its day, long before had taken a stake in an obscure little bank, beefed it up with the pensioners' funds—and, lo and behold, it blossomed into Triumph Investment Trust, and into a fat capital gain for the Courtaulds' old boys and girls. Where these trustees had trodden the ground first, others rushed in; and the Crown Agents, naturally, were deeply committed to Triumph when its later career ended in inglorious failure.

The ultimate irony is that when the Bank of England, confronted by the crisis of the secondary institutions like Triumph, put together its fleet of lifeboats to save the City from drowning in bad debts, the Crown Agents were among the first asked to man the boats. They put up £50 million for the general support fund: as remarkable a case of the blind helping those who have no sight as the annals of finance record. Indeed, a detailed history of the Agents' investments would cover most of the territory involved in the rise and fall of London's financial whiz-kids and later washouts.

The involvement goes right back to one of the first such sagas, when an automobile insurance firm, Vehicle and General, collapsed, leaving thousands of motorists covered by suddenly worthless policies.

The fall cost the Agents a mere million—peanuts compared to what was to come. But the story in outline was much the same as those that were to follow: new men bursting into an old industry, with much grandiose talk and with adept encouragement of personal publicity, seeming to glean great and growing profits where the old-established farmers found only moderate crops.

Like the founding genius of Triumph Investment, Tom Whyte, such men sprang from obscurity and tiny scale to a status of big name in the City: for example, the pair of bankers, with none too gentle a reputation for the collection of debts, who parlayed their Dalton Barton Bank into key management positions and eventual near-destruction of the merchant bank Keyser Ullman. There, too, the ubiquitous Agents popped up: their involvement at Keyser Ullman was to the tune of £5 million. Indeed, the ubiquity of the Agents was so prodigious as to encourage speculation, even in the least suspicious of minds, that more than coincidence explained the trail of woe.

The British government, at any rate, was sufficiently curious about the Agents' uncanny instincts for failure to appoint a judicial inquiry into their affairs. The director of public prosecutions was also looking for possible fraud, while the Agents themselves were busily examining every transaction, trying to uncover the last of the "horrors," and slowly restoring the operation to solvency and credit in world eyes. New men were in most of the key positions, naturally enough. As far back as the autumn of 1974, the man in charge of the £350 million "sterling money book" had been removed from his post and, a month later, suspended. In the genteel way of the British, the suspension was on full pay, and was kept secret until an investment magazine spilled the beans.

Whatever other factors were involved, knowledgeable City hands were sure that two innocent crimes played a key part in the downfall of the Crown Agents (apart from the central fact that, as their 1833 title of Crown Agents for the Colonies implies, they were never geared to the banking role they later assumed). The first failing was susceptibility to being flattered. The rich luncheons staged in discreet City dining rooms, at which large financial secrets would be freely discussed while the aphrodisiac effect of fine wines and wealth did its work, made officials feel less like flunkies and more like money warlords in their own right. Moreover, great financial acumen is needed to pierce a facade of fine figures that conceals an empty building; men far better trained in money matters than the Agents failed completely to see that the banks in which the Agents invested so heavily were purely *papier-mâché*.

The innocence of at least some of the officials employed by the Agents might explain the idiocies of the one deal that hung most threateningly over their heads as the clear-up continued. Some of the situations could be cleaned out with relative ease; for instance, the Texas

Commerce Bank, partner in the banking subsidiary of the stricken Burston Group, took over the entire bank. But no easy solution was available in the case of Abbey Capital, the Agents' Australian venture and a prime example of how to obtain maximum exposure with minimum sense. This company was committed to a £174 million property development program; and the Agents, although only one of the partners, had undertaken to provide all the finance—a cool £120 million.

The implications, when the Australian property boom, like its cousins around the world, collapsed, were frightful. The portfolio sounded fine and fancy: first-class office blocks in Sydney and Melbourne, the Sydney Hilton, and so on. But the Agents were committed "to provide or procure" £100 million, half of which was nowhere in sight. By late 1975, this singularly ill-judged investment already had cost the Agents £15 million, including the total writeoff of the equity stakes in the companies undertaking the development. Nor did anybody know where the damage would end. The comptroller and auditor general, Sir David Pitblado, a civil servant whose strictures sound a stern accompaniment to the unfolding of the whole Crown Agents' story, noted that "it seems doubtful whether the provision . . . already made will be adequate to meet losses that may fall on the Crown Agents."

Since an annual revenue deficit of £5 million loomed ahead, Sir David's doubts needed no explanation. The accounts that he audited for 1973 and 1974 were the first since 1971. The latter had been glossy, decorated by beautiful and inviting pictures of the projects by which the Agents had set so much misplaced store; in contrast, the two subsequent productions were sober documents of over thirty pages, stuffed with figures and small print. Seldom had any official body managed to create so complex and ramified a confusion by its ventures into the private sector. And never (or so the government must have hoped) would one be allowed to do so again.

Just as the Bank of England in the extremity of the secondary banking crisis had held the bridge like Horatio faced by the Tuscans, so the government gritted its teeth and saw the battle through. The miffed ministers, after all, had the ultimate powers of the purse and Parliament—and would use them. It was made clear that any liquidator who tried to rob the Agents of their due by using the lack of proper banking status as a lever would be robbed in turn by new legislation. This didn't seem to be in the best traditions of British justice—a government passing a retrospective law to recover debts to which otherwise it might not have been entitled; but having made a total mess of supervising its Agents, the Crown now barred no holds in the fight for their survival.

It would not be survival in the same form. Proposals for the restructuring of the Agents were aired as soon as the extent of their mismanagement became known. The cardinal error was to allow a public body of uncertain, hybrid status to develop a dangerous life of its own. The mistake had cost the government and the financial prestige of Britain a great deal more than the £85 million hastily proffered as a grant. And even that saving contribution was beset by the same confusion and incompetence that had caused the crisis of the Crown Agents in the first place. It turned out that the £85 million lacked statutory authority and was thus technically irregular—just like the Agents themselves.

9. Beyond the Fringe

THE Greatest Story Never Told—that is the appropriate title for the extraordinary, interlocking series of scandals and shocks that gave the City of London its most harrowing time since the Great Depression, and which, but for hasty and wholly unprecedented emergency measures, would certainly have led to a wide financial collapse. As it was, the collapses were several and large. But the British public, whose vital interests were at stake, received minimal information about what was happening, whether to threaten or protect its money. Even long after the event few people outside the world of banking knew that another Battle of Britain had been fought and won.

The root of the crisis, to paraphrase Winston Churchill, was that never had so much been owed by so few to so many. The collapses were confined to the secondary banking sector, also known as the "fringe." The latter name, with its intimations of something short of respectability, just beyond the pale, gave the better guide to the true nature of these outfits.

Starting in most cases from tiny bases, they built up in incredibly quick time astounding aggregations of assets. But in banking, assets equal liabilities. The fringe banks took their deposits wherever they could be found, for as short a period as they had to, and lent the money wherever borrowers prepared to pay on onerous terms were gathered, for as long as the borrowers wanted—the classic recipe for banking failure.

The focus was predominantly the property market. Initially the action had also been heavy in shares, but the bull market in equities came to an end while the boom in all kinds of real estate was still working up to full steam. The property developers could afford to pay any interest rates demanded (or so they thought) because of the gigantic capital gains that accrued effortlessly to their developments. Uncompleted buildings changed hands at huge profits. Some were the equivalent of the herrings in a famous Jewish business story—not for eating, but for buying and selling.

What had been created, under the eyes of the Bank of England, was a simulacrum of the lethally unbalanced Wall Street of the late and roaring twenties. Like the stock prices of that era, those of real estate were supported primarily by borrowed money, with only an inadequate base of equity.

As then, the balloon could only stay aloft for so long as the hot air continued to rise. Once prices sank, the need to bolster up shrinking collateral would cause further sales, which would reduce prices still further, which would require further reinforcement of collateral—and so on, until the financial last trump was sounded.

The crisis unfolded so slowly that it was by that token easier for the British authorities to conceal the full horror of events. The recognized starting point was the crash of the fringe bank London & County Securities, later shown to have been flagrantly mismanaged, in November 1973. Probably the last skeleton clattered out of the cupboard in October 1975, when the Bank of England secretly put up £110 million to rescue a shattered Slater Walker Securities—the most famous and prominent of the fringe banks, and the epitome of their multifarious failings. In between these dates, so-called bank after so-called bank either disappeared completely or was kept tenuously alive in a semi-embalmed condition.

The amount of money pumped in by the Bank and the healthier members of the banking system had reached something like £2 billion before the ship could be said to be securely afloat. Plainly somebody, somewhere, had been guilty of monstrous errors of judgment and control. But who were the guilty parties?

Tom Lester—writing in *Management Today* in October 1974 in what remains by far the fullest account of the catastrophe—gave a long and highly plausible list of all the possible causes, starting with the unquestionable profligacy and mismanagement of the secondary banks themselves.

But that wasn't all, by any means. The weakness of the property market, while encouraged by the avid lending of the fringe banks, was not entirely their doing, yet it was a fundamental factor in the latter's fall. Then, the London money market had blossomed (if that is the right word) into newly vigorous life, which saw fringe banks successfully bidding for funds by offering interest rates slightly above the odds, and moneybrokers making quick fortunes by dealing in short-term funds at spiraling interest rates. The whole process was aided and abetted by the treasurers of industrial companies, who found that they could win golden reputations by lending out their surplus funds for the highest rates the market would pay.

None of this, of course, would have been possible had the Bank of England brought its full interventionist weight to bear. But the Bank was preoccupied with its own policy of Competition and Credit Control, which held that healthy competition, including that of the secondary banks, was the very thing required to restore the financial sector of Britain's ailing economy to a rude health that would benefit the entire country.

Unfortunately, the Bank's enthusiasm coincided with a similar enthusiasm in Nos. 10 and 11 Downing Street, where the Heath government was dead set on its now infamous dash for growth. The newly competing banks were consequently primed with the high-octane fuel of an explosive rise in the money supply. Between mid-1970 and early 1974, M3 (currency, current bank accounts, and deposit accounts) rose by the previously unthinkable amount of 270 percent.

It was in this swollen pool of credit that the secondary banks cavorted. They were not alone. In the two years from 1970, total bank advances shot up from an average of £12,400 million to nearly £24,000 million by the end of 1972, largely as a result of the efforts of the large and now liberated clearing banks. But the secondary competitors had grotesquely enlarged their still small market share.

In 1970 London & County's balance sheet totaled a mere smidgen of £5 million. Three years on, the total was £129 million—an expansion of over twenty-five times. Cedar Holdings, another of the disasters, did only half as well. It rose from an £11 million total to £128 million in the same time span. Not only were such second-line banks lending avariciously, into the property market in particular; they were also borrowing heavily themselves, for example, from foreign banks with London operations. By November 1973, the latter were lending £3,850 million into the sector, a figure whose awesome proportions can be assessed from one fact alone: it was hardly less than the clearing banks at that moment were lending to the whole of British manufacturing industry.

Property developers were the most favored borrowers, simply because both their appetite for funds and their willingness to pay exorbitant interest rates were apparently insatiable. Interest rates went as high as 30 percent. Although the lenders might also greedily insist on a 50 percent equity stake in the developments they financed so voraciously, they offset this double greed by readiness to finance, not just the normal prudent 60 or 70 percent of a project, but more than 100 percent. This unusual arithmetical result was achieved by throwing in as extras architects' and surveyors' fees, and other nonbankable goodies.

The high interest paid on property loans by no means marked the end of the fringe bankers' usury. London & County first ran into strong public criticism (which one of its directors, the then Liberal Party leader, Jeremy Thorpe, could especially ill afford) by charging interest on second mortgages that effectively added up to 280 percent. With interest charges like that being exacted, it hardly seemed possible for the fringe banks not to make fortunes from their fast-growing assets. But such a conclusion failed to take proper account of the fringe bankers' inexhaustible capacity for business error.

A basic failure, common to nearly all the failed, was to confuse hopelessly the banking and nonbanking activities of the group. The banking side customarily financed the other investments, so that if they went sour, the bank was stuck with a bad debt—none the less bad for being internal. Since the inhabitants of the fringe had a touching, but misplaced, faith in their ability to turn all they handled into gold, the risks became intolerable. Tom Lester quoted as merely one example of the mad diversification along the fringe a company called J. H. Vavasseur, which increased its assets fourfold in the two years to 1973, acquiring interests in banking, property, foreign exchange, unit trusts, life insurance, film production, a crocodile farm in South Africa, etc., etc.

To this complexity, the directors added that of interlocking deals. Thus Vavasseur's life assurance company had too much of its assets in one office building; so the parent obligingly agreed to buy the block if need be. Need was—but by then the parent was in no position to buy anything at all.

At London & County, the last half-year profit figures it ever issued were found to have arisen entirely from the sale of shares in one of its associated companies, in a deal that had been financed by London & County itself. It was the kind of sharp practice in which the fringe bankers specialized—all unbeknown to the investors who owned their shares, the depositors who placed their money in the banks, and (presumably) the regulatory authorities who were supposed to guard the purity of the City of London.

All the key directors of the banks had large share stakes in the companies, and thus had strong vested interests in keeping the share price on the boil. The shares were often acquired in the easiest manner imaginable. Thus, bundles of 70,000, worth as much as £170,000 in the inflated values of the period, were handed out to the favored few. Shareholdings were not the only way in which nests were feathered. One London & County director probably holds the all-time record: a loan of £1.2 million was extended to this single fortunate individual.

In the banks on which these persons battened, one cardinal sin was committed every day, which, even if the directors had not been addicted to complication and mild corruption, would almost certainly have proved fatal sooner or later. Take Cedar as a conspicuous example. At the end of 1973, the bank held 85 percent of its deposits for less than three months; only 4 percent of the entire portfolio was for more than a year. This money was locked up, moreover, not only in longer-term property loans, or in the aforesaid usurious mortgages, but also in consumer loans repayable over as long as three years.

The ability of these spectacularly unsound banks to attract deposits from greedy industrial treasurers would not have been enough to finance their mushroom growth. They also opened many and generous lines of credit with the respectable clearing banks; the National Westminster, for example, had two dozen secondary banks among its customers; only two of its wild bunch did not have to be rescued from drowning. Still more important was the money market, where great quantities of money, let loose by Competition and Credit Control (Uncontrol would have been a better title), and by the government's abortive dash for economic freedom, were sloshing around.

In a mere couple of years, the liquid funds traded between banks quadrupled to £8 billion, and the secondary banks dipped freely into this lake—either at first or second hand. The stage had been set, wholly inadvertently, for a terrible disaster. Yet even when London & County collapsed, nobody read the signs as portending widespread calamity for the whole fringe—not even the Bank of England. The sole regulatory financial institution in Britain demonstrated its ignorance of the true situation by choosing First National Finance Corporation as its proper partner to rescue the battered hulk of London & County. No bunch of beleaguered officials has ever jumped out of the frying pan into the fire with more alacrity.

FNFC had been built up by Pat Matthews, an overbearing entrepreneur originally seduced away from the furniture trade by the greater attractions of installment purchase finance. Like many of the fringe operators, Matthews was not content merely to exploit his profitable corner of the financial world. He wanted to get to the center of the stage, to become a *real* banker. The ambition was a trifle quixotic, given that the U.K. authorities were none too precise about what a bank was. The fringe banks nearly all had the word "Bank" in their various company titles somewhere; yet the bank of banks, the Bank of England, had not authorized them as banks at all. They could only claim "123" status.

The numbers referred to a section of the Companies Act that exempted the concern from the restrictions of the Moneylenders' Acts. (The British have a long historical dislike of moneylenders, who are not entitled to enforce collection of their debts unless they are registered.) Any nasty little outfit that had its "123" certificate could open its office, usually in the West End, safely remote from the supervisory eye of the Bank in Threadneedle Street, and do business. But ambitious operators like Matthews of FNFC were after grander game—and the figures chart the astonishing degree to which they were apparently able to succeed.

Back in 1965, FNFC had just over £4 million of deposits and £9 million of long-term loans. By far the biggest deployment of the funds was in installment debt: £7.5 million. The company earned a very respectable after-tax profit of £480,000. Move on to 1973, and FNFC is a very different animal—an elephant. Deposits now total £346.5 million, an amazing rise of eighty-two times; the company's liabilities, other than those to depositors, are now £98 million; the installment debt, although it too has swollen mightily, is a mere drop in this ocean at £40 million; the debts and deposits, just over five times the ordinary capital in 1965, now represent a staggering multiple of thirty-seven times the equity.

This was the jerry-built structure on which the Bank of England rested its hopes for a tidy conclusion to the mess at London & County. Not only that: when the Bank actually went in as Matthews's partner, it was "a . . . move which," as Tom Lester commented in 1974, "gave FNFC more status than any authorisation which the Bank could devise, and which raised several eyebrows in the City." Before long the eyebrows had lifted right off City foreheads. FNFC's reported profit of £9.8 million for 1973 turned into losses of £8.3 million in 1974, and a horrendous £82 million in 1975 as the rescuer's plight proved to be no more enviable than that of the rescued.

In the first half of 1975 alone, FNFC managed to lose the remarkable amount of £73 million, when £91 million had to be written off the value of its loans, mainly in the property sector. By the time all the damage had been counted by the dismayed authorities, £140 million of the £350 million that FNFC had committed to property loans had disappeared.

Committed was the right word—FNFC's deposits had gone into house-building, commercial development, flats, house conversion, and even hotels. With losses like that to be accommodated, it was small wonder that an unhappy deputy chairman admitted to the world that the company was "advancing to a position of technical insolvency."

Few more delicate formulas for the indelicate business of going bust have ever been devised. It meant that the support organized for the company by the Bank of England (whose own prestige would hardly allow its erstwhile and brief protégé to go under) had to be arranged all over again. The total bill was £360 million: of that, £50 million was in subordinated loans, £120 million was extended to the fortunately profitable consumer credit division, while the massive sum of £190 million would only attract interest as and when the shattered remnants of FNFC had any profits from which payments could be made.

The degree of shattering can be measured by one vicious vital statistic. Between December 31, 1974, and October 31 the following year, FNFC's deposits collapsed from £356.5 million to only £40.7 million. The whole grim experience merely repeated on a somewhat larger scale what two banks that actually were allowed to crash demonstrated in miniature; but the miniatures themselves were far too large for comfort. Thus, Cannon Street Acceptances went down for the third time with a total deficit of £24.1 million. The run on the bank in just twelve weeks had totaled £45 million, and not even £20 million from the Bank of England's rescue scheme could save the shareholders and unsecured creditors from their fate.

Over at Triumph Investment Trust, where the total deficit was £48 million, some £14 million of shareholders' capital went out of the window. It wasn't just indiscreet corporate treasurers and wild-eyed investors who put too much faith in presiding genius Tom Whyte. The afflicted included Lloyds Bank, one of Britain's finest, whose total involvement was put at £30 million, including a debenture shared with a consortium bank of highest caliber (the shareholders included First National of Chicago, Crédit Lyonnais, Commerzbank, and the Banco di Roma, as dignified a collection as there ever was).

The debenture holders had the wry consolation that the depositors got repaid under the Bank of England scheme (by which £30 million had been put up); so long, that is, as their deposits were "shown to the satisfaction of the Bank of England to have been taken direct in the course of banking business from persons unconnected with the [Triumph] group." The proviso becomes understandable when you learn that the crashed Triumph contained no fewer than 216 companies within its ample embrace. (They had a book value of £22 million, which had crumbled to a realizable £4 million at the end of the day.)

By the spring of 1975 the out-of-business banks, including the two mentioned above, added up to over £400 million of one-time assets; that does not include two operations—Burston Finance and First Maryland —whose asset totals were unavailable. Another eight banks had disappeared into larger institutions for amounts ranging from the £34.7 million that Standard and Chartered paid for Hodge Group to the "nominal" (i.e., minuscule) sum that Williams and Glyn's paid for a sad affair named Cripps Warburg. And Philadelphia National Bank, in a typical story of the epoch, was forced to buy for £1.5 million the majority stake in the Western Credit consumer finance operation, an enterprisingly run joint venture which also proved unable to withstand the adverse tides.

Such fiascos were demonstrably and pathetically true of the fringe as a whole. Nothing like this manifestation of all the vices to which banking can succumb is likely ever to be seen again, if only because the Bank of England has woken up to the dangers its officials were courting. The innocent onlooker may well wonder how on earth the authorities could hope to be authoritative if they were that ignorant beforehand. The answer is plain as the blush which should have been on their collective face. Had the knowledge been at hand, and acted on, the Greatest Story Never Told would never have happened.

10. Women and Children First

THE disaster which struck the City of London in 1974 was sedulously presented as an accident on the fringe, if not beyond it. In truth, as the previous chapter noted, the primary institutions of the City were involved as bankers to the afflicted and as lenders of last resort (a delectably abstract phrase that became embarrassingly concrete) to the devastated property sector. But that was by no means the end of their involvement. Some members of the City in good standing created their own private financial hells. And all the dignitaries of London's financial world got dragged along willy-nilly when the fringe disaster passed the point of no return.

The Establishment has always been uneasy about the success of relative newcomers. Its policy, by and large, was the well-tried principle, If you can't beat 'em, buy 'em. This habit was best illustrated when installment credit companies began to show the banks a fairly clean pair of heels. The big banks dealt with the problem by buying into the credit firms on the grand scale. In fact, installment credit (hire purchase to the British housewife) is an industry of checkered recent past.

When Britain's consumer economy began to develop a real head of postwar steam, the credit firms were so eager to enlarge their business that Donald Duck would have had scant trouble negotiating a loan at one stage of the game. That phase culminated in a welter of bad debts, giving the industry so severe a shock that, you might imagine, prudence would have been seared into its collective soul.

Not so: worse excesses by far were in store. Before these materialized, however, the installment credit firms had again become desirable financial properties. The apotheosis of First National Finance Corporation was only one example. Another was a vigorous stock market battle for the business of Bowmaker: the chalice, won by the C. T. Bowring insurance and shipping business, turned out to be poisoned.

So dire was Bowmaker's emergency (even though it was less extreme than that of other houses) that no normal means of saving the company and its once-proud parent could have worked. In this situation the Bank of England showed much the same presence of mind as an onlooker snatching a baby from a sinking vessel with a boat hook: it noted that only abnormal means would save a situation that was so far gone.

Bowmaker's rescue proved the most successful of all the millions upon millions of loans that the Bank of England duly sent in the direction of sinking or sunk companies. As late as the autumn of 1976, Bowmaker was the only recipient of emergency aid (£90 million had been needed) to repay its loans and escape (after a 30 percent staff cut) from a global rescue operation unprecedented in either scale or necessity.

The operation became known to posterity as "the lifeboat" (the full title, invented by some desperate banking wag, was "The National Joint Stock Bankers' Lifeboat Institution"). The original notion was that those manning the lifeboat would merely recycle funds: as deposits fled from the sinking secondary banks, etc., the money would head for the big clearing banks, who would promptly redeposit the loot whence it came. The theory was engaging, but foundered on the reality of the victims' heavy involvement in property—Bowmaker's single stroke of good fortune was its "quite insignificant" stake in property, meaning that, unlike its shipwrecked brethren, it was not crucified by high interest charges outrunning the negligible or nonexistent income on properties whose market value had slumped by 30 percent.

The full measure of the catastrophe can be seen from the grisly experience of United Dominions Trust (UDT). In a single year, UDT, the doyen of the installment credit business, managed to lose £32.4 million before tax, to drop £6 million from its investments, to write off £25 million from its assets (including a one-quarter reduction in the value of its head office), and to bring its total cut in reserves to no less than £59 million. The company had to slash its payroll by 1,000 jobs, and to close 30 "money shops"—mini-banks opened in Britain's High Streets. To survive even in this reduced state, UDT required a scarcely credible amount of assistance from the lifeboat—£450 million, or a clear billion in dollars at the prevailing rates of exchange.

The tragic reflection is that none of this disaster was necessary. UDT's managers had come to the exciting conclusion that the world of finance offered far juicier rewards than the ones they were currently enjoying. It was thus positively incumbent upon them to encourage pseudo-banking initiatives in all directions, nearly all of which misfired in so explosive a manner that, even when the chairman (a new one, naturally) announced that after a "salutary year" the company had "wiped the slate clean," UDT's slate still carried intact the £450 million owing to the lifeboat consortium.

About the only consolation which UDT could draw from its experiences was that it had so many companions in misery. Mercantile Credit, for example, was taken over by Barclays Bank; otherwise this company too, it was said, would have needed £100 million-plus of lifeboat aid to stay afloat. In theory, at the sight of another drowning passenger the lifeboat would have refused to sally forth, given the reluctance of the Establishment banks, with £1,200 to £1,300 million and thirty salvaged wrecks in the lifeboat, to advance any more.

Ever since the recycling mechanism had failed to revolve, the great clearing banks (and their boatmaster, the Bank of England) had found themselves at an impasse. If they withdrew support, the existing lifeboat loans would have been of dubious value—and these represented *half* the capital and reserves of the clearers. If the latter stayed in, they would still lose money, but not so much.

The brutal fact lent added poignancy to the remark by one highly placed source to the effect that "you can't go into an operation of this kind and fail." The bankers had a tiger by the tail. But not only did they keep the public largely uninformed about the perilous situation: those responsible shrouded themselves in mysterious verbal cloaks such as "somebody close to the lifeboat committee"—a personage who made several appearances in contemporary reports of the crisis, during which the committee was in almost continuous session. He was presumably one Jasper Quintus Hollom (later Sir Jasper), the Bank of England official who at the end of 1973 launched the lifeboat on its dangerous voyage.

It wasn't just that the crew found itself carrying debts not of its own choosing as depositors fled the sinking secondary ships. The problem was that the unchosen debts were so often bad. From the very first, it was clear that the banks would have to write off part of the lifeboat loans, but they hoped to limit the damage to £30 million. In the event, the provisions had to be four times as high; and, even so, that total was "less than expected" when the sirens were at their loudest.

The burden had been shared around the City as equitably as possible; still, some of the individual loads were huge. Both Barclays and the National Westminster, for example, were in for £300 million. The smaller Lloyds got by with half this exposure, with the Midland handing over more than Lloyds and the Scottish banks dutifully bringing up the rear. Not only were these loans like the celebrated curate's egg ("bad in parts"), but the institutions in receipt of the largesse were often in no position to pay any interest, so some of the interest had to be added to the debt or "rolled forward." The process is far less comfortable than it sounds, and threw a curious light on one bank chairman's argument that the losses on its part of the support operation would probably be covered by the profit on the lending itself. He didn't say *when*.

By the spring of 1975, some of the lenders who presumably were actually paying their interest had begun to complain quite bitterly about the cost of the loans. But neither bankrupts nor beggars can be choosers, and the lenders for their part had cogent reasons for exacting the highest price the traffic could (or rather couldn't) bear. The extent of their pains can be seen from the figures that the National Westminster was obliged to parade. The amount set aside against doubtful loans was £40 million. Nor was this simply the cost of manning the lifeboat. The chief executive, Alex Dibbs, admitted that his bank's lending on property had exceeded the average by 7 percent. That small number meant a massive commitment of £110–115 million more than Dibbs's bank would have lent to this sector had it adhered to the banking norm.

But the consequences of normality were not such as to inspire great confidence in Britain's bankers, either. The property boom which they had directly and indirectly helped to finance had piled up a collective property company debt of not quite £3 billion (owed by the real estate developers and their unhappy creditors). This represented 13 percent of all advances, a full quarter of the loan portfolios of non-clearing banks: and its value became increasingly putative as the crisis rolled on.

The joke of it all (though the joke's point would have been lost on the victims) was that the property boom, both at the time and during its miserable aftermath, was the supreme symbol of capitalist exploitation under the Conservative administration of Edward Heath. The indignation against the gigantic profits made by the developers grew so intense that the Heath government was itself moved to clap a levy on a property bonanza whose capital gains, nine times out of ten, were purely on paper. The government, with the impeccable timing characteristic of British statesmen, acted at exactly the point when the market, like all booms, was about to bust.

Just so did Harold Macmillan appoint an ex-admiral to alleviate the post-Suez tanker shortage, and James Callaghan, in 1976, nominate his minister of sport to take action to save Britain from drought. In the first case the tanker shortage promptly turned into a glut overnight; in the 1976 instance, the heavens opened forthwith, and flooded the dry land. The deluge which similarly descended on the property market not only swept away profits and all hope of profits, so that years later developers were still losing enormous sums; it also threatened to undermine the foundations of British finance, since industrial, commercial, and residential property provides the collateral for most lending.

The situation became so threatening that a Socialist government under Harold Wilson was forced to take action to relieve the Conservative squeeze on a property industry whose very existence was anathema to the "Left." But no moves within the government's power could improve the basic equation that had destroyed the industry's finances.

Like any income-producing investment, an office block has only one underlying source of value—its yield. That, in turn, depends on what rent can be charged for the space. But the chargeable rent is not infinitely high (though some developers in the City of London tried their best to disprove this eternal truth). If the finite rents provide a yield that is unattractive in relation to other investments, then the value of the property must fall until the yields come into line.

Any first-year economics student will at once conclude that if interest rates rise, property values will drop—unless rents rise in step. As the bough breaks, in other words, the baby must fall. Not only were rents frozen in Britain, but much of the property littering the city centers was either unlet or uncompleted, and thus its carrying charges went up while its potential value went down. Suppose you have an investment of 100, four-fifths of which is financed by debt at 15 percent, with a potential yield of 8 percent when let. What happens if interest rates rise by a couple of points?

Your equity is wiped out, for a start. You are still paying interest on loans that are only just covered by the collateral, and any deterioration will put you still deeper into jeopardy. Since the liabilities of all property companies were many times their equity base, the classic bottomless pit had been created—no matter how much money had been poured in to fill up the hole, more would still have been required so long as the market went on falling. It would not have taken long for nearly every property developer in the land to have become insolvent —and with them, no doubt, much of the British banking system.

It says something for the caution of the British merchant banks that their property involvement—so far as it came to light—was generally restrained. Over the years the influence of these blue-blooded investment houses has declined, partly because their financial strength has steadily fallen in comparison with that of the large clearing banks. In addition, the latter have used their greater brawn to muscle in on old merchant banking territory. Despite competition from above and below, where the fringe banks boastfully nibbled at the merchant banks' territory, few of the latter succumbed to contemporary lures. Their blunders were mostly on traditional ground, like tanker finance, where sums as elementary as those in the property market were ignored or miscalculated at hideous cost.

Two gross exceptions were Keyser Ullman and William Brandt's; the grossness which afflicted both was the collapse of the property market, in which they were heavily overlent. Brandt's bank was a member of the inner circle, one of eighteen banks that comprise the Accepting House Committee and thus revel in a special relationship with the Bank of England. In the wake of its awful losses (£19 million of provisions against a £90 million property portfolio, a £15.3 million deficit on a year's trading, plus other provisions of £15.4 million), Brandt, no longer independent, left the Committee; it looked like an officer being stripped of his epaulettes before being cashiered.

The practical result of the disgrace was that Citibank increased its large holding in Brandt's parent company as prelude to a refinancing operation in which the total needs were put at £30 million. In the circumstances, the statement of a spokesman for the U.S. bank was worthy of the stiffest upper lip ever sported by an Englishman. A contemporary report noted that ". . . a Citibank spokesman said in London last night that the bank was not worried by the situation" at Brandt's.

At that, there were even more worrying City horrors than the Brandt's imbroglio (which ended with its virtual disappearance into its parent company, National and Grindlays). Among those worries, none was a more spectacular story of hubris leading to nemesis than the sorry saga of Keyser Ullman (KU).

In the postwar period KU had by and large minded its manners and kept its place below the salt as one of the lesser merchant banks. The fourth generation of a founding family, Ronald Franklin, and his brother-in-law, Ian Stoutzker, were in day-to-day charge, and a leading Tory politico and unit trust pioneer, Edward Du Cann, was chairman. There was thus nothing in KU's stars that hinted at the incredible transformation to come. But mainly thanks to Wagnerian expansion in the single year of 1972, the lesser KU became the largest merchant bank, measured by assets, in the entire City. Two whopping deals—the £69 million purchase of a property company, and the £58 million acquisition of a fringe bank—plus the backing of the mighty Prudential Insurance, had apparently taken KU permanently into the big leagues.

The impression was only confirmed when KU sold on its property purchase for cash and netted a £28 million profit in the process. (The purchaser, another property company, despite excellent management and connections, had to struggle to keep its head above water.) But anybody who thought that KU had successfully negotiated the hazards of the property market was sadly misled. A staggering four-fifths of its lending was on property—the fringe bank sin *in excelsis*. KU's buy, Dalton Barton, was run by a couple of sidekicks named Jack Dellal and Stanley Van Gelder. Of Dellal, known to the satirical magazine *Private Eye* as Black Jack, it was said that he was "a great lender of money." The remark was certainly true quantitatively; quality was another matter.

In the 1974–75 financial year, provisions against bad debts came to £82.5 million, bringing the total to £119 million. The lifeboat had to provide £65 million of loans to keep KU afloat, and it appeared that almost half the money lent out so vigorously might never come back home. Dellal and Van Gelder were first to leave the wreck (with their bruises gently plastered by a £27,000 payoff). Franklin and Stoutzker followed: "Their departure marks a break. I think that break must now be demonstrated," said Derek Wilde, the new chairman. Wilde was a transfer from Barclays. The big banks, in fact, provided most of the desperately needed new blood for lifeboat passengers, a process that gave the careers of some long-service company men a presumably agreeable and totally unexpected change—and, indeed, uplift.

Wilde stood out for a certain crispness of phrase and a rigorous attitude toward debts. He blamed the bad debts of the bank on "a mistaken policy within one short but disastrous period of its history," and insisted on providing in full against all doubtful loans, unpaid interest, and the cost of carrying loans. A columnist for the *Sunday Times* (London) measured the scale of the disaster at KU by noting that, had the same calamities struck a bank as big as the National Westminster, a sum of £4 billion would have disappeared. It was lucky that no larger institution had fallen into the hands of the Fearless KU Four.

KU's catastrophe was an elemental example of the bad business that had ruined companies good and bad. A year after the main wave of collapses, the deputy chief executive of Natwest opined that the recent events were not simply a passing difficulty but "a serious and deep-seated crisis in the secondary banking system." The conclusion the speaker drew from all this was that ". . . sound banking rests not on the financing of transactions as much as on an understanding of the total circumstances of the customer and a continuing relationship with him." But had the secondary crisis and the unsound banking of its creators been impenetrable mysteries before the collapses?

Did the City Establishment know what was going on? If so, why was nothing done to warn the politicians and the public of the death-watch beetles in the City's woodwork? After the crash, a Machiavellian explanation was advanced—naturally, from the fringe sector itself. The big clearing banks, so it was said, had only waited for their small rivals to fall in order to stab them in the back. Not so much a lifeboat, in other words; more a dinner party at the Borgias. Like most conspiracy theories, this one was inherently implausible. You don't take a sledgehammer to crack a nut—and then drop the thing on your own big toe.

The truth of the matter is that the City has always divided into two utterly different zones. By far the largest, wealthiest, and most significant are the great banks and insurance companies, which in their ponderous, unimaginative way go about their business with reasonable efficiency, never making any mistakes that cannot be decently and invisibly interred (although Lloyds certainly broke that rule by its foreign exchange fiasco in Lugano). Outside this inner zone cluster the lesser houses, most of them eager to get in, some of them so noisy that they, rather than the inner denizens, get publicly identified as "the City"—which they are not.

A few outer-dwellers come inside, by dint of proving themselves as respectable and reliable as the original inhabitants. A few others blow up and disappear from sight, leaving more or less damage behind them. The rise and fall of the fringe only differed in its spread and scale. The size of the phenomenon was the factor that cracked the City's code. Because of the law-abiding nature of the inhabitants of the inner zone, it is as easy to police as the Forbidden City of Peking. The citizens are highly unlikely to misbehave in the first place, and nods and winks, rather than whips, are enough to check any rare tendency to stray.

In the outer zone, conduct unbecoming to officers and gentlemen is commonplace, which in itself is enough to persuade the inner gentlemen to avert their eyes. Knocking the competition is not the done thing; even noticing the competition is a trifle unnecessary. But nods, winks, and *noblesse oblige* were totally inadequate to control the fringe phenomenon or to prevent its overflow from engulfing the inner zone banks as well. In manning the lifeboats, the latter were not actually saving the fringe: most of the fringe's overlords were lost overboard, anyway, and hardly any of their institutions survived in recognizable form. No; the inner City, in the last analysis, put out to sea to save itself.

The lack of an effective policing system for the City, in which the big banks connived because informal regulation suited their own books, proved disastrous in a situation where the main action was taking place outside the inner zone and beyond the direct influence of the inner banks. Hindsight says that the Establishment could have done far more to arrest and criticize the excesses beyond, far less to finance those excesses by extending the usual financial facilities. Hindsight ignores the pervasive influence of an atmosphere inimical to that kind of interference. All the same, it was partly the Establishment's own fault that the lifeboat put to sea on a voyage that lasted so much longer and cost so much more than the crew had ever expected in its blackest moments.

11. Lax Old Lady

No central bank luxuriates in so appreciative a reputation as the Bank of England. Possibly no British institution receives so much respect from both the knowing and the ignorant. Its honesty and technical competence are taken so much for granted that the Bank has survived onslaughts in the seventies that would surely have demolished a lesser and less well-guarded fame.

Some of the main accusations against the Bank have already appeared in these pages: that it was the prime mover in the fateful relaxation of controls that helped to unleash the secondary banks; that it allowed a catastrophic expansion of the money supply, which created a disastrous hyper-inflation; that it showed woeful ignorance of who was who and what was what in the early days of the crisis.

These allegations are not the only ones. Time and again, the Bank has been accused of bungling its job when managing the value of sterling on the foreign exchanges. To cap it all, in 1976 the Bank was sued by Burmah Oil on the grounds that the former had in effect cheated shareholders of hundreds of millions by buying their shares in British Petroleum under duress. And an official of the supposedly incorruptible Bank had to be suspended as reports spread that profits running into the millions had been made by elementary abuses of the exchange controls administered by the Bank.

That loophole has since been closed. But even this closure typifies another criticism of Britain's central Bank: that it never locks any stable doors until far too many horses have bolted. All in all, even if the above accusations are only half-true, they add up to a damaging enough roster. How is it, then, that the virtuous reputation of the Old Lady of Threadneedle Street has survived so largely unscathed?

The answer lies partly in the secrecy that has always surrounded the Bank, and that is symbolized by the blank walls its famous building, in the heart of the City of London, presents to the world. Its officials do give interviews, more now than ever in the past, but the interviews are incognito. It publishes an annual report which never fails to show a profit (hardly surprising, since the Bank has a monopoly of England's banknote supply) and which also records the occasional embarrassment —like the £9 million-plus which the Bank had to write off as its share of the lifeboat loans that saved the secondary bank sector from instant extinction.

The Bank is the better able to preserve its secrecy because of its public ownership. In theory, nationalization (visited on the Bank by the first postwar Labour government) should result in less secrecy, not more. But the Bank's own reticence is wrapped up in that of an almost equally taciturn organization, the treasury. Between them, the two have conspired to keep as much daylight as possible from reaching the dark backrooms where British economic policy is misconceived. In fact, the treasury for years refused even to make public the economic forecasts on which it was basing its misjudgments, while the Bank, in addition to the regular release of manifestly cooked figures for Britain's official reserves, equally shied away from naming any figures from which its policy on monetary control could be derived.

The secrecy is only typical of British government in general. So is another curious aspect of the Bank's affairs. There is no regulatory agency for Britain's commercial banks. This believe-it-or-not situation may have some advantages over that in the United States, where there are too many regulators; but the resulting vacuum is filled by the Bank. This regulatory role, flexible to the point of looseness, is combined with two others (the plurality of role is also typically British). The Bank has all the usual national functions of a central bank. And it is also supposed to be the arbiter, guide, and voice of the City of London.

Until the secondary bank crisis exposed the weakness of its arrangements, the Bank did not even have an established department responsible for the regulation of the banks. A senior subordinate of the chief cashier was in charge, aided by a handful of officials, and operating under the title "principal of the discount office." (The archaic names of an institution that is headed by a Governor and a Court have a more than symbolic significance.) After the crisis, the Bank at last split the Discount Office into two. The old job of running relations with the London discount market was separated from bank regulation, which became a separate function.

The move was coupled with the observation that the number of banks in London had doubled to 300 in the previous 7 years, which had obviously increased the regulatory load. But this expansion cannot have gone unnoticed by the Bank—why had it persisted so long with an anomalous and dangerous system?

The best answer seems to be that the Bank in the first place prefers to let sleeping dogs lie; and in the second, needs overmuch convincing that the dogs, far from being asleep, are charging around the place, frothing at the mouth, and biting everybody in sight. The second defect is especially obvious in the Bank's behavior as custodian of the City's good name; it has sometimes shown an apparently woeful lack of knowledge about what is actually going on.

The proofs are plentiful enough. As the fringe banks burgeoned, not a hint came from the Bank that the practices of the secondary banks were causing it any concern; in fact, by going into partnership with the crippled and grossly overlent First National Finance Corporation for the first of its rescue operations, the Bank revealed a total lack of the inside information that outsiders would suppose it to have. Equally, only after Lloyds had laid its £30 million egg in Lugano did the Bank send out instructions telling the 260 authorized foreign exchange banks in London how to behave themselves. Either the Bank simply didn't know, pre-Lugano, that hairy dealing was going on in the foreign exchange markets; or it knew, but decided that intervention was unnecessary. Either way, Threadneedle Street was culpable.

As for the property boom, which would have been impossible without the heavy financing from the banking system, the Bank's sole reaction was a mild directive to the banks in the autumn of 1972, requesting them to make credit less freely available to property companies and for nonindustrial purposes. In the conditions of the time, which the Bank had helped to create, the request had about as much effect as Canute's celebrated injunction to the tides.

The most significant and fateful of those contemporary conditions was the expansion of the money supply by 60 percent in two years, an unprecedented surge that made hyper-inflation inevitable. Whether the Bank approved of this amazing phenomenon or not, history fails to record. But there is some reason to believe that the Bank may not, odd though it sounds, have been fully aware of the development or its implications before it was too late. Part of the evidence came in October 1976, when the Bank was apparently caught unawares by figures showing that in the three months to October the money supply had again zoomed upward at an annual rate of over a quarter. The implication was that for three months the Bank had not been performing its single most crucial job—and didn't know it.

But 1976 was a bad year for the Bank's technical experts in other fields as well. The extraordinary sterling collapse that year could not be blamed on the Bank—ultimately, the fall was the inevitable result of the government's huge spending deficit. But at various points the Bank's management of the market in sterling created more confusion and problems than it was designed to resolve. The most notorious example came in the late spring, when the Bank, apparently wishing to prevent a small burst of support for the pound from carrying the price too high, sold sterling itself—and let the fact be known to the market.

The market, not surprisingly, thought that if the Bank wanted the pound to go lower, lower it would go: and thus began the Great Sterling Slide. From then on, nothing the Bank could do stabilized the currency. If it supported the pound, precious reserves (all borrowed from other countries) were lost without trace. If it didn't support the pound, the rate dropped sickeningly. Somehow or other, the Bank had maneuvered itself into a no-win situation; and maybe a fatal insensitivity to the mood of markets had played a part.

Insensitivity of another kind was certainly shown in the case of Burmah Oil. This company was the British equivalent of the Lockheed/W. T. Grant/Penn Central lending disasters in the United States. The directors had become bored with a soft and comfortable position as a small oil producer with a vast, trouble-free 25 percent stake in British Petroleum and a smaller but also rich chunk of Shell. They exchanged their life of ease for a hopefully dynamic future as an integrated oil company, diversified industrial conglomerate, and tanker entrepreneur rolled into one.

The shareholders who protested at this swap, which was accompanied by a buildup in loans from banks and others to £182.2 million in 1972, against £142.7 million of ordinary capital, were treated with scant respect. The maltreatment was nothing, however, compared to what the Bank of England meted out when Burmah, paralyzed by a £30 million loss on its tanker operations, was directed to Threadneedle Street for salvation. The deal included the purchase of Burmah's entire B.P. holding for £179 million.

The Burmah board was in no position to argue, since it needed (and desperately) Bank guarantees for $650 million of borrowings which financed its ambitious expansion in the United States, where Burmah had bought Signal Oil & Gas. But within months the Bank was showing a paper profit of over £100 million on its purchase; and as the B.P. share price went on mounting, so did the indignation of the Burmah shareholders.

The old board's indifference to shareholders' complaints was not shared by the new directors. Their task would plainly be much easier if they, rather than the Bank, could get their mitts on the B.P. capital appreciation. On October 6, 1976, Burmah duly issued a writ, almost certainly without precedent, requiring that the Bank forthwith return the shares at the price paid. By that time the paper profit was heading toward £300 million. Although it couldn't help looking like one of the biggest rip-offs in history, there was one offsetting factor: Burmah was still in debt to the Bank for £85 million of standby facilities and $100 million of dollar loan guarantees.

Still, it could not do a central bank's image any good to extract the principal asset of a beleaguered client when the latter was flat on its back, and then to cling to a profit that was quite plainly not envisaged at the time. But the Bank had shown some disregard for commercial fine points before.

When London & County led the fringe bank collapses, the Bank refused to accept that £1 million owed to the Fidelity Life insurance business was a deposit. The chairman of the parent Fidelity Corporation of Richmond, Virginia, threatened to close the insurance company, much to its policyholders' distress, on the grounds that "since the Bank of England will not stand behind its English subsidiary, we are not prepared to stand behind ours." In the Burmah case, but not the Fidelity one, the Bank could argue that it was acting at the government's behest, and that the B.P. share windfall was a side issue compared to the central one of whether the government (which already owned half of the oil giant) should enlarge its control. This is a familiar pose for the Bank's defenders. In most of its external functions, it operates as an agent, not a principal.

If the government has not made up its mind about whether or not to support sterling, the Bank must dither too. If the government is running so large a budgetary deficit that its financing needs cannot be met by selling so-called gilt-edged stocks, then the Bank will find it impossible to curb the growth of the money supply. If the government sees energetic monetary expansion as the key to a growth breakthrough for the economy, how can the Bank refuse to operate the policy decreed by its political masters?

Even if the above points are conceded, few now doubt that the Bank made a unique contribution to the shambles in the City by its introduction of the Competition and Credit Control policy. For years monetary policy had been run on ultra-traditional lines, with its cornerstone the Thursday announcement of the mystical figure known as Bank Rate. In its rough and ready way, the system worked well enough; but piece by piece it was taken apart. Bank Rate was itself abolished, to be replaced by something called Minimum Lending Rate, which in due course, as the sterling crisis deepened in 1976, came to be announced on Thursdays—when to all intents and purposes it was indistinguishable from Bank Rate.

That process, too, was typical of postwar British history: the wheel of change turning full circle, back to where it started. Insofar as the Competition and Control movement had a rationale, it lay in the belief that the commercial banks were too cozy, competed too little with each other, and never would wake up and fight unless they were freed from the official cartel that strict Bank of England control necessarily implied. Freedom to compete, it was believed, would turn back the rising tide of competition from foreign and fringe banks, and produce unquantifiable but highly desirable benefits for the banks' industrial and private customers.

In their commercial innocence, the Bank's officials had failed to realize that the big banks were hidebound more by their responsibilities than by any artificial restraints. It was the newcomers who reveled in the freedom as the money spawned by the Heath government's overexpansionary policies flooded forth.

Whether the Bank's new ideas would have worked in an atmosphere of controlled monetary growth, nobody will ever know. In the context of unrestrained credit, the ideas proved disastrous, and the Bank's attachment to them no doubt played a part in slowing down its never lightning reactions.

At a time when governments are contriving to obtain the worst of both worlds in their economic policies, no central bank can be expected to perform any better. But in more successful economies than Britain's, the central bank does have more clearly defined independence from the government and is able to act as a restraining influence, and sometimes as a spare rudder, on economic policy. Because the Bank of England is not independent, however, it is not an effective restraint; nor is it accountable. Whether or not any of the charges against the Bank are wholly true, one thing is wholly certain: no Bank heads have been seen to fall in public, and probably none have fallen in private, as a consequence of the failure.

The results of this catalogue of divided and unclear responsibilities, of miscalculations and misjudgments, of oversights and slow reactions, have appeared in previous chapters. The collapses and near-crashes of British and London-based banks do not reflect credit on the Bank of England's supervisory function. True, as a leading monetary analyst put it later, the rescue operation organized by the Bank averted "a financial crash of 1929 dimensions." But prevention is much better than cure in monetary matters, especially since the cure cost the sound banks large losses and the unsound banks calamitous ones.

The cure did not, true again, cost genuine depositors anything more than some desperately anxious moments. The crashes, remarked one banker, "have been very easy deaths." It is doubtful whether shareholders would have agreed, or would have been overjoyed by another banker's observation that providers of risk capital have nothing of which to complain if they lose the lot. A well-run financial system does not allow thirty or more institutions, both significant and insubstantial, to move simultaneously into positions so overexposed as to stretch credulity. The lifeboat loan to United Dominions Trust, for example, was half as big again as the largest sum ever raised in the City by an industrial company—presumably for a better purpose than cleaning up the damage after some woeful mismanagement.

For the losses incurred, the dangers run, and the disaster threatened, the Bank must take its share of the responsibility. The informal methods that it preferred (and still prefers) proved adequate when the crunch came, although it isn't easy to fail in a financial operation when you have unlimited funds. But every time the Bank, in the post-crisis period, demanded information from more banks, and more information from all banks, it implicitly criticized its own previous requirements. Did it really need the biggest crisis since 1929 to persuade the Bank that fringe banks, too, should be obliged to supply detailed returns to Threadneedle Street? Or that banks should provide details of deals with associated companies, provisions made for bad or doubtful debts, and standby facilities available to back up capital and reserves?

The elementary nature both of the new requirements and of spreading the net to cover other deposit-taking organizations lays the Bank wide open to the charge that it presided over a lax system laxly administered. Small wonder that the horses were always bolting through so wide open a stable door. Nor was it only with domestic banks that the Bank left too many openings, which were apparently only noticed after trouble struck. Take the story of the consortium banks.

The consortium idea was one of the ways in which East and West, or rather Europe and America, were brought into potentially unhappy harness. Banks got together in powerful international combinations to grab their share of the booming Eurocurrency operations of the time. So long as the boom continued, the consortia had easy pickings. But when the bust came, especially after the collapse of Bankhaus I. D. Herstatt, the consortia found themselves particularly suspect. They might have prestigious shareholders galore; but what did that add up to in real, reliable backing?

In the deepening crisis, some of the consortium banks suffered a grievous loss of deposits. As Jocelyn Hambro, chairman of Western American Bank (Europe), put it in succinct bankerese: "Banks became acutely aware of balance sheet, leverage, liquidity and bank credit evaluation, and reduced their activities in foreign exchange dealing and in the interbank deposit market." In other words, having expanded too fast by methods that were partially unsound, the banks were terrified by circumstances into cutting back sharply on their commitments and their exposure.

Nowhere was the cutback more obvious than at Western American, whose shareholders were of immaculate pedigree—Bank of Tokyo, Hambros, National Bank of Detroit, Security Pacific National Bank, and Wells Fargo Bank. Overheads had mounted so excessively that the consortium was forced to reduce its staff numbers heavily and close some of its branches, along with effecting some dramatic, even melodramatic, cuts in its loans outstanding. The balance sheet total shrank like Alice after nibbling the toadstool: from £565 million on January 31, 1974, to £133.3 million a year later. Over that same dismal period loans for more than a year dwindled by two-thirds, from £188 million to £67.1 million.

Even in 1973–74 the consortium had only made £906,000 of profit on its half-billion of capital, which is not the kind of return to which bankers are accustomed. Plainly something in the state of Western American, if not rotten, was cause for great concern. This time the Bank reacted to the alarm before the fire had spread. It wrote to all twenty-five of the consortium banks to seek the promise of their mighty and less mighty owners that at all times and in all circumstances they would stand fully behind their partly owned children.

Since something like £5 billion was deposited with the consortium, the Bank's nervousness is easily explained. But it says something about both the uneasiness in big league banking and the risks which had been allowed to develop that the Bank—the arch-apostle of informality—felt compelled to seek these formal guarantees. Some of the consortium were notably less blue-blooded than others. Yet for banks of the ilk of the Chase Manhattan, the National Westminster, and the Royal Bank of Canada to be asked to state that they would not shelter behind minority shareholdings if trouble struck—that was not the most dignified moment in international banking history. It was, however, a necessary one.

In the various moves to bring international banking under control, the Bank of England played its traditional leading role. Sterling went on sinking; the British economy ran into deeper and deeper trouble; the evidence of the Bank's own slips of omission and commission piled up —but Threadneedle Street, at home and abroad, paradoxically retained its prestige. No doubt there were other facades in the City of London concealing episodes that the owners of the houses would rather nobody noticed. No doubt, too, the Bank will remember the shocks of the seventies in the unlikely event of another fatal combination of monetary mania, rampant speculation, accelerating inflation, and overabundant loopholes.

But the hard fact remains that, however well the Bank handled its pivotal role in the cleanup, the era had not seen its most glorious hours. If the inglorious moments are ever repeated, next time somebody might notice. And that could mean an end to the cloistered privileges of the most British institution of them all.

PART III

THE LENDING
SPECTACULARS

12. The Wrong Side of the Tracks

IN the days when the robber barons built the substructure of twentieth-century capitalist America, the banks combined with the railroad moguls to forge the transportation system on which all else depended —not forgetting to bilk the public of as much money as possible along the line. By the seventies of this century, the railroads were palsied wrecks of their former selves while the banks were mightier yet. All the same it took a railroad, embodying the one-time pride of the Vanderbilts, to show how shaky the foundations of banking strength could be.

In March 1976, the Penn Central Railroad, after close on six years of arduous puffing up the steep gradient of receivership, finally made it. The suffering railroad became the largest component of the Consolidated Rail Corporation (Conrail, for short), whose seven bankrupt Northeast carriers constituted the biggest, shakiest corporate reorganization in U.S. history, and whose names read like a roll call of past glories. Sharing the calamity with the Penn Central—which contributed some 20,000 miles, or about 80 percent, of the total track— were the Boston and Maine, the Lehigh Valley, the Erie-Lackawanna, the Reading and Ann Arbor railroads, and the Central Railroad of New Jersey.

None had been able to pay its way. All survived only because much of the nation's transportation and most of the commuters in the Northeast megalopolis depended on the Seven Weak Sisters. By seeking to combine them into a single system, the United States Railway Association—the quasi-state agency responsible for operating Conrail—was seeking to head off a national crisis. But the Penn Central's disappearance into Conrail was not just another demonstration of the uncompetitive economics of fixed track systems. The collapse was also, and far more worryingly, a financial mismanagement fiasco of the highest class, which the Conrail solution could do little to solve.

The super-railroad was going to be no economic flyer, even by its own admission. It would be several years before it turned a profit; a decade before the holders of the preferred shares might begin to collect dividends; while, for the owners of the common stock, that hope would be deferred until the twenty-first century. Even these forecasts were considered sublimely optimistic by many reputable railroad analysts. Almost nobody had a good word for Conrail, and many used bad ones. Among them were the bankers who had financed the Penn Central throughout the wild ride that finally ended in derailment and bankruptcy in June 1970.

The afflicted included Citibank, Chase Manhattan, Morgan Guaranty Trust, Bankers Trust, First Pennsylvania Banking and Trust, Girard Trust, Philadelphia National Bank, Provident National Bank— great names all—and many others; each was madder than a hatter over the Conrail solution. The angry banks led 100,000 or so institutional and individual investors (also including such leading life insurance companies as Metropolitan Life, Equitable Life, and Connecticut Mutual Life) in resorting to the courts to prevent implementation of the Conrail project. They argued that the scheme made no provision for their claims as secured creditors, which amounted to no less than $3,000 million, of which a thumping $800 million was owing to the banks.

The defendants in this unprecedented suit were the U.S. Railway Association, the U.S. secretary of transportation, and the chairman of the Interstate Commerce Commission. All three were attacked on the grounds that the Regional Reorganization Act violated various articles of and amendments to the United States Constitution, especially the Fifth Amendment, which (among other things) prohibits taking over private property for public use without just compensation. Specifically, the banks and other claimants charged that the $471 million offered for the roadbed and basic equipment of the Penn Central represented only a "fire sale" valuation. As a going concern, they estimated the railroad's worth at more than $7,000 million, or over double the $3,000 million which the creditors were so desperately trying to recover.

But the bankers who fumed over Conrail should by rights have been angrier at themselves for helping so largely to produce the shoddy circumstances that made an emergency solution inevitable. The Penn Central finally went bankrupt only after several years of gross mistakes and consequent misfortunes, faults of which the banks, which continued to give financial backing almost to the moment of ultimate smashup, should have been fully aware but which they in fact did precious little to rectify, let alone punish. Moreover, their responsibility in the matter was all the greater because of the close-knit ties between the railroad and its banks. Prominent bank directors sat on the board of the Penn Central, and vice versa.

This cozy arrangement extended back to the days when the Pennsylvania Railroad operated as a separate system. That was before the 1968 merger with the New York Central, an earlier exercise in amalgamation which signally failed to conjure a single pulsating railway out of the two twitching systems. The Penn Central was until 1968 the largest corporate marriage in U.S. history; it also produced the largest railroad, the sixth largest corporation in the country, and the largest insolvency —an event that occurred exactly two years after the merger.

The dominant coterie on the board of the Penn Central, as earlier on that of the Pennsy, was perfectly at home on the boards of some of the country's leading banks. Thus, the chairman of the board as the railroad rattled to ruin was Stuart Saunders, also a director of the Chase Manhattan and First Pennsylvania Banking and Trust. David Bevan, finance director for the railroad, filled a similar role at Provident National Bank; Paul Gorman, president, was with Bankers Trust Company; Alfred E. Perlman, vice chairman, graced Marine Midland Grace Trust; Thomas L. Perkins, counsel, enjoyed the blessings of Morgan Guaranty.

The nonexecutive directors further extended the money Mafia. They included prominent businessmen such as Walter A. Marting, president of Hanna Mining Company and a Bankers Trust director; R. Stewart Rauch, Jr., president, Philadelphia Saving Fund Society (Girard Trust); R. George Rincliffe, chairman, Philadelphia Electric (Philadelphia National Bank); Robert S. Odell, president, Allied Properties (Wells Fargo Bank); and so on. These interlocking business relationships were fortified by personal ties. Many of the Penn Central pals belonged to the same exclusive clubs in Philadelphia; in some cases they were near neighbors along the exclusive suburban Main Line.

After the crash, these interlocking directorates aroused lively controversy, especially in the Congress, where the late Texas Democratic Representative Wright Patman, a baiter of banks, charged that this was a conflict of interest situation in which the railroad had been corrupted by the banks. According to Patman, contamination by the banking environment was the main cause of the Penn Central's demise. In 1972, his House Committee on Banking and Currency charged that the management had embarked on a "disastrous diversification program," pouring into other ventures, especially real estate investment, money that should have been used to maintain plant and equipment. Patman had a point: in 1973, the Penn Central suffered 3,779 derailments, 40 percent of the total for all railways in the United States. Two years before, the regulatory Interstate Commerce Commission had criticized the Penn Central management for devoting "a considerable amount of time and resources to the diversification program at a time when all their energies and corporate finances were desperately needed to cope with serious problems" posed by the 1968 merger. These nonrailroading activities were said to have caused a cash drain of more than $200 million.

It was and is common for an individual to serve as a director both of a giant corporation and of an institution from which the company borrows huge sums of money; but it is quite uncommon for so many to bob up on one board. The obvious problem, given a conflict of interest situation, is which interest would get priority? In the case of the Penn Central, such a conflict did indeed arise, and on a massive scale.

However, the bankers were not to blame for the crash of the Penn Central. From the start, the merged enterprise was in all probability doomed by the laws of economics. There was really no sound reason to believe that two railways, which had scarcely made a penny of profit for two decades, could miraculously pull off the depressingly difficult trick by merger: zero plus zero still equals nought. To complicate matters, the two systems were as incompatible as Punch and Judy. Nothing matched: the backgrounds and personalities of the top management at the Pennsy, Stuart Saunders and his cronies, who belonged to starchy, conservative, old-line Pennsylvania families, were supposed to mesh with the boss of the New York Central, Alfred E. Perlman, a self-made railroad man, and Jewish to boot. Even their respective computer systems couldn't handle each other's data.

Furthermore, the conditions under which the merged system found itself obliged to operate were pernicious. Essential labor economies were frustrated by union insistence that no worker should be compelled to leave his job by the merger. Notorious featherbedding (including the obligation to man diesel engines with firemen, with no fires to stoke) was still condoned in a number of states in which the Penn Central operated. Subsequently, despite consistent operating losses, the unions with equal consistency demanded wage hikes, backed by naked strike threats. When the end came, the work force of close to 100,000 was said to be at least 10 percent heavier than necessary for efficient operation, and wage costs, at some $1,100 million per annum, accounted for two-thirds of all expenses.

Increases in the charges for shipping freight, the main source of income, regularly lagged behind increases in wages. Rates were artificially held down by the federal Interstate Commerce Commission and the state regulatory agencies, on the grounds that a public service was involved (also, preferential terms were enjoyed by large corporations including those with representatives on the Penn Central board). The railroad had to absorb an annual deficit of some $6 million on passenger services. Lucrative mail-carrying operations were progressively transferred to trucks and the airlines. Penn Central's management never ceased to complain that competitive means of transportation gained from subsidies that were denied to the railroads.

The excuses ran on and on. In the last six months or so before failure alone, there was a bitter winter, which disrupted services and compounded losses, followed by a tight money situation in the spring and a stock market slump which dragged down the share prices of the Penn Central and its listed subsidiaries. But there were other factors, acts of neither God nor outsiders, which the railroad directors should have spotted and reacted to long before the crash; for instance, the matter of the subsidiaries.

The Penn Central had diversified outside its basic business of running a railroad into operating a pipeline and an air transportation service, as well as its real estate development concerns (whose activities even ran to amusement parks). The floundering managers justified these ventures on the grounds that they produced net income that helped offset the losses sustained in railroading. In the case of the pipelines, this notion worked out. Not so with the real estate fliers, which made the Penn Central one of the largest property owners, with hotels in New York, Philadelphia, and elsewhere, and large developments in Florida and Texas. These assets apparently did produce earnings and dividends for the parent; but did the earnings actually exist?

Dubious accountancy had been at work. In 1974, the Securities and Exchange Commission charged that Penn Central officers (including Stuart Saunders and David Bevan), desperate to create the impression that their failing enterprise was sound, had sold off real property at inflated values, in return for overly modest down payments and excessively long-term mortgages, to purchasers whose ability to pay even over the unjustifiably extended period was debatable. At the same time the entire gross proceeds of the sale were reported as current income. Other critics claimed that the Pennsy and its successor company had kept going only by gradually liquidating nonrailroad assets.

The Penn Central's involvement in the air with Executive Jet stirred up the murkiest storm. The acquistion was illegal, anyway, since a railway was forbidden to enter air transport. When the management finally heeded the repeated orders of the Civil Aeronautics Board to divest, the loss came to some $21 million, which does not include the $70,000 fine, the second largest ever handed down by the CAB. The rotten publicity surrounding the affair cannot have helped the Penn Central's credit with the banks, especially since the Executive Jet prime mover was the chief financial officer, Bevan.

That was not the only situation into which Bevan blundered. He got other executives at the Penn Central, their families and friends, and Charles Hodge, a partner in a huge Wall Street investment banking firm, to set up a private investment club known as Penphil at the time

Bevan was also responsible for investing the assets of the railroad's pension fund. The conflict of interest was obvious. In yet another financial controversy (so charged the U.S. Department of Justice in a suit filed in 1974) some $4.2 million out of $10 million, loaned to the Penn Central by West German bankers to pay for freight car repairs, meandered its way into the Liechtenstein bank account of Fidel Goetz, a German businessman who claimed that the railroad owed him money.

But in the spring of 1970, when Bevan could no longer count on any more money from the banks that had financed the suffering company through thick and (mostly) thin, neither these nor other alleged personal peccadilloes of Bevan's explained the slamming of the door. It was shut because at last even the bankers could no longer ignore the fact that the railroad was hurtling toward disaster. Their very last act of misplaced faith was committed in the spring of 1969, when a group of fifty of the country's leading institutions, headed by Citibank, put together a $300 million revolving credit.

This handy sum was supposed to be used to improve the efficiency of the railroad; actually the millions went largely not into rolling stock but into rolling over commercial paper. The Penn Central had amassed enormous bundles of this unsecured, short-term credit, in transactions that did not have to be reported to the SEC, after the well-founded doubts about its creditworthiness had begun to circulate. A $59 million loan conceded by a group of Swiss banks at the end of 1969 went the same sorry way. This uncharacteristically foolish investment by the sages of Zürich was doubtless encouraged by the news that the Penn Central intended to perpetuate its record of never passing a dividend for 122 years (back before the Civil War) by disbursing $56 million to the shareholders at year end. Of course, the dividend was a far, far way from being earned.

A run on the loosely issued, much-rolled commercial paper ultimately sent the railroad hurtling off the track. The critical period ran from April 21 to May 8, 1970, when redemptions of the paper exceeded sales by $413 million. Another $75 million had to be rolled over by the end of June; and close to $200 million was looming up for the entire year. The corporation simply had no funds to meet the by now inevitable demands for redemption. The banks were solicited; but almost as one grim, groaning body, with Citibank taking the lead, they refused to renew their virtually exhausted $300 million credit. As usual, one bank was a dismal exception: Chemical Bank, which recklessly offered another $50 million unilaterally to the Pennsylvania Company property subsidiary, not to the transportation company.

Chemical Bank's management, looking ineffably foolish in the aftermath, claimed this was short-term financing, intended to tide things over until Pennco could complete a projected $100 million bond issue.

That issue never rose an inch from the ground. It was stymied by the news that first-quarter losses on railway operations, in part because of the fierce winter, had piled up to close to $102 million—more than twice the $49 million predicted by the management. About the same time, the slump on Wall Street drastically reduced the share price of Great Southwest Corporation, the strongest component of Pennco's portfolio, so that its total value plummeted from $980 million to $230 million.

Confronted by such dismal omens, the shareholders in the Penn Central itself began to dump their stock. Several of the directors were the first to leave in this way—which led to subsequent charges that they had unfairly taken advantage of inside information. From a peak of $86, the quote fell to under $10 on the New York Stock Exchange (it was down to not much over $1 by the time the Big Board delisted the shares in the summer of 1976). The situation was by now truly desperate, and a last vain, agonized fling was tried. The resistant banks were urged to provide another $200 million, on condition that the loan would be guaranteed by the federal government under a 1950 law, passed in connection with the Korean emergency, which sanctioned such aid to firms that were vital to national defense. The Nixon administration turned thumbs down, mainly (it was said) through the adamant refusal of the then deputy secretary of defense, electronics millionaire David Packard, to set such a precedent. (Ironically, similar scruples were later waived to help out Lockheed.)

This sealed the Penn Central's doom. On June 21, 1970, the transportation company filed the papers that set going the largest business failure in U.S. history. The bankrupt firm owed $248 million in taxes, interest, and rents, plus $1,800 million on outstanding bonds, equipment contracts, and other sales agreements. It would take another six years, until July 1976, for the parent outfit, Penn Central Company, to follow its chief subsidiary down the drain. By then this was necessary to stave off the legal proceedings falling on its head from all directions.

The railroads have a special Section 77 of the U.S. Bankruptcy Act, which was designed to let them suspend payment of most of their debts while reorganizing under the supervision of trustees and continuing to provide service. Under these most accommodating of bankruptcy terms the Penn Central kept its trains running for nearly six years, until it was absorbed into the Conrail system in the spring of 1976.

Meanwhile, a subsidiary drama had been enacted, including enforced settlements. Here those alleged to have behaved unfairly or illegally in their dealings with the company were obliged to make restitution; settlements were also worked out by which some creditors clawed back at least part of what they claimed. But while the Penn Central Railroad advanced into a new and dubious future as the major constituent of Conrail, a mountain of controversy and litigation over-shadowed the system, including the not-to-be-forgotten suit by the bankers and others to enforce their vast claims.

The presence of the banks before, during, and after the last rites was fitting. It was difficult to separate them from the disaster to the railroad; all those directors with bank connections, all those vast sums of money outstanding in debt, forged a heavy set of links. The wreck of the Penn Central did not leave its bankers in a flattering light. In their lively and fascinating study of the crash, Joseph R. Daughen and Peter Binzen quoted "one of the directors" of the railroad in a revealing tale. When the full scope of the disaster was nakedly revealed, Walter Wriston, president of Citibank, was "furious at his loan officers for get-ting his bank so deeply involved without knowing what a hole the Penn Central was in. . . . Wriston was not the only banker that was mad. They were all mad." That was all very well; but if the bankers of the Penn Central had cause to be mad with anyone, it was above all with them-selves.

Conrail's expansion of the combination to seven, with the whole bloated and creaking system rattling along on the backs of the state, was, to tell the truth, the type of "solution" on which everybody con-nected with the whole Penn Central disgrace had ultimately been counting—especially its bankers. That, and that alone, was why such perfunctory attempts were made to establish the creditworthiness of the company (or lack of it), or to demand adequate security for loans. The bankers, if they could ever be so honest with themselves, would have to admit that in the last resort they had assumed the Penn Central system would not be allowed to abandon services. The railroad was too important to the economy to cease operations, whatever happened, and the bankers equally assumed that, as usual, they would fall into the first come, first served category when the state's tax money came to the railroad's aid.

Under the circumstances, the denunciation of the Conrail set-tlement and the suit filed to try to reverse it were somewhat less than admirable, somewhat more than ambiguous. The big creditors, certain of retrieving something from a wreck they helped to create, appeared to want the lot. As for the small investors, who held the Penn Central's common shares, they had a one-way ticket to no-where.

The banks can argue convincingly enough that they had no re-sponsibility for the shareholders. But their faults were heinous anyway. The obligation of a bank to protect its depositors' money is not bounded only by the promise to return as much as was deposited. What happens to that money in between times is also the bank's responsibility. In the case of the Penn Central, it was not exercised in any reasonable degree. By allowing, even encouraging, a rogue management to ruin so large and heavily indebted a company, the banks jeopardized the interests of the whole industrial community. The robber barons would not have been proud of their successors.

13. The Naked City

In June 1975, the beleaguered Mayor Abe Beame appeared on TV to announce what he described as a crisis for the next fiscal year. He was making an inevitable response to the ineluctable financial troubles that were falling on his New York City like hailstones. With the far from uncanny instinct that politicians always show in times of trouble, Beame went after an external enemy (external, that is, to his administration). He bitterly attacked the big banks with headquarters in his bailiwick, accusing them in language worthy of Tammany Hall at its ripest of "poisoning our wells" and conducting a whispering campaign "to denigrate our fiscal integrity."

Not many people had ever suspected New York of having much fiscal integrity to denigrate, as it happened. But those with faith must presumably have included Beame's unloved banks, since they held such mountainous amounts of the city's bulging debts in their portfolios. They had earned Beame's abuse solely because, with the cupboards full to bursting, they had refused to underwrite any more of the city's bonds. Not only did this belated prudence draw the mayor's scorn; municipal workers (no doubt discreetly encouraged by the municipal government) were demonstrating before the main Manhattan office of the largest of New York's banks, Citibank, and their unions were urging the rank and file to withdraw their money from the accursed institution.

For all the sound and fury, with Beame even demanding a congressional investigation into the unseemly behavior of his bankers, he protested too much. The banks' behavior over New York's debt was scandalous, true. Yet the scandal lay not in turning down the mayor, but in the past financing of the profligate overspending that had brought the world's richest city to the brink of ruin. By their indiscreet lending, the big city banks (which meant a good proportion of the largest banks in America and the world) had compromised their own welfare, risked the security of their depositors and stockholders, and (by no means incidentally) jeopardized the economic futures of the citizens of New York—including the incumbents of the overpadded municipal payrolls.

102

The money at risk was in mind-boggling quantities. In January 1976, there were 954 banks in 33 states of the Union which collectively held some $6.5 billion in various kinds of debt obligations from New York City and the scarcely more prudent New York State. These voluminous holdings accounted for over half the total capital of 234 of the afflicted institutions; between 20 and 50 percent in the cases of the rest. The technical distinction between debt owed to the city and to the state was hardly worth making, since their destinies were and are interlinked to a potentially fatal degree.

If Humpty Dumpty City had fallen off the wall, all the state's armies and all the state's men would have fallen right after it. The city's drain on state funds was the prime factor behind the state's own precarious financial position in the mid-seventies—although the politicians in Albany had shown little more wisdom than those in Manhattan when it came to fitting expenditure to the revenues prudently available. The resulting horror show frightened money men far beyond the boundaries of the state and even the nation; from West Germany, for instance, Chancellor Helmut Schmidt felt moved to warn the Americans that the collapse of New York City could have a domino effect worldwide.

Not content with its too friendly neighborhood bankers, the city owed money wherever it could find the stuff. In Illinois, Missouri, Florida, and Alabama, you could find New York debt in the bank vaults —as you could in Britain and on the continent of Europe. The owners of the debt, as the crisis deepened, certainly felt little sympathy for the far greater anxieties of the big New York banks, which were naturally stuck with the biggest bundle of potentially worthless paper. At the end of 1975, according to figures that they were then compelled to publish by law, the seven largest bank holding companies between them held in their Wall Street and uptown skyscrapers about $1.9 billion in the debt of their impecunious home town.

The Chase Manhattan led the group in its civic devotion, with $408 million, followed close behind by Chemical Bank's $378.8 million. The third was Citibank, with $340 million. Similar gigantic sums were owed all the way down the line of leading banks. The Chemical Bank had succeeded in having 44 percent of its total equity covered by this one huge debtor; Citibank was best off on this score (although "best off" is hardly the appropriate phrase), with a 15.6 percent exposure. Thus, the entire banking system of the city, which meant the state, which meant the United States, which meant the world, was tottering on that fateful June 9 when an emoting Mayor Beame blamed the banks for their lack of willingness to ingest more financial poison.

His appearance was prompted—indeed, necessitated—by the uncomfortable knowledge that within two days of his broadcast some $790 million of debt was scheduled to mature; and that the city was in no better position to pay off the money than a Bowery bum without a cent is able to purchase a bottle of the hard stuff. Just like the latter, Beame held out his hand. The panhandling and the pressure resulted in the creation by the state legislature of an agency now known to the world as "Big Mac" but officially christened the Municipal Assistance Corporation—a clever-seeming device for enabling New York to borrow more money without having to use its own nonexistent credit.

Big Mac's debts are backed by certain tax revenues garnered by the city, which are paid over to the Corporation. It was the only possible answer to the impasse that began to build up in the autumn of 1974, when the city went to market with the biggest tax-exempt bond offering ever laid before an uninterested public. The $475 million sale was an unmitigated disaster. Many of the underwriters lost money and love for New York City in equal proportions, and the stage was set for the next calamity.

That duly appeared in early 1975, when the syndicate underwriting $260 million of tax anticipation notes, headed by the Chase and Bankers Trust, began to suspect that the offering exceeded the permitted legal limit. The operation was canceled. A short time thereafter, all but six of the biggest New York banks, plus the huge brokerage house of Merrill Lynch, Pierce, Fenner & Smith, withdrew from a syndicate offering $537.3 million of similar notes, after a Brooklyn Law School professor (of all people) had sued the city to prevent its incurring any more long-term debt.

The professor lost his case. But his action prodded the New York State controller, Arthur Levitt, into an investigation which showed that the city had erred well beyond the bounds of impure but simple improvidence. In order to boost its borrowing power, the city had overstated its receivables—just like any dishonest company promoter. Some $1,275 million of the obligations issued over a fourteen-month period might be of doubtful legality. The Securities and Exchange Commission was no happier with New York's vaunted "fiscal integrity." It investigated possible fraud in connection with the sale of some $1,600 million in the city's notes, reconstructing the circumstances in which investors (including the allegedly shrewd banks) had bought them to see how far the buyers had been made aware of the deplorable state of the city's battered finances.

The crisis could not be staved off indefinitely. Finally, a $1 billion offering in high-yielding short-term notes was received by the investment community like an attack of smallpox. In the aftermath the banks, as the major creditors (or suckers), declined in the future to renegotiate borrowings as they matured; that meant beginning with the little matter of the $790 million scheduled to fall due on June 11, 1975. Big Mac stomped into the breach with stopgap aid.

The new agency was empowered to begin converting up to $3,000 million in short-term debt into long-term bonds. Its intervention enabled Mayor Beame to resume negotiations with the state about raising some $330 million in new taxes, including, rather ironically, levies on bond sales and bank and corporate franchises, which added insult to injury for the stuck financiers. This was one remedial measure. Others included scheduled cuts of 20,000 in the city's work force (some of which cuts, to nobody's surprise, were later restored); a three-year pay freeze; and other operating economies of the kind that banks are accustomed to demand from defaulting customers.

Big Mac did manage to place the first two tranches of $1,000 million in city bonds in July and August 1975. But that September the banks and other investors refused to take up the third. The prices of the first two issues had slumped in market trading, reflecting the investment world's lack of confidence that the economy measures and the crisis budget would really save New York City from its own indiscretions. As the new crisis erupted, yet another agency was invented—the Emergency Financial Control Board, with the remarkable task of supervising the city's finances to ensure that income would actually match outgo. This new encroachment on the city's "home rule" went much further than Big Mac; five of the seven members of the Emergency Board came not from the city but from the state.

The Emergency seven committed themselves to a three-month crash program to pull the city from its hole. It included fresh borrowings by the state on the city's behalf; contributions from the state insurance fund, plus a $400 million commitment by the big New York banks to roll over short-term notes and buy some Big Mac bonds too. Property owners, for their part, pledged to prepay $150 million in real estate taxes, and amid bitter protest from New Yorkers, the subway fare was raised from 35 to 50 cents. The extent of the crisis, however, was shown not just by the severity of the measures but by their inadequacy. In exerting itself to save the city, the state had damaged its own already tarnished reputation; lenders began to shy away from Albany's debt as well. As the end of 1975 approached, New York City was as far from financial salvation as ever. Since the New York banking crisis could no longer be kept under local control, there was only one more place to turn: Washington, D.C.

Ever since New York City's dreadful problems had been exposed, President Gerald Ford had adamantly refused to commit a red cent toward their solution. It hardly matters whether this was to embarrass the Democratic majority in Congress (as opponents claimed), or to warn other U.S. cities such as Chicago, Philadelphia, Cleveland, Detroit, and Boston to mend their own profligate ways before disaster struck. The president, with the enthusiastic backing of his secretary of the treasury, William Simon, and with Congress lukewarm on the issue, was fighting the good fight for fiscal rectitude. The only trouble was, he couldn't possibly win.

The largest and best-known city in the United States could in theory go broke, and for real; but could it be allowed to? That well-known financial forecaster, Mayor Beame, argued vehemently that his city's fall would have repercussions in all the other cities in potential trouble (which meant nearly all the biggest ones) and upon the entire United States economy. The Consolidated Edison Company of New York, no stranger to financial troubles itself and with a monopoly in supplying light and power to the community, warned of a possible deliberate blackout (not an accidental one, like its earlier celebrated overload and shutdown) if the city, the utility's biggest customer, could not pay its bills.

The stuck banks bellowed as loudly as anybody. The biggest of them had, of course, already written off large losses on New York City paper. Arthur Burns, head of the Federal Reserve Board, had also publicly promised that the Fed stood ready to provide all necessary aid to any bank that might be threatened by a New York default. Nonetheless, neither New York bankers nor any others could be sure whether the structure would endure the shock if the Ford administration and the Congress did nothing and the city consequently collapsed.

Naturally, the president capitulated, against his own better judgment, and swallowed an arsenal of words. The administration guaranteed $2.3 billion a year in federal aid until mid-1978; thus backstopped, New York State pledged itself to additional aid totaling some $9 billion over the same period. So disaster was again averted by the public's billions, and the bankers were able to breathe more easily—for a spell.

They could less easily rid themselves of the embarrassment, the downright indignity, of pestering the federal government to adopt a policy that as bankers they knew was morally reprehensible and financially unsound. If ever a debtor deserved to go under, it was New York City. As rich and privileged members of the community, the bankers had been ringside spectators as the Big Apple (the phrase with which citizens of New York, encouraged by some vigorous public relations, like to describe the place where they live) rotted to the core; or as Fun City, to use the other funny title, had exhausted its finances with some fairly riotous civic living. Since the degenerative process had been going on for well over a decade, it can be fairly asked what the bankers thought they were up to.

Their acquiescence in the destruction of a city's credit really started in earnest when John Lindsay was mayor from 1966 to 1973. True, his long-term predecessor, Robert Wagner, was no fiscal puritan either; under the Democratic regime, the city had already slipped into fatally sloppy ways. In Wagner's last year in office, the budget showed a cool deficit of about $100 million. But Lindsay's spendthrift spree went on nonstop until he was succeeded by the former city controller (who thus participated in the responsibility), none other than Abraham Beame.

Lindsay's particular contribution was to escalate the city's labor bill out of sight. Greeted by a strike of transit workers when he took office in early 1966, he bowed to their demands, setting a pattern from which (a paragon of consistency, if nothing else), he never deviated thereafter. The municipal workers exploited to the hilt and beyond their monopoly stranglehold and the weapon of the strike—even though it was supposedly illegal. They succeeded in pushing the Big Apple's pay scales, fringe benefits, and pensions to the highest levels for any city in the United States. By the time they were (temporarily) through, labor costs, at some $7 billion a year, accounted for around 60 percent of the total city budget.

A banker might well have admired the business acumen of the unions, which had achieved some sensational bargains. After three years on the force, for example, a cop would earn close to $17,500 a year, and get four weeks' vacation; a sanitation worker (the modern euphemism for a garbage collector), close to $17,750. A secondary school teacher's salary could go as high as $20,000; that of a college professor up to $38,000. More than one-third of the 107,000 or so employees of the Education Department were so-called administrators, which meant they never taught a class.

The pension program, which financiers should especially have understood in all its terrifying implications, was something else. By 1975 it was already costing a billion a year, and was scheduled to rise to $3 billion by 1985. After twenty years of service, our New York cop could retire on half-pay; he could go on drawing his pension even if he took another full-time job; if he lived on for thirty years, as he had every actuarial expectation of doing, he would draw more money in pensions than he had ever earned while protecting the citizenry against crime. Just to gild the gingerbread, the pension was not based on average earnings over a period of years, but on pay in the final year, including overtime; many cops, naturally, took good care to work a great deal of overtime in that final year.

The same kind of terms were extended to all the city's employees. Thus the transit workers, after they gained a startling increase in pension scales in 1970, retired from their jobs in droves, and at once took on better-paying jobs in private industry. In that one year, New York lost 70 percent of its subway car maintenance supervisors in this slick manner. The massive Lindsay welfare programs were another nail in the city's financial coffin: equal opportunity projects for the less privileged minorities, the blacks and Puerto Ricans (i.e., a full third of the citizens), day care centers, drug treatment programs, youth services, bilingual teaching, job training. By the end of Lindsay's term of office, about 1 million people (around 13 percent of the total population) were on welfare, at an aggregate cost of $852 million a year.

The bankers were also financing a bonanza in higher education. The 270,000 students at the City University of New York were, for the most part, charged no tuition fees; some even received subsidies. An apparently wide-open admission policy was still further broadened by Lindsay in 1970 to allow any high school "graduate" (whatever his or her grades) to enroll. The score of hospitals operated by the city, too, were overstaffed and also underutilized, sometimes by as much as 20 percent.

The whole bureaucracy of municipal workers swelled over the decade 1966–75 by 37 percent to 338,000, even though the city's total population was in decline; it fell to some 7.5 million as private citizens and large corporations fled the city, driven out by high taxes. The imposts included property taxes, which were constantly being raised, a city income tax piled on top of the federal and state income tax, and an 8 percent sales tax. Between 1969 and 1975, some 420,000 jobs were lost in the private sector, a trend that accelerated with the onset of recession in 1970.

To finance its prodigious outlays, the Lindsay administration resorted more and more to "funny money" techniques, which should have raised the eyebrows of the creditor banks, but apparently failed to produce any reaction at all. In the days when balanced budgets were in vogue, even for Fun City, New York had been let off the hook in two ways: it had been allowed to issue revenue anticipation notes (or RANS) against forthcoming grants from the federal and state governments; and tax anticipation notes (TANS) against certain uncollected taxes and fees.

However, the city was forbidden to borrow against taxes unless they were actually due and payable during the same fiscal year as the borrowing; and the issues against federal and state aid could not actually exceed the amounts received from those sources in the previous year. Toward the end of Mayor Wagner's term in office, the rules were changed to allow borrowings against certain fees and taxes not scheduled for payment during the year; the city could also borrow against the mayor's estimate of the amount of federal and state aid that would be forthcoming during the current fiscal period.

Before he stepped down, Wagner had raised some $56 million in

RANS and TANS. Mayor Lindsay eagerly grasped at this remarkable fiscal opportunity. In just five Lindsay years, these borrowings swelled over sevenfold to some $420 million; by the end of 1971, they had doubled again to a bloated $965 million. Even so, Lindsay's administration was strapped for money. So the mayor began to shift a growing proportion of his operating costs out of the expense budget into the capital budget, which was supposed to be used only for construction projects. By 1975, a total of some $800 million had been diverted by this ingenious route—with, so far as anybody knows, not one word of complaint from the city's bankers.

Then there was the so-called rainy day fund, into which the city was meant to deposit $20 million a year to meet emergencies. By 1975, not only was this fund almost drained of liquid resources, but it was found that the city had skipped making the mandatory contributions for about seven years. Yet for all these jiggery-pokery efforts to conjure money out of thin air, the great city's financial situation turned progressively more sour. By the mid-seventies, the city was having to lay out some $1.9 billion a year simply to service its debt; that is, 17 percent of the total fiscal 1976 budget of $12.3 billion, which was expected to show a deficit of about $800 million.

By that same date, New York City, in its own single, astonishing right, owed 18 percent of all the money due on all the municipal bonds of the entire United States—not to mention 39 percent of everything owing on tax-exempt notes. Even the strangely permissive banks were now sufficiently shocked to cry, "Hold, enough." Nor was it a case of better late than never; it was by no means certain that the hour of reckoning had not already passed. The federal government had warned that not one dollar more in help would be provided after mid-1978— not that, after President Ford's earlier *volte-face*, the promise meant anything. That was the issue in a nutshell. The politicians, the banks, the unions, the citizens all assumed that, in the end, a New York bankruptcy would not be allowed, that their skins would be saved.

When Jimmy Carter became president in 1977, they seemed to be betting on an even rarer thing, as he had promised more help than his predecessor during his election campaign. Sure enough, in March, when default again threatened and the banks vowed they would put up "not a penny" more, the new treasury secretary, Michael Blumenthal, came up with another $255 million in aid, after the conjurer Beame suddenly "discovered" $600 million in spare cash.

Many disillusioned critics of the government bodies, of the city itself, of the banks, and of everybody else involved in the affair reckoned that a cynical attitude was exactly right, that the back-to-the-wall promises made by Mayor Beame about cutting the labor force, freezing wages and salaries, closing down schools and hospitals, charging tuition at the City University, however genuinely intended, would never stick in the face of political pressures and militant municipal unions. Sure enough, a cut of 32,800, or 12 percent, in the number of workers directly employed by the city in the second half of 1975 saved only 5 percent in payroll costs. Why? Because those policemen, firemen, and others still in jobs naturally had to receive pay increases negotiated before the fiscal crisis.

But without economies on the grand scale of $1 billion or more, the Big Apple's finances in mid-1978 would be as rotten as in mid-1975. The General Accounting Office, the bookkeeper of the U.S. Congress, feared as much. The Senate Banking Committee, which had had to approve the program of federal aid, thought so too. It warned in mid-1976 that the city's budget cuts were too shallow, and urged further restrictions on city spending, such as a ban on direct loans from the state, and cutting off all federal aid unless the city met its target reductions in municipal spending of $379 million in the year beginning July 1, 1976, and of $483 million in the following fiscal year.

If the city fails to achieve solvency at any date in the future, then all the arguments used to avert bankruptcy in mid-1975 will very likely be trotted out again—and with the same result. It would, of course, be a different matter if the banks got really tough; as tough, that is, as they would be on a delinquent consumer or corporate borrower in the same feckless, foolish circumstances. But the banks' extraordinary indulgence toward New York City, like that of other banks to other municipalities and states, demonstrated that ordinary standards do not apply when politics beckon.

No doubt the banks' insurance—so their directors felt—was the impossibility of a major governmental bankruptcy. If so, sight was never shorter. Their complacency and complicity encouraged the very policies that threatened the value of the banks' portfolios of city securities; mortgaged for years in advance the tax revenues on which those securities depended; and weakened the economic base from which those taxes and the banks' own custom derived. The New York banks, like it or not, were big worms in the Big Apple.

14. Heedless Lockheed

BANKS like to boast that they support their customers in time of need —and no doubt one day the Lockheed Aircraft Corporation will be wheeled forth as a proof of this generous zeal for the welfare of the afflicted. Cynics might counter that the first slice of bank aid for the plane manufacturer only encouraged it in the stupendous folly of building the TriStar jetliner, and that the second installment was only proffered after the Nixon administration came up with federal guarantees. More—such cynics can now point out that what business the bank-supported company did achieve had its way greased by bribes of quite stupendous size and brazenness.

It was summer 1975 when the world got the news that Lockheed, a $3,250 million corporation, had been paying bribes to promote its overseas sales of military and commercial aircraft, and that the slush money had gone to airline and government officials, right up to cabinet ministers, even heads of state. The scandal touched the great and powerful in West Germany, where Franz Joseph Strauss, former defense minister and potentate in the Christian Democratic Union, was named; and in Italy, where two former defense ministers, Mario Tanassi and Luigi Gui, were mentioned along with other leaders of the Christian Democratic Party, which had ruled that country since the end of World War II—including no fewer than three prime ministers, Aldo Moro, Mario Rumor, and Giovanni Leone, later president of the republic.

In Japan, the ruling Liberal Democratic Party was traumatized by allegations of massive payoffs to high politicians in high places, effected through the agency of the party's behind-the-scenes maestro, Yoshio Kodama, and culminating in the arrest of former Prime Minister Kakuei Tanaka. The sensation was no less than that caused by the earlier charge that Prince Bernhard of the Netherlands had taken some $1.1 million from Lockheed between 1961 and 1972 via the Swiss bank account of one Fred C. Meuser; the latter was Lockheed's European sales director, then busily soliciting the purchase of the firm's F-104 Starfighter by the Dutch government. The prince denied everything at

111

first. But after being reprimanded by an inquiry commission for "showing himself open to dishonorable requests and offers" and taking completely unacceptable initiatives, Bernhard had to resign all his business and public posts.

All in all, the mighty aircraft manufacturer—for many years the largest defense contractor in the United States—had paid some $38 million (from a total of some $165 million spent in export promotion between 1970 and 1975) as bribes to prominent personalities in customer countries. Congress launched an investigation; the SEC conducted a probe; the Internal Revenue Service audited the books. But Lockheed's bankers could do nothing but fume. Their client had besmirched its image—and that of U.S. industry in general—at a moment when they were desperately striving to keep the company in business, at considerable risk to their own banking pockets. The scandal even touched off a rare row between bankers as they argued whether the corporate delinquent, which the banks had been bailing out for years, should still be kept afloat or allowed to sink in its sin.

The great Lockheed bribery scandal had one long-overdue benefit. It finally forced the bankers to get rid of the autocratic, intransigent top management whose obstinate persistence in the hopelessly uneconomic L-1011 TriStar had landed the company in its original mess—a plane whose grotesquely insufficient sales, it now transpired, had only reached that indifferent total with the aid of bribery and corruption. Even then, but for the hardheadedness of just one of the two dozen banks belonging to the save-Lockheed consortium, the management purge might never have taken place.

The virtual war between the banks erupted from longtime skirmishing into full-scale combat early in 1976, when Robert Abboud, chairman of the First National Bank of Chicago, demanded that Daniel Haughton, the Lockheed chairman, should go, and swiftly, on the pardonable grounds that he headed a lousy management which had almost ruined the company by building a plane that hardly anybody wanted.

Arrayed against Abboud, in the beginning, were most of the other twenty-three banks. In particular, Frederick Leary, executive vice president of Bankers Trust Company, of New York, it was said, "worked day and night to keep Lockheed alive." Leary's quixotic support for the Haughton management reached its climax at a head-on confrontation during negotiations to work out new terms for the consortium's life-sustaining loan of $595 million to the struggling airplane firm. Battle was joined in the privacy of boardrooms, over transcontinental telephones, at bankers' conventions, at staid receptions and plush cocktail parties; even breaking out in a furious public shouting match between two well-known bankers, so the *Wall Street Journal* affirmed. Yet what were they fighting over? The continued privilege of supporting the insupportable with their depositors' money.

Abboud's lonely refusal to sanction the outpouring of any more funds to help sustain Lockheed's tottering edifice, unless top management was replaced, only won substantial support after the bribery scandal flared across the world's headlines. Several of the leading New York banks shifted to the Chicago tough guy's side, including Citibank, Chase Manhattan, and Morgan Guaranty. This defection was decisive; these three banks had each contributed 7.5 percent to the consortium loan, compared with only 3.75 percent (a mere smidgen that nonetheless amounted to $22 million) from Abboud's First National of Chicago.

That left the opposition effectively reduced to Bankers Trust and Bank of America, which jointly administered the loan on a day-to-day basis. Even they gave in after the scandal had utterly wrecked Haughton's credibility; in February 1976, the chairman was ordered out, and with him went his deputy and designated successor, A. Carl Kotchian, long known as Lockheed's super-salesman, soon to be revealed as the go-between in the negotiations that landed Japan's former prime minister in jail and acutely embarrassed several other world leaders.

Haughton's temporary replacement, Robert Haack, a former chairman of the New York Stock Exchange, had the kind of impeccable reputation that bankers look for in their nominees. It was a job that Haack should never have held, because the affairs of Lockheed should never have been allowed to deteriorate so far or so long. The crucial decision of firing the bosses came about five years too late. As early as 1971, the sustaining banks must already have had good reasons to believe that precisely the same management had set Lockheed on a course that threatened the company's survival. However excellent the reasons, the bankers collectively ignored them.

Not individually, however. Even that far back a number of the bankers were reluctant to commit themselves any further. A restive Congress felt much the same way when asked to guarantee close to $200 million from the total $600 million on loan from the banks. Congressional arms were twisted by Nixon's secretary of the treasury, John Connally (the Nixon administration always proved intensely solicitous toward the Burbank company). The banks were dragged along in the wake of Congress mainly by the crusading Frederick Leary. Misgivings in both camps were based on a common calculation that Lockheed had no hope in this life of reaching the sales targets for the TriStar 1011 commercial airliner on which break-even depended—even using Lockheed's own ludicrous underestimates of that level. Selling some 300 TriStars by the 1980s, which alone would make the project viable on more realistic assessments, was the other side of the moon. Moreover, the L-1011 was only the latest in a series of flying Edsels to emerge from Lockheed.

The fifties saw the turboprop Electra airliner appear and flop disastrously after others had captured a market that promptly vanished before the competition of the pure jet. The C-5A Galaxie military transport, while a marvel of large-scale technology, exceeded its original cost estimates by so many billions as to force the government to come to the rescue with a massive infusion of taxpayers' money. Even the money-making F-104 Starfighter, sold so successfully and corruptly to European air forces, became known to Germans as the "widow maker" after 178 (by spring 1976) had crashed, killing many of the pilots. When the scandals erupted, the logical conclusion was that part of the $24 million in bribes had smeared the palms of officials and politicians who otherwise would not have pressed for the purchase of weapons so lethal to the users.

The TriStar, at any rate, had no defects in service. Its drawbacks were the engines, made by Rolls-Royce in Britain, and severely delayed when that company went financially bankrupt and technologically astray. But above all, the problem was the competitive reputation of the Douglas DC-10, designed for exactly the same niche in the wide-bodied market, yet produced by a company that already had hundreds of planes in service, earning it an excellent reputation with the world's airlines. The motive for Lockheed's entering the competition was obvious: frozen out of the first round of commercial jet production, desperate to offset declining military sales and profits, it didn't want to be left out again from the only civil game in town.

So Haughton jumped in with the TriStar without having a single order on the books, in defiance of every tenet of airliner marketing. Kotchian's claims that his company could capture at least half of the total market were only the first of several inane and ferociously costly exercises in wishful thinking, all of which the company's bankers were asked to swallow (and did) as they advanced $400 million, more than the entire stockholders' equity, to finance Haughton's folly.

After spending some $1.2 billion on developing the plane, by the spring of 1976 Lockheed had come near to the end of the TriStar's tether, with deliveries and firm orders for only 158 planes, tentative orders for an additional 49, and not a single new order booked during the whole of 1975 (not to mention the added difficulty of trying to sell new TriStars while some customers were already selling off their used planes). The longer Lockheed went on, the more money it lost. The deficit in 1974 was about $50 million; in 1975, it climbed to nearly $95 million. On its flight to nowhere, moreover, the TriStar had wreaked all manner of havoc, including the financial destruction of Rolls-Royce.

The British Isles rang with premature rejoicing when Rolls-Royce won the competition to supply the engines for the TriStar, with the British government using every argument in its power (including money) to clinch a deal that was a disaster from start to finish—primarily because, like Lockheed itself, Rolls-Royce had grievously underestimated the costs and grossly overestimated its own financial and commercial capabilities. In accepting these errors, the British government, which later poured in millions to maintain the Rolls-Royce aero-engine output, was no wiser than the Rolls-Royce company's own bankers (who raised money which was immediately used to pay dividends to the stockholders it borrowed from), or bankers in America.

The U.S. bankers had made the elementary banking mistake of pouring good money after bad, becoming progressively sucked into the Lockheed quagmire until they were immersed so deep, up to their very necks, that they could not afford to get out. They had started modestly enough in 1967–68, with an initial infusion of $75 million, later raised to $125 million. Then, in 1969, the company came back, cap in hand, asking to up the commitment to $400 million. Haughton & Co. were applying a procedure dear to the hearts of defense contractors. You put forward a project, the original cost of which you underestimate, and take it step by step to the stage where you can argue that the cost of cancellation will be greater than providing the money (underestimated again, of course) needed to complete. And you throw in, naturally, the economic and political cost of laying off all the workers whose services will no longer be required.

In the mid-seventies, Lockheed had some 68,000 workers on the payroll, a good number of whom were employed on the TriStar project at the company's California facilities; supplier firms also had thousands of jobs at stake, mostly, again, in California. The state not only sends more politicians to Washington, D.C., than any other, but during the TriStar era it had a president in the White House; and both Richard M. Nixon and Lockheed had connections with the secret political and money power of the late, legendary Howard Hughes.

Pressure from the administration partly explains why the banks—some of them very reluctantly—upped the ante to $400 million. It lasted a scant two years. This time only the federal government guarantee of the additional $200 million or so stopped the institutions from slamming the door. And sure enough, five years later the good money, having joined the bad, had been contaminated by it. Lockheed was back to square one again, with zero TriStar sales for 1975. Haughton, an ace at negotiating from a weak position, was again calling for help. The difference this time was that the cry, instead of being for more loans, was for relief from the commitments already on Lockheed's back

—interest payments alone were running at some $75 million a year, and few of the bankers can genuinely have believed that their battered client could afford such an outflow of cash.

At this point, the smoldering resentment of the more disenchanted and clear-sighted bankers flared up. A few favored outright bankruptcy; on the company's deserved demise, they might even recover their entire investment. They could take over the profitable Missiles and Space Company and Lockheed Georgia Company subsidiaries (which enabled Lockheed Aircraft, in spite of everything, to report and maybe even to make a profit of some $45 million in 1975), and then sell shares to the public. But America's No. 1 defense contractor (unlike Britain's Rolls-Royce) could not be allowed to go into bankruptcy.

Other banks favored a merger between Lockheed and some strong company, in aircraft or anything else. At one point it looked as if Textron—a conglomerate so highly diversified that it practically was in everything else—might come to the rescue. That deal collapsed (to Textron's great good fortune) in 1975. As no new partner seemed in the offing, the bankers had to abandon their almost instinctive merger twitch (banks revere amalgamations, partly because of the massive fee income they generate) and fall back on some other expedient.

The proposals they adopted are of interest to ordinary bank customers mainly because they show the fantastically preferential treatment a large and semi-bust borrower gets, as compared to even the solvent borrower-in-the-street. Go into default just once, and the bank will very likely nail you to the floor—unless you are a Lockheed, and have stuck the banks for millions instead of hundreds or thousands. The agreement by which Lockheed was charged a low, low interest rate of 4 percent on that part of the consortium loan not guaranteed by the federal government was extended until the end of 1976, after which the rate was to rise to the prime rate plus 1 percent. Judged by those terms, anybody would think that Lockheed was being rewarded for good conduct.

Then the banks would convert $43 million in loans and $7 million in accrued interest into $50 million of a new 9.5 percent preferred stock. The $350 million left in nonguaranteed loans was to be extended until 1981, and converted from the highly inconvenient form of revolving notes (which needed reconfirmation every ninety days) to a term loan for the full period—another important concessionary reward for Lockheed's sins. As their recompense, the participating banks got ten-year warrants to let them acquire 3 million Lockheed common shares at $7 a share, and another 500,000 at $10.

The company's stock and debenture holders had actually, at that point, not met since May 1974. A shareholders' meeting had been scheduled when the bribery scandal erupted, but was put off when the SEC at first refused to approve Lockheed's proxy statement until the company disclosed everything "material" about the foreign payments, including the names of recipients. The tale that emerged grew steadily more horrendous, as Lockheed revealed enormous commission payments, running at several times the confessed bribes, which made even hardened observers wonder how the company ever expected to make any money on its sales, or, if it did, just how vast the true profits of aerospace business might be.

On the second point, the answer was plain—nothing like vast enough to remove Lockheed's financial position from the critical list. The General Accounting Office, which had shown more sense than many of the alleged financial wizards throughout, warned that Lockheed might have difficulty in repaying the $195 million lent under federal guarantee by the deadline of 1978. Dr. Arthur Burns, chairman of the Federal Reserve Board, apparently believed that the original loan was a mistake; any other opinion would have placed his own credentials as top U.S. banker in grave doubt. The company's own auditors were perplexed and bothered by the uncertainties—such as some $515 million in deferred TriStar charges which might never be recouped. Nor could they guess at what might be the outcome of various legal and other disputes relating to the commissions and bribes disbursed so liberally by the company.

But Lockheed stayed in business, though that too was hurt by the scandals. The Canadian government, ordering a fleet of anti-submarine aircraft, came back to the store: too big to go bust, Lockheed was far too important a merchant of death to be left out of the wheelings and dealings of the military-industrial complex. That did not help the TriStar. Early in 1976, Lockheed was storing an inventory of planes at Palmdale in California, as deliveries were delayed or canceled. One customer, the British Court Line travel operation, had collapsed; TWA and Eastern Airlines had postponed purchases; Pacific Southwest Airlines had not taken delivery of a plane; other potential customers were extending the service life of existing equipment, or expanding its seating capacity, not buying new machines. Even the successes, like beating the Douglas DC-10 to the state-owned British Airways order for a long-range version (a victory no doubt aided by the Lockheed-Rolls connection), had a drawback. They committed the company to TriStar activity still further ahead.

But the new management, more realistic than the old, drew up a schedule for gradually phasing out the TriStar: the $500 million in outstanding costs would be written off by 1985, and more sales would trickle in (three for Saudi Arabia, one for Delta, the three for BA, and so on). Yet the banks with so much at stake in Lockheed could take little heart over these modest improvements in the company's fortunes, and certainly no credit. It took twenty-four of the biggest banks in the United States five years to get rid of a management that had staked the very life of a great company on a no-win bet. It should have taken the bankers five minutes.

15. A Grant in Aid

WHEN a giant corporation hires a chief executive on terms which virtually guarantee him an income of $100,000 a year for life, one of two preconditions must apply. Either the man or his assignment must be terrific. Probably both—as appeared to be the case when the W. T. Grant Corporation, a huge chain of stores, bid for the services of Robert Anderson, then vice president of retail merchandising at Sears Roebuck, in the spring of 1975. The glittering offer was needed to woo Anderson away; he was at the peak of his career with one of the great retailing enterprises and had a first-class reputation as a merchandiser. Why sacrifice all that to join a rival, especially one in desperate straits?

But the W. T. Grant board used its princely offer so to twist Anderson's arm that eventually he ceased to resist. Nobody on that board twisted harder than De Witt Peterkin, the director representing the interests of the Morgan Guaranty Trust Company. Peterkin knew better than anyone how much the interest of his own bank, and of twenty-six others belonging to a consortium that by then was struggling frantically to keep W. T. Grant alive, depended on working a miracle.

It is bad business to reckon on wonders, or on wonder-men. A miracle on the scale demanded was beyond Anderson's powers, or anybody else's. In the spring of 1976, a year after Anderson had sidled into the most uncomfortable seat in retailing, W. T. Grant went into total liquidation. The seventeenth largest retail enterprise in the United States, which at its peak operated close to 1,200 stores and employed 82,500 staff in forty states, with an annual turnover of some $1,800 million, went as thoroughly bankrupt as any East Side novelty shop.

It was the worst disaster in retailing history, and second only to the demise of the Penn Central on the scale of modern corporate failures. The banks, which in their unbankerly despair had been hoping for a miracle, became victims of their own misplaced faith, or misapplied money. Grant failed owing the banks some $600 million in short-term debt and another $100 million in long-term loot. In a gesture that

119

became distressingly routine, as American banking counted the cost of past excesses, the banks collectively wrote off $234 million of Grant debt. A fortune had gone with the wind.

The bigger the financial institution, the bigger the bashing. Morgan Guaranty, Chase Manhattan, and Citibank, each with $97 million outstanding, said sad farewells to $50 million apiece. The damage was proportionately lower for Manufacturers Hanover, Bank of America, and Continental Illinois, which had about half as much at stake; and so on down the line to Chemical Bank, Bankers Trust, and others who were less deeply involved. The losses were retribution for a series of miscalculations of mounting and baffling size and stupidity—right up to the extraordinary act of faith in Robert Anderson and his supposedly magic wand.

The clear truth is that when Anderson came on the scene, no rabbits were left in the hat. In rueful retrospect, Anderson himself mused to *Fortune* magazine: "I'd say there never was a chance of saving Grant. But I didn't know that when I took the job." Since he was not an insider, perhaps Anderson can be excused. But those who were on the inside, or at least inside the boardroom, knew little better. After the event, the main reason for the debacle emerged as an appalling lack of information, a communications gap of awe-inspiring dimensions. Other factors contributed, including poor management, personality clashes among top executives, overhasty expansion of retail outlets, overambitious trading up, credit policies that bordered on the macabre. But the root of all evil was that the Manhattan headquarters (since rechristened "Grant's tomb") lacked the basic figures necessary for control; indeed, no meaningful numbers seem to have penetrated that corporate grave.

Morgan Guaranty's vice chairman, John P. Schroeder, the mastermind behind the Grant loans, has subsequently admitted that the bankers had already sensed trouble in 1974; they had agreed to help out, " . . . because Grant looked sound if they received some bank help." The claim deserves closer examination—and such study unfortunately indicates that Grant could only have looked sound to someone with exceptional myopia.

Some myopia was inevitable, given that the figures which management fed to the board, and which the board in turn fed to the bankers, in Schroeder's words, "all turned out to be wrong—continually." Which means that $700 million was lent to a management that, with over 1,000 stores and $1,800 million a year in turnover, had gone on year after year serving up gobbledygook in place of sound operating data. It also means that a group of allegedly sophisticated, smart bankers had equally consistently swallowed the lot.

Grant was no headstrong newcomer. It dates back to a store established in Lynn, Massachusetts, around the turn of the century by William T. Grant. For the next sixty years or so, there was no trouble as the enterprise expanded gradually to a chain of a few hundred traditional five-and-dime stores, catering mostly to blue-collar workers and their families, and located mainly in the northeastern part of the country. The turning point was 1960. At that key date in the Kennedy go-go era, Grant embarked on a massive expansion program designed to take it onto a new plane, that of a nationwide chain. The crucial influence was Edward Staley, brother-in-law of the original William Grant. Staley took control when Grant stepped down in 1952 and effectively dictated policy thereafter.

It was a policy that threw traditional retailing precepts to the winds. Between 1963 and 1973, the chain opened 612 new stores and enlarged 61 others—in an all-time record, 15 new Grant stores were opened on the very same day. This was flying in the face both of providence and of the retailing rule of thumb that it takes, on average, three to four years for a new outlet to move into profit. It follows that when a chain like Grant has almost half of its stores less than five years old, the business is most unlikely to make much money.

No doubt, the need for profit helps explain the passion for trading up—selling higher-priced goods. For nearly three-quarters of a century Grant had supplied working people with such basics as textiles, clothing, and household furnishings. Now they were to be encouraged to use Grant for such big-ticket purchases as furniture and household appliances. The policy took the chain into new and formidable areas of competition, for which it was ill-prepared, and into selling on credit, about which Grant was woefully ignorant. "If a customer's breath fogged a mirror, he was given credit," is how Robert Anderson mordantly summed up what he found on taking over. Furthermore, New York headquarters launched an all-out drive to promote store credit cards. Sales personnel were awarded a premium of $1 for every credit card holder they signed up; store managers wise enough to protest at the improvidence were warned to "hush up or quit."

The debt outstanding on credit cards zoomed to around $500 million; in the final accounting, only about half of this looked as though it would ever be collected. This wholly indecent exposure, a key factor in the firm's downfall, was one manifestation of a total loss of control. It was only to be expected, given the helter-skelter pace of store expansion. Opening the premises was the least part of the problem. Finding the qualified personnel to staff the stores, and training them to the necessary competence, was beyond the powers of an organization whose whole structure was makeshift, with authority undermined and communications haphazard at best. The 1,000-plus managers of the individual stores had an exceptional degree of autonomy. They could order directly about four-fifths of all their merchandise, price the goods as they saw fit, and simply forward the invoices to New York. Not surprisingly, different Grant outlets in the same area might cheerfully charge different prices for the same item.

To make bad even worse, New York required each store to report only total sales. So the head office had no idea what was selling well, or what was overstocked; some stores became so cluttered up with slow-moving flops that they had no space for new and possibly more attractive merchandise. Without any effective inventory control at either local or national level, Grant walked straight into a liquidity crisis of its own making.

Its inane credit policy forced the company to wait longer for more and more money due from the customers, while the chain itself came under ever greater pressure to pay its suppliers for expanding amounts of merchandise. For a time the gap was closed by borrowing, at heavy cost; in 1973, as the friendly bankers obliged, interest costs jumped to $51 million, up from $21 million a year earlier. But the seventies' credit squeeze, compounded by recession, forced management's back to the wall.

In the summer of 1974, Grant failed to pay a dividend for the first time in its sixty-nine-year history. By now, the discredited management was prepared to confess its sins and to seek absolution. The search for a new chief executive ended at home: the poisoned chalice was handed to James J. Kendrick, veteran of an excellent record at running W. T. Grant's Canadian subsidiary. Endowed with the rank of chairman, president, and chief executive officer all rolled into one, Kendrick had the first and melancholy task of revealing to an unsuspecting public the full extent of the carefully concealed mess at Grant. Actually, the signs should have been visible to even the mildly suspicious. In 1972, earnings of some $38 million had been reported on turnover of some $1,600 million; the next year, although volume increased to $1,800 million, net income plummeted by 78 percent.

One might have thought that so startling a fall in profit margins would have alerted a less knowledgeable soul than a banker. But worse was to come. Now Kendrick had to tell the world that in the nine months ending October 31, 1974, Grant had incurred a loss of some $22 million. Worse still, the full fiscal year was projected to record, at some $175 million, one of the most grievous deficits ever reported by a U.S. retailer; of the loss, two-thirds was attributable to credit operations.

On a year-to-year basis, the Grant janissaries had more than doubled inventories to some $450 million; while the expenses attributable to credit operations had escalated on a Homeric scale, from $6 million to over $160 million. These wondrously bad figures had two immediate and perfectly foreseeable consequences. Suppliers became accountably shy about shipping merchandise to Grant; and the chain's sales of commercial paper to finance inventory began to dry up.

At this point, Kendrick sought succor from the firm's now less friendly bankers. Grimly (and in some cases, reluctantly) the bankers gave aid—to many, there seemed to be no real choice. The devastating publicity that the banks had received when the Penn Central collapsed became a strong argument against allowing a similar debacle to develop at W. T. Grant. The crisis was every bit as acute as the Penn Central's: the chain was unable to roll over some $400 million in commercial paper. The banks came up with $500 million in unsecured short-term credit to fill the hole, shoveling good money after bad as if to the manner born.

No fewer than 143 corporate suckers participated in the $700 million loan agreement ($600 million short-term and $100 million long) which replaced the original half-billion. Morgan Guaranty corraled the victims, who took as collateral W. T. Grant's receivables, plus a 51.3 percent interest in Zeller's, the Canadian business once run by Kendrick. With his rearguard thus temporarily secure, the latter started to hew, hack, and saw at the dead wood cluttering up the business. An emergency blueprint was designed to shrink the chain to a "hard core" of about 900 stores by 1977; to lop capital spending by 90 percent in 1975; and to retire or release 12,600 of the 82,500 employees.

Still the losses went on. By the spring of 1975, the estimates showed a stupendous deficit of $18 million a month. Against that background, management's extraordinary offer to Robert Anderson must have seemed like petty cash. He was guaranteed, at the age of fifty-six, $2.5 million in salary and pension rights over a five-year period, which effectively set him up for life. Moving into Grant's tomb, Anderson worked at tremendous seven-days-a-week pressure. He fitted out a "war room" worthy of the real General Grant, and launched a campaign to close down 123 unprofitable stores, eliminate big-ticket, big-money losers like furniture and appliances, lay off tens of thousands of workers, and institute long overdue basic inventory controls.

No "war chart" on the wall spoke more eloquently than that which listed the 90 or so suppliers who, out of some 8,000, were proving least eager to deliver to Grant stores. Some were demanding cash on delivery, if not in advance; Anderson used an unheard-of tactic—sending out his buyers armed with certified checks. The suppliers' revolt was the real danger area, so Anderson persuaded the uneasy banks (now reduced to a nucleus of twenty-seven larger institutions after the claims of the rest had been settled for $56.5 million) to subordinate $300 million of their outstanding debt to claims by suppliers.

Even this did not work. The suppliers were still wary; many were notably undercapitalized themselves, and couldn't risk the evaporation of the money owed by W. T. Grant. The recalcitrants included some of the greatest names, and the stores were thus left deficient in merchandise at vital moments like the back-to-school promotions in the fall of 1975; Christmas that same year; and spring of 1976. As late as October 1975, the chain owed about $1 billion to some 3,500 unlucky suppliers. At this same point, Grant's management was obliged to tell the banks ("stunned" at the news, so they claimed later) that the corporation had a negative net worth that would reach the magic $100 million by the end of 1975.

The end was near. Early in October, W. T. Grant filed for bankruptcy under Chapter XI of the U.S. Bankruptcy Act. Here a technicality should be explained. Chapter XI proceedings assume that the afflicted enterprise can be salvaged by reorganization, and at the same time allow the creditors to play an active part in trying to work out a solution. The chapter avoids complete breakup of the bankrupt firm. A committee of Grant's creditors was duly set up, consisting of six bankers and five merchandise suppliers, with a banker (the vice chairman of Citibank) in the committee's chair. That of the company continued to be occupied by Robert Anderson, also chief executive officer in charge of operations.

But the committee was plagued by the same disease that had invalided out the previous managements—the absence of any figures worth even the paper they were written on. At the beginning of 1976, Anderson projected sales for the year of some $659 million, and a loss of $25 million. Well before the end of the first quarter, the sales calculation had moved in one direction and the loss in the other. Now, sales would be $647 million, and the loss $36 million. But the revision's life was no longer than that of the original figures. Somebody had come up with the right, if belated, idea of introducing objectivity into the calculation by calling in outside consultants.

This team projected the 1976 loss at $50 million, without, it turned out, having had the advantage of knowing just how much inventory Grant had on hand. Invited by management to choose between a high and low estimate of $115 million and $45 million respectively, the experts opted for a guesstimate of $60 million. On that basis, the banks were asked for a further $160–200 million (on top of $90 million already volunteered) in emergency aid urgently required to beef up the inventory.

The latest plan, on which the appeal was based, was for a "new Grant," a preshrunk model of 359 stores confined to the original northeastern region, specializing in soft goods and supposed to achieve an annual turnover of $700 million. The consultants reckoned, however, that it would take between six and eight years to get even this sadly diminished chain viable; and at this news the once indefatigable lenders gave up the ghost.

Early in 1976, the creditors' committee finally decided to liquidate the entire tottering enterprise. Despite all the revelations of the past, the liquidation had a traumatic impact. Until only a few weeks before, the official line had been that Grant would emerge from the tomb. The collapse also unleashed angry controversy. The Internal Revenue Service queried the basis of some $57 million in earnings reported between 1966 and 1971. The SEC questioned the profit and loss figures—and other matters besides. But these official doubts were nothing compared to the anger at the equivocal and even unsavory aspects of the final ignominious days of W. T. Grant, including the declaration of bankruptcy itself.

In the United States, a bankrupt enterprise can choose to file under Chapter X instead of Chapter XI of the Act, as used in the Grant case. Under Chapter X, the reorganization is entrusted to a court-appointed, independent body of trustees, pledged to treat all creditors equally and alike, instead of the creditors themselves participating, as under Chapter XI in the case of Grant. It was the bankers who first urged filing under Chapter XI; and it was the bankers again who insisted on bankruptcy in a 6 to 5 vote, which found the supplier creditors in the minority. The latter were protected by $300 million in Grant assets, which made them more willing to slug it out with fate.

The bankers undoubtedly wanted to liquidate in the end. The wrecked chain had $320 million in cash deposits and other liquid assets in the till at the moment of liquidation. These, if the banks could get hold of them, would cut the banking losses to some extent, leaving the devil—or the unsecured claimants—to take the hindmost. In the final agony, Morgan Guaranty and its allies showed far more alertness to arithmetic in their own interest than they had done during the long and grisly decline of W. T. Grant. It is a pity that they didn't start adding two and two a great deal earlier.

PART IV

THE NIXON
MAGIC CIRCLES

16. All the President's Money

THE love of money that is by repute the root of all evil was without doubt the origin of Richard M. Nixon's catastrophic, unprecedented decline and fall. Lucre, true, had played a crucial role in Nixon's phenomenal rise. But just as his collapse blotted out all previous Nixon wonders, so the trail of money in, up to, and around the Watergate scandal surpassed all the previous known or suspected involvements of the ex-president. It wasn't just money for himself, though the extravagance of his palatial homes, and his blatant avoidance of taxes, did more to turn the country against Nixon than anything except the fatal tapes. The key to the unmaking of the president was the money he sought to finance political activities—ranging from open election expenditure to the covert operations (the "dirty tricks") for which this politician seems to have had a unique taste. The treasure and the tricks helped win two elections to the presidency; then they destroyed the president.

Carl Bernstein and Bob Woodward, the now world-famous *Washington Post* reporters, were advised by "Deep Throat," their undercover contact, that the money held the key. It was excellent advice. The trail to Nixon's resignation started with the discovery of a cashier's check in a Watergate burglar's bank account and its tracing back to the Committee to Re-elect the President. Along the subsequent trail Nixon's point of no return came when he fired the chief Watergate investigator, Archibald Cox, presumably in a last desperate effort to stop Cox's discovering the whole truth about the notorious burglary of the campaign headquarters of the Democratic Party. Yet one mystery still remains unanswered—why was CREEP so eager to bug the Democratic headquarters that it took such a terrible risk?

Follow the money, as Woodward and Bernstein were told. And the most plausible answer is that the Nixon gang feared a leak about the secret $100,000 contribution made to the reelection campaign by the billionaire industrialist and longtime Nixon backer Howard Hughes. The connection could have been made all too easily. Larry O'Brien, the Democratic national chairman, had once worked for Hughes, and it wasn't difficult to foresee that the Republican candidate would have suffered from any such revelation in the mounting battle for the presidency—even at the hands of a bumbling candidate like George McGovern.

But the Hughes donation of a mere $100,000 was only the tip of a mountain of millions: dollars paid over in secret, illegal, and often extorted contributions by individuals and business enterprises, which thought they had something to gain from the reelection of incumbent President Nixon, or feared they had much to lose from his revenge.

The uncovering of Nixon's illicit cash gave the American public its first open instruction in how the banking system can be used, by mobsters as well as unscrupulous politicians, to hide their financial tracks. Systematic steps were taken to "launder" the Nixon funds by both donors and recipients. Money that is in some way "dirty," either because of its origin or the purpose for which it will be used, is processed through various channels, mostly banks, so that it finally emerges as "clean"—without a speck of suspicion attached to it. The banks are the most convenient and efficient laundromats for this cleansing, whether the managements are innocent of the process or not.

Money-laundering is part of the stock in trade of the Mafia and other underworld interests, crooked dictators, tax evaders, "hot" money manipulators, embezzlers, and other shady characters—which must mean that it accounts for a significant amount of the traffic passing through respectable banks. Handling illegal campaign contributions had not generally been included in the traffic until CREEP crawled along.

Just how much money "went through the laundry" during that campaign will never be known. Nixon's campaign managers were said to have raised some $60 million in all, much of it, no doubt, by fair means as opposed to foul. The tally of illegal payments by its very nature can never be complete, although the three main secret funds unearthed in the course of the Watergate investigations, each set up to ensure the reelection of Nixon and to frustrate the efforts of the Democrats, were large enough.

The fund that actually resided in a safe in the White House itself was known as the Haldeman Account, because it was supervised by H. R. (Bob) Haldeman, the president's chief of staff. Subsequently, the $350,000 or so involved was turned over to CREEP and joined a much larger bundle of cash kept in a safe in the office of Maurice Stans, former secretary of commerce, and chairman of the Finance Committee of CREEP. The exact size of this second fund has never been definitely established; estimates had it ranging all the way from $500,000 to over $1 million.

A third fund, put at around $500,000, was looked after by the president's personal lawyer, Herbert W. Kalmbach. Less trustful of safes, the attorney kept the money in the Newport Beach, California, branch of the Bank of America. It was alleged to have been used, in part, for Nixon's personal benefit, including the improvements to the winter White House (Nixon's later St. Helena) in nearby San Clemente. All three funds were kept in cash. Allegedly a fourth fund, containing anywhere up to $1 million, had stayed hidden in a bank in Switzerland, where its purpose was to facilitate "offshore" contributions to Nixon's reelection by people who wanted to avoid prying eyes in the United States.

A number of very big corporations had the same secretive desire. They had backed Nixon with donations, and these, large or small, were completely illegal under a law (dating back to 1902) that forbade business firms to make political contributions and politicians to accept them. These corporations, too, had urgent need of laundry services, and their subsequent confessions gave an exact description of the methods used. Thus, former American Airlines president George A. Spater, whose company passed over $55,000, admitted that the payment was made by means of a false invoice to a Lebanese subsidiary. The latter transferred the funds through a Swiss bank back to the United States. Phillips Petroleum and the 3M Company were alleged to have opened Swiss bank accounts for the same purpose, and Gulf Oil was said to have laundered contributions amounting to some $12.3 million over a period through a subsidiary in the Bahamas.

The most notorious examples involved the Associated Milk Producers, Inc. (AMPI)—a cooperative of dairy farmers—and International Telephone and Telegraph (ITT). In both cases the contributions were clearly accompanied by the granting of valuable favors. The Milk Producers, with assets of around $170 million, represent some 40,000 large and lesser milk producers in 22 states, mostly in the Midwest. They offered as much as $2 million to Nixon's reelection campaign, much of it illegally. This huge sum, what is more, was only part of a "war chest" that AMPI was willing to disburse over five years to candidates of both the main political parties, in order to protect, promote, and pamper the interests of its dairy farmer members.

Their outstanding interest at the time was to squeeze higher milk price subsidies from the federal government. Whether it was over $500,000 or a little less than $1 million that CREEP pocketed in March 1971 is unclear. But shortly after the first contribution was made, Nixon reversed a decision of his own secretary of agriculture to announce an increase in the price of the milk subsidy. The reverse put an extra $300 million into the pockets of the dairymen, at the same time effectively extracting a similar amount from the pockets of the taxpayers. When the murky affair was illuminated in the harsh light of Watergate, the cooperative got a light rap over the knuckles in the form of a $35,000 fine.

The affair, which caused a sensation after the Watergate revelations, had in fact been fully known long beforehand. A chapter in a 1971 book entitled *How the Government Breaks the Law* by Goddard K. Lieberman was actually headed "President Nixon Takes a Bribe." The author gave full details of the milk deal. Nobody, in the lax and sleazy political atmosphere of those days, took the blindest bit of notice. Not so in the case of ITT. Here the spotlight of unfavorable publicity became even more glaring after it was alleged (perfectly correctly) that Nixon had intervened personally on the company's behalf, instructing his Department of Justice in 1971 to lay off its pressure on the conglomerate in an antitrust case after ITT had pledged a contribution of $400,000 to the Nixon reelection campaign. When an earlier request from the White House had no effect, Nixon got on the phone to Richard Kleindienst, then assistant attorney general, storming, "You son of a bitch, don't you understand the English language?" (Kleindienst compounded the felony later by testifying before the Senate Watergate Committee that no pressure had been put on him by the White House to drop the case.)

None of the president's illegally gathered money could be put into banks in the normal way. Some was stashed in office safes; some found its way into the banking system by devious methods, which backfired disastrously in the Watergate burglary itself. The first positive break linking the burglary with the Nixon apparatus came in the summer of 1971, when *The New York Times* published a story (with a Mexico City dateline) that four cashier's checks to an aggregate amount of $89,000 had been paid into the Miami bank account of one of the burglars, Bernard L. Barker, through the Mexican Banco Internacional.

This was the lead that took the *Washington Post* reporters into the heart of the case and on to fame and fortune. Bernstein discovered the deposit in the same account of an additional check for $25,000, payable to the order of one Kenneth H. Dahlberg who, the reporters discovered, had been Nixon's campaign manager in the Midwest in 1968. Under questioning, Dahlberg revealed that he had sent the check to Maurice Stans at CREEP. This was the key that eventually unlocked the large "slush fund" in cash that Stans kept in his office safe; the secret payoffs in connection with activities such as the Watergate break-in; the "dirty tricks" that disrupted the Democratic campaign; and all the other illicit undercover operations.

In *All the President's Men*, Bernstein and Woodward give an account of the "Mexican laundry" caper, which traces a path followed by many similar dirty money movements. In this case, the trigger was a new campaign finance law that made it an offense not to disclose the source of election contributions. Shortly before then,

> Stans had gone on a final fund-raising swing across the Southwest. If Democrats were reluctant to contribute to the campaign of a Republican, Stans assured them that their anonymity could be absolutely ensured; if necessary, by moving the contribution through a Mexican middleman whose bank records were not subject to subpoena by U.S. investigators.
>
> The protection would also allow CRP to receive donations from corporations, which were forbidden by campaign laws to contribute to political candidates; from business executives and labor leaders having difficulties with government regulatory agencies; and from special interest groups and such underground sources of income as the big Las Vegas gambling casinos and mob-dominated unions.
>
> To guarantee anonymity, the "gifts," whether checks, security notes or stock certificates, would be taken across the border to Mexico, converted into cash in Mexico City through deposit in a bank account established by a Mexican national with no known ties to the Nixon campaign, and only then sent on to Washington. The only record would be jealously guarded in Washington by Stans, kept simply to make sure the contributor would not be forgotten in his time of need.

The sources from which this account was derived estimated that $750,000 raised by Stans and his two principal fund raisers in Texas had moved through Mexico in a single week. A few months later, the General Accounting Office (the auditing agency of the U.S. Congress) claimed that Stans was keeping a $350,000 slush fund in his office; later, the estimate was raised to $500,000. *The New York Times* lifted the figure to $900,000; some claim it must have reached at least the $1 million mark.

On one of the incriminating tapes, Nixon can be heard telling aides that there would be no problem raising a million dollars; he knew where the money could be found. This so-called security fund was demonstrably used to buy the silence of the Watergate team.

The General Accounting Office's investigations identified eleven apparent and possible violations of the new law on campaign contributions. In due course, Maurice Stans pleaded guilty to five charges of misdemeanor, including failure to report campaign contributions of $40,000 and $30,000 from Goodyear Tire and Rubber and 3M Company, respectively; of $39,000 from the former governor of Montana; of $30,000 from the former Philippine ambassador to the United States; and of disbursing $81,000 to Frederick LaRue, a CREEP official who arranged some of the Watergate payoffs.

But Stans was lucky, at that. He and John N. Mitchell, the former U.S. attorney general and later head of the Committee to Re-elect the President, were acquitted on earlier charges of conspiracy, perjury, and attempting to obstruct justice, in a case that was tried before the main Watergate evidence, so highly damaging to both men, had come to light.

The loot this time was offered by one Robert L. Vesco, a financier who bobbed up apparently out of nowhere to take over the battered rump of the Investors Overseas Services group of mutual funds, and then looted what was left in the IOS bag. Vesco should have stood trial alongside Mitchell and Stans, together with the go-between, Harry L. Sears, Vesco's lawyer and a prominent Republican politician in New Jersey; but Vesco had absconded to a hideaway in Costa Rica. According to evidence at the trial by Sears, who testified for the state in return for immunity, $200,000 in cash was given secretly, plus another $50,000 openly by check, to the Nixon reelection campaign.

Vesco did not even contribute the money out of his own pocket; it came from a corporation in which he was the major stockholder, International Controls Corporation. In delivering the contribution, Sears indicated that Vesco expected Stans and Mitchell to put pressure on William J. Casey, at that time chairman of the SEC, to call off the investigation into his affairs. Later, Vesco tried to blackmail the two high CREEP officials with threats of exposing the $200,000 secret.

In any event, Vesco was too dirty to be laundered. Three weeks after Nixon had been reelected in November 1972, the SEC charged Vesco and forty-one other individual and corporate defendants with converting to their own use some $224 million in IOS funds. A few weeks later, in January 1973, CREEP belatedly returned the entire $250,000 to Vesco, with a covering letter referring to the SEC indictment. The fugitive financier, in potential danger of twenty years in prison and a fine of $25,000 should he ever leave the expensive comforts of Costa Rica to stand trial in the United States, provided a poor illustration of political bribery but another excellent demonstration of how money can be laundered through the banks.

The secret $200,000 originated in the Bahamas Commonwealth Bank controlled by Vesco. It was instructed to transfer the money to the branch of Barclays Bank International in New York. From there the money was picked up in hundred-dollar bills by an associate of Vesco, with an office in the same building as the bank. He took the money in an old briefcase by car to the headquarters of International Controls in Fairfield, New Jersey. The notes, wrapped in brown paper in the same briefcase, were delivered, according to Sears, to Maurice Stans in his Washington office. No receipt, he alleged, was given or asked (Stans himself was said to have requested the money in cash), but presumably another sharp hint about calling off the SEC watchdogs was dropped.

Large wads of currency seemed to have a habit of wandering around the Nixon world. The infamous $100,000 from Howard Hughes, for instance, which was entrusted to the care of Richard Nixon's good true friend "Bebe" Rebozo, was kept, according to the latter's barely credible account, for three years in a safe in the bank he owned in Key Biscayne, Florida. At the end of the period, Rebozo said, he returned the very same greenbacks to Hughes. Skeptics prefer another version: that the funds had been used for Nixon's political or personal benefit or both; and had been hurriedly replaced when the fact of the donation came to embarrassing light.

Once again, as with the payoffs from contractors that brought down the corrupt Spiro T. Agnew, an element in the mystery was the relative smallness of the sums. Could $100,000—the price of a suburban residence—really bribe the president of the United States? Maybe the Italian financier Michele Sindona had less intimate knowledge of the money-grubbing ways of American politicos. He allegedly offered ten times as much, a hot $1 million, toward Nixon's reelection, at a time when the government was opposing his plans to merge the Franklin National Bank with the Talcott National Corporation (both of which Sindona controlled). The bank merger remained blocked, and the million was turned down. Had it been accepted, Sindona's operations in Italy, Switzerland, Luxembourg, Liechtenstein, the Bahamas, Panama, and who knows where else, would have placed him in an ideal position to play laundryman.

How many other launderings never became known because they achieved their purpose cannot be told. Without the accident of a botched burglary, very few people would have believed that henchmen of the president of the United States were using circuitous banking routes to conceal the origins and uses of illegal money. It seems that in most circumstances, for those who need to launder money, you really can trust your bank. Whether that makes the rest of us any happier is doubtful. But if the circuit is broken—as it was by the Watergate burglary—the fact that banks record the fall of a sparrow, monetarily speaking, means that the cover-up can be stripped bare in seconds. Thus did a single cashier's check pave the way for the downfall of a president.

17. C. Arnholt Smith Takes a Dive

AT Richard Nixon's moment of narrow triumph over Hubert Humphrey in November 1968, the exclusive group of private celebrants in a New York hotel suite, before the official victory party, included Conrad Arnholt Smith—wealthy San Diego banker, many-sided businessman, and longtime close friend of the new chief executive. In the well-worn way of political friendship, Smith had cemented the relationship with money. His $200,000 personal contribution to the election campaign was only a particle of the cement. As fund raiser, and open persuader of others to donate much more, the San Diego entrepreneur carried on a tender loving care for the Nixon finances that dated way back to the president's first ferocious race for Congress in the forties.

Nationally obscure, C. Arnholt Smith was a big deal in San Diego —as chief shareholder and executive officer of the city's United States National Bank (USNB), and also as supremo of the Westgate-California Corporation, a conglomerate in agriculture, tuna fishing and canning, air transportation, taxicabs, real estate, life insurance. Altogether he ruled over an empire supposedly worth a couple of billion dollars: a titan of finance, apparently, a self-made wonder, worthy to stand side by side at the summit of electoral success with the most prodigious politician ever to emerge from California.

Half a dozen years later, the pair were companions at the nadir of disgrace. Nixon's Watergate was matched by C. Arnholt Smith's Westgate. As Nixon was deposed, so had his crony been removed, losing the presidency of both the bank itself and Westgate-California under a dark Nixonian cloud. Smith too had been accused of manipulating his office to enrich himself and betray his constituents—in this case, the creditors and shareholders of his businesses.

The parallel between the two pals went even further. Obviously, both had striven to cover up their misdeeds; in neither case did the authorities uncover the crimes with much evidence of efficiency or zeal. In the Watergate case, the *Washington Post* proved far more dogged and effective than the Justice Department and the FBI. In the affair of C. Arnholt Smith, the authorities responsible for the regulation of banks (the comptroller of the currency and the Federal Deposit Insurance Corporation) not only knew of irregularities long before USNB's collapse in October 1973, but were even alleged to have conspired in the cover-up.

Thus charged a suit brought against the two agencies at the beginning of 1976 by the trustees for thirty-two companies affiliated with the British Columbia Investment Company, which blamed its own failure on Smith's manipulations. The nominal owner of this blowout was a Kansan called M. J. Coen, a veteran business associate of Smith; the latter was said to have actually directed day-to-day operations of the whole caboodle. The suit itself was testimony to the complexity of Smith's affairs, naming as co-defendants Smith and no fewer than seventy-three companies owned by him, his relatives, his friends, and his business associates—all said to be "completely and absolutely" dominated by the financier, who "controlled their credits, assets and liabilities."

The two federal regulatory agencies managed to arouse the ire of bilked financiers on two continents. By letting the Crocker National Bank, of San Francisco, pay some $90 million for the sixty-four branches, and all the deposits and other assets and liabilities, the agencies safeguarded the depositors (and incidentally avoided a costly payout of deposit insurance by the FDIC). But the action jeopardized the chances of aggrieved creditors seeking to recover their investments. None were more affronted than a couple of dozen foreign banks, who had some $74 million at stake in letters of credit with USNB. On its collapse, international howls of protest arose as the FDIC indicated that foreign claimants would be excluded from the settlement.

The affronted included National Westminster Bank and Barclays Bank, two of Britain's Big Four; the vastly influential Société Générale of France; Banque Interunion; the unlucky and inept Westdeutsche Landesbank-Girozentrale of West Germany; and the Belgian Crédit Générale. The FDIC's tactic was thus exceedingly ham-handed. These and other banks also sued to try to reverse the Crocker deal. Banks are great litigants—they can afford the bills. Later, however, the foreign claimants got their hands on at least part of their claims; Natwest and Barclays, for example, recovered the respective totals of $14 million and $4.5 million at risk.

The overseas claimants were drops in an ocean of litigation. Some 150 lawsuits were pending at the time of the collapse; in one, victims of the affair accused the two Washington agencies of perpetrating a "bureaucratic cover-up." The suit claimed that the supervisors of banks had known of irregularities (and possibly illegalities) in Smith's conduct of the bank dating all the way back to 1960. The alleged shenanigans were quite spectacular: buying companies of questionable value at grossly inflated prices; transferring these assets to companies under Smith's control, and then using them as collateral for loans from USNB; selling Westgate-California assets at bargain prices to Smith companies, with the help of loans from Smith's handy bank; manufacturing false profits for Westgate-California by selling assets (or lending them interest-free) to nominee purchasers, who then used these same assets as collateral for USNB loans which paid for the purchases; and much else besides.

It followed that false and misleading financial statements were issued to the shareholders, the general public, the SEC, and other interested parties (so the suit asserted). As for Smith, like Nixon, he was The One, directly controlling about 38 percent of USNB and, through the medium of shares held by kin and cronies, effectively exercising 80 percent control.

The way in which the bank was run was a monument to laxity. Not to be outdone, the FDIC filed a lawsuit itself—this time against the directors of USNB, claiming that $400 million in loans were made "in contravention of sound, safe and prudent" banking practice; that loan officers were not properly supervised (some loans were said to have been made on Smith's personal appraisal); that bank records were incomplete or inaccurate about such germane matters as the purpose of loans, and the source, manner, and schedule of repayments; that the directors had failed to exercise control over the internal auditors, and even to establish an audit committee; that dividends had been illegally distributed in the absence of profits; and so on.

After years of sharp and shoddy practices, USNB arrived at breaking point when its portfolio of risky loans exceeded the amount in the capital account. In a desperate attempt to replenish its capital, the bank bid around for short-term money wherever large quantities could be found, from corporations, labor unions, private investors, the open market (where USNB apparently bought up money in lumps of $100,000 and more). To attract these blood transfusions, USNB had to pay well above the going market rate. By the autumn of 1973, the burden of interest had grown intolerable and the bank was clearly cracking under its weight.

The comptroller of the currency and the FDIC stepped in to place USNB in receivership; Westgate-California followed it into bankruptcy the following February. (Arnholt Smith, together with his associates, was removed from the bank's management in spring 1973.) The bank was not one of the country's or even the state's greater banks. Yet at the time, its collapse, with assets of some $1,200 million at stake, ranked as the biggest in U.S. history (later to be eclipsed in the roll of dishonor by the crash of the Franklin National Bank, of Long Island). Given the machinations of the Smith gang, it is doubtful whether the crash could have been prevented, once the pattern of improper banking had been set. And that was the most worrisome aspect of all. Smith's financial wheels and deals had produced the USNB's downfall, and that fall had exposed the banking misdemeanors. But could a bank whose officers were not feathering their own financial nests have banked equally atrociously without the regulatory agencies' making a move?

The answer alleged in one of the lawsuits is an appalling Yes: In 1960, in a routine examination of the bank, Jack Baker, chief national examiner for the comptroller of the currency, uncovered evidence of "unsound and illegal" USNB practices. He confronted Smith with the violations, and exacted a promise that the malpractices would not be repeated. But when Baker came back for another review in 1963 he found the offensive behavior still going on, and on a substantial scale. USNB had made loans beyond the legal limit to a single individual or company, to certain other enterprises under Smith's control, without requiring adequate collateral or keeping necessary records. At that time, Smith was apparently the only man in the bank who knew what was going on; so Baker called a meeting of the board to inform the other directors.

In his official report, Baker described the condition of the bank as "unsatisfactory"; he also took the further extraordinary step of writing to both the FDIC and the comptroller of the currency, filling in more details of the grisly situation. The FDIC was sufficiently moved to put the bank on its "problem" list, designating it a bank "with substantial weakness requiring prompt corrective action to avoid a risk of loss to the FDIC insurance fund." So the aggrieved parties claimed.

The second report went to the comptroller of the currency, James E. Saxon; he, too, was aroused, sending his chief Washington assistant, Justin T. Watson, out to San Diego. Watson reached a "cease and desist" agreement with the management, restricting loans by the bank to Smith-related companies, including Westgate-California. Now the whole board should approve any loans of this kind; audits were to be made by independent accountants; and audited statements were to accompany any unsecured loans to Smith-connected enterprises. In addition, complete and current reports of Smith's interest in or affiliation with any company borrowing from the bank had to be submitted to the chief regional bank examiner.

Back came the assiduous Baker to carry out yet another examination in 1966—and to find that Smith was neither ceasing nor desisting. He again described the bank's condition as "unsatisfactory," and specifically warned both the regulatory agencies that their instructions were being disregarded. This was Baker's last stand. His diligence was rewarded by a post examining banks in Alaska (which can't be much warmer than Siberia, where Russians who rock the boat eke out their penance). Baker's successor, Richard Spencer, who had also been a member of the Baker examining team, found nothing to criticize about the running of USNB for the next decade; his superiors, in spite of the knowledge at their disposal, appear to have accepted his reports without challenge and no doubt with relief. At the end of that period, in 1973, Spencer ended up, not in Alaska, but in appointment by Smith as a vice president of the bank.

The best interpretation that could be put on the weird conduct of the regulatory agencies was that they gambled on the possibility that USNB might escape from its difficulties by contrived bank mergers, by dumping certain liabilities of the taken-over banks into enterprises controlled by Smith, and by keeping the "clean" loans to improve the business of USNB. If the regulators did condone these operations, as charged, they had aided and abetted the cover-up of massive irregularities by Smith and his bank. In any event, the merger scramble failed.

But if the watchdogs, for whatever reason, were turning a blind eye, others probed. In 1969—that far back—the *Wall Street Journal* questioned certain activities of USNB, Westgate-California, Smith himself, members of his family, friends, and business associates. The report stimulated the comptroller to order a special examination of the bank, but the findings were never divulged, and no action was taken. Two years later, in 1971, Haskins and Sells, the well-known accountants, voiced qualms about Westgate-California's investments in hotels, a horse-training facility, and Air California, and the company's relationship with USNB to boot. In November that same year, the SEC started investigating the convoluted affairs of the conglomerate.

But the real crunch came in 1972, when a tough new examiner was appointed by the currency comptroller's office in place of Spencer —William Martin, an official worthy of the Baker inheritance. After a thorough going-over, Martin found that all the old, condemned practices were not only going on but had been magnified. Martin ordered operations tightened up, but on returning to USNB's premises in January 1973, he found that Smith had removed all the accounts of his "captive" corporations.

The most critical report yet on Smith and his bank found Martin accusing the financier of engaging in the "deceptive and improper use of bank records that could be construed as criminal violation." He specifically charged that USNB had exceeded its legal lending limit of $233 million; questioned the creditworthiness of loans equivalent to a stunning 370 percent of the bank's capital; and opined that its contingent liabilities on letters of credit could result in a severe liquidity crisis.

This time the bad news was communicated to the attorney general, the Criminal Division of the Justice Department, and the FBI in San Diego, together with a view that USNB was in "grave condition." The law enforcement agencies were also alerted to twenty-five separate transactions by the institution "which might have violated criminal law." What happened? Nothing—or nothing much. Decisive moves were made neither to curb the abuses nor to take legal proceedings against the perpetrators.

In spring 1973, the SEC joined the chase. In the light of evidence turned up by its investigation, the SEC told the federal regulator that it was set to move against USNB for financing fraudulent transactions on behalf of Smith and Westgate-California. The comptroller's office responded by privately urging the Commission to lay off, for fear that a fraud suit might trigger a run on the bank. Passing all belief, the comptroller still actually thought that the bank's problems could be sorted out, that, "with the exception of Westgate and British Columbia Investment self-serving loans, the bank appears to be operating with due regard for the depositors' and shareholders' interests . . . the internal weaknesses in the bank's assets can be corrected without receivership and subsequent losses to depositors and shareholders."

Faced by this astonishing (and utterly misleading) assertion, the SEC stayed its hand. Not that USNB won any respite. It was already five minutes to twelve for C. Arnholt Smith. A month or so after issuing the gratuitous vote of confidence, the comptroller's office ate its newly mouthed words by issuing a cease and desist order, curtailing the lending activities of the bank, and booting Smith from office. Shortly thereafter, the SEC finally filed its threatened suit.

Still the saga of official stupidity, or worse, was not over. At this point, when midnight had already struck, the most extraordinary episode occurred. The delinquent, devastated bank was allowed to market some $5 million in debentures to improve its capital position. This resulted in a further charge that by permitting this travesty, while knowing that the bank's financial reports were a sham, the regulators themselves had violated the anti-fraud provisions of the law.

By this time, with his friend Richard Nixon paralyzed by the long agony of the Watergate revelations, C. Arnholt Smith began to be crushed by the USNB investigation. Ironically but justly, in view of his history of political financing, his first penalty had no connection with his banking and business affairs; in March 1975, he was found guilty of making illegal contributions to the reelection campaign of former California Senator George Murphy. The jury could not agree on charges involving contributions to the 1972 Nixon campaign. Smith was fined $10,000.

Three months later, he pleaded no contest to four charges of fraud, out of an original twenty-five, involving the misapplication of millions of dollars of USNB funds by ninety-seven loans and letters of credit; eleven promissory notes; fifteen falsified credit memos; and eighteen special accounts set up at USNB in the names of Westgate subsidiaries. The plea, the dismissal of all but four of the charges, and the light sentence imposed hardly fitted the crime—Smith got only a two-year suspended sentence and a $30,000 fine. The extenuating circumstance of age (the promoter was seventy-six) presumably helped. Had he been found guilty on all the counts, Smith could have been imprisoned until his nineties.

The affair could not end on that false note, however. Early in 1976, Smith was indicted by a grand jury in San Diego County, on fifty-eight charges of grand theft and the misapplication of bank funds. The first trial had been in a federal court. Now the state was bringing its own charges, alleging the violation of California laws that did not enter into the earlier case. The state's attorneys got U.S. Supreme Court consent to have access to secret testimony before the federal grand jury that handed down the first indictment; and that included testimony by representatives of the comptroller of the currency, the SEC, and the Internal Revenue Service (which was busily dunning Smith for unpaid taxes dating back to 1969).

Prosecution apart, Smith faced forty suits involving claims of thousands of millions of dollars, including one for $1,500 million filed by the trustees of Westgate-California; a $150 million action by USNB stockholders, alleging fraud; and seven suits by government agencies seeking more than $300 million in damages and claims on loans. In the financial world, the disaster paralleled friend Nixon's Watergate. Birds of a feather, it seems, do flock together. The president had been helped by Smith, and very materially, when running for office; while in office, did Nixon repay the debt by restraining government bureaucrats who otherwise might have made trouble for his friend?

Smith himself had a remarkably different version: that the difficulties which finally caught up with him resulted from "bureaucratic zeal," caused by resentment of his friendship with Nixon. One thing is sure. If it were true that a hidden hand stopped the bank regulatory agencies from doing their duty in the affair of the U.S. National Bank of San Diego, that would be less discreditable—though still discreditable enough—than if the dereliction had been all their own sloppy work.

18. The Bountiful Bebe

AMERICA has its superabundance of banks for a very simple reason: because Americans have a great, an irresistible yen to open them. That is what happened in the autumn of 1973 at Key Biscayne. A group of prominent local citizens, businessmen and lawyers in this lush Florida community, decided that what they would like best, next to a few more millions, would be to open a bank. There was already one bank serving a population of only 8,000 to 9,000, but the group considered there was room for another, especially theirs, in view of their faith that within a few years the population would about double.

If you, too, want your very own bank, this is how you go about it. Simply apply for a charter to the department of the comptroller of the currency. He will appoint an examiner to consider the application and recommend that the charter should or should not be granted. In the Key Biscayne case, he turned thumbs up. But somewhere aloft in the hierarchy of the agency, the examiner's decision was reversed; the community had to go on managing with just one bank, the Key Biscayne Bank and Trust Company.

Its would-be competitors were naturally aggrieved. But when it came to friends in high places, influence, and clout (as they publicly grumbled), the latecomers were hopelessly outscored by the chief shareholder, chairman, and president of the Key Biscayne Bank—none other than Charles Gregory "Bebe" Rebozo. The local millionaire of Cuban descent, famous only by virtue of his bosom friendship with the president of the United States, Richard Milhous Nixon, was then still at the height of his power and prestige.

True, any banker in Rebozo's position would have taken a similar line at the hearing in Atlanta, Georgia, arguing against the opening of a rival institution on the grounds that the future population of Key Biscayne had been grossly overestimated, and that his own bank was quite capable of taking care of the needs of residents for the foreseeable future. There's nothing a banker likes more than a nice, secure monopoly, and Rebozo, a man always ready to throw his weight around, especially if his interests were threatened, was no ordinary banker or businessman—because his relationship with the president was no ordinary friendship.

So Bebe Rebozo retained his monopoly as a banker in Key Biscayne. Nixon's indebtedness to the banker took many forms, not all of them monetary. But money runs like a vein, or an artery, through the Nixon-Rebozo story. Bebe may indeed have been the only man with whom Nixon could talk quite frankly, with total security, the only person with whom Nixon could relax under pressure, the ideal and totally silent companion for the long boat trips on which Nixon recharged his nervous batteries. After Nixon lost to John F. Kennedy in the 1960 presidential election, Bebe was the only outsider to stay with the family in a Los Angeles hotel suite while they absorbed the bitter news.

The other aspect of the indebtedness, a far more practical turn than kindly sympathy, was especially in evidence after Nixon reached the political Valhalla of the White House. Rebozo was always on hand if the president needed money, for seemingly any purpose. His was a key role in setting up the relatively poor Nixons in the multi-millionaire style to which America's First Family reckoned they should become accustomed, in rich villas in the Rebozo territory of Key Biscayne, and in San Clemente, the president's future California exile.

Rebozo was not just a banker. He also ran a lucrative real estate business; that, too, was only part of the variegated financial interests built up by the emigrant from Havana, brought to Tampa by his parents as a child. Known as "Bebe" because a brother had difficulty in pronouncing "Baby," Rebozo went to Miami High School, then found work as a chicken plucker, a chauffeur, and a mechanic. Eventually he opened his own gas station in 1935. Its financial success redoubled after Rebozo went into the business of selling recapped tires during World War II while also flying as a pilot for Air Transport Command. With capital now behind him, Rebozo entered the small loan and acceptance business, potentially lucrative because of its high rates of interest, and requiring a tough attitude toward customers who neglectfully fell behind in their loan repayments.

In this same period, Rebozo became involved in a number of real estate deals, many of them with former Senator George Smathers, to whose Democratic star Rebozo hitched his own. Several of their deals were financed with the help of public funds, such as loans from the Small Business Administration. It was Smathers who introduced Bebe to Nixon (then a senator and shortly to become vice president to President Eisenhower) in 1951. The friendship which matured down the years reached its apotheosis in 1968. Soon after he became president, Nixon adopted Key Biscayne, at the tip of the Florida Keys, as a spot in which to relax from the cares of office.

He bought a house owned by Smathers in an exclusive community, adjacent to Rebozo's, for $125,000; and then the house next door for $127,000 to ensure privacy. Another neighbor was Robert Abplanalp, a financially helpful multi-millionaire who played a prominent part in the subsequent Nixon story; his home was leased to the federal government to house the Secret Service officers guarding the Nixon family. Abplanalp was the largest producer of aerosol can valves in the United States, outdoing Rebozo in the little matter of big money.

The purchases caused the president no cash strain; he acquired them with a loan of $65,000 from the First National Bank of Miami and a $189,000 mortgage. But almost from the moment of his arrival in Rebozo-land, Nixon began to improve his asset position through real estate deals that owed far less to the president's business acumen than to the guiding hand of his resident friend. In 1967, before he became president, Nixon had bought 185,891 shares in Fisher's Island, Inc., a Miami-based development firm in which Rebozo was a major stockholder, for $1 a share. Two years later, the president sold them back to the company for $2 a share, making a profit of $185,891, before capital gains tax.

Also in 1967, the president bought two undeveloped lots in Florida for $38,000, which he sold at the end of 1972 for $150,000. This was the notorious deal supposedly financed with the help of a $20,000 loan from his daughter Tricia on the condition that she would receive back the face value, plus 40 percent of any profit her father realized from the sale of the property. She eventually grossed $65,000, on which she dutifully paid capital gains tax of $11,617.

Nixon's Californian eye had also lighted on an estate owned by a widow in San Clemente, on the coast between Los Angeles and San Diego close to the U.S. Marine base of Camp Pendleton. Nixon agreed to buy the house and immediate surroundings for $100,000, plus a $240,000 mortgage; but the owner wanted to sell all 26 acres. The president financed the purchase with a $400,000 loan from Abplanalp, plus a $1 million mortgage. This, too, was in 1969. The following year, Nixon sold the excess acreage, keeping 6 acres of choice beach property, to a firm known as B. and C. Investment, which actually meant Messrs. Abplanalp and Rebozo. The purchase price was close to $1.3 million. This remarkably convenient deal for the president enabled him to repay his loan to Abplanalp, plus interest, and to enter into possession of the sumptuous winter White House for a relative song.

When the Watergate scandal broke wide open, this deal was among the odors released. Nixon never paid tax on his huge capital gain; the division of the property was never recorded officially, so that it never really passed out of Nixon's control (Abplanalp allegedly said he would hold the extra land for the president); and the payment Nixon received was in truth a gift. The details of this carefully negotiated wheeling and dealing, so handy for Nixon and making him so beholden to his two friends, only came to light through the Watergate investigations. Banker Bebe was charged with no offense, but the blaze of unwelcome and unfavorable publicity reached its peak of intensity in a separate controversy: the $100,000 Howard Hughes payment, bribe, campaign contribution—call it what you like—to the Nixon coffers.

Rebozo became involved because the money—proffered in two equal installments in 1969 and 1970—was deposited in his bank at Key Biscayne. Nobody denied that, including Rebozo himself. The point of contention was what happened to the cash thereafter. What happened to Hughes after the deposits is clearly established. Two separate government agencies were giving him irritation and trouble at the time. The Civil Aeronautics Board was opposing his acquisition of Air West, a small West Coast airline; and the Justice Department was trying to prevent Hughes from adding the Dunes Hotel and casino to his other gambling centers in Las Vegas. Both agencies finally ruled in Hughes's favor.

According to Rebozo, if the money was meant as payment for services to be rendered, it singularly failed—because it never reached the intended beneficiary. The faithful banker simply put the bills in the safe, left them there without earning any interest for three years, and then returned the same bills in the original wrappers to the donor. Rebozo offered no explanation for this behavior. It is as unlikely a story as a banker has ever told, starting with the assertion that the $100,000 returned to Hughes was the same as he had handed over in the first place. A much more convincing theory was that the bank had simply acted as a laundry; later, when the Hughes largesse came to light during a suit brought against the multi-billionaire industrialist by his disgruntled ex-employee Robert Maheu, somebody (so the unauthorized version runs convincingly) must have quickly replaced the loot in the bank safe.

Physically, the opposite of laundering seemingly took place. Crisply clean bills from the Las Vegas casinos were replaced by grubby ones as from long storage in a vault. Senate investigators thought they knew whose: the Hudson Valley (N.Y.) National Bank, whose general counsel, William E. Griffin, allegedly reimbursed Hughes against cash from associate Robert Abplanalp. An account tells of a May 1973 meeting at the presidential retreat, Camp David, between Rebozo, Richard Danner (Hughes's emissary in turning over the money), and Nixon himself, at which arrangements were concluded with Abplanalp to replace the missing sum, and for the generous donor to take it back.

What had the original $100,000 been doing if it was not in Rebozo's bank safe? A team of investigators appointed by the Senate

Watergate Committee, after conducting some 300 interviews and poring over innumerable documents, found evidence to suggest that some or all of the Hughes donation had been used for the benefit of the president and his family, including the purchase of jewelry for Mrs. Nixon. Herbert Kalmbach, personal attorney to both Nixon and Rebozo, told of a meeting with Rebozo in April 1973; the latter had asked advice on what to do about the Hughes contributions, saying he had given part of the money to the president's two brothers, and part to his secretary at the White House, Rose Mary Woods. In Kalmbach's version, he counseled Rebozo to return what was left of the funds, and to submit a list of the names of any people who had received any of the money, and how it had been used. Rebozo, of course, flatly denied the whole tale.

Curiously, the Kalmbach lead was never followed up; the investigations into the allegations were purely perfunctory, lost among the other reverberating scandals of the Nixon regime, even though another key figure in the Watergate scandal, Charles Colson, the president's special counsel, charged that Howard Hughes had given $100,000 and more to the president and his family for their own private use. That could conceivably have covered part of the purchase and improvements of the properties in Florida and California; the total outlay on improvements alone was some $187,000. One compromising development was the report that Rebozo received the second $50,000 Hughes contribution while actually at the winter White House in San Clemente, negotiating with the president about further financing for the property.

The figures involved make for some fascinating coincidences, too. (1) Nixon acquires 26 acres of property, aided by a $400,000 loan from his pals and a $1 million mortgage. (2) A little later, Nixon gets the chance to pick up another 2.9 acres; $20,000 was to be in cash and the other $80,000 in the form of a mortgage—adding up to $100,000. (3) Nixon has, ostensibly sitting in a safe in Bebe Rebozo's bank, a sum of $100,000.

Or did that $100,000 from Hughes simply get submerged in the general pool of slush money, from which nearly $500,000 in payoffs passed over to buy the silence of the Watergate burglars and cover up the White House involvement? If so, was banker Rebozo the custodian of contributions other than those of Howard Hughes? Did that explain a notable passage from the White House tapes (Nixon is speaking): "I told B-B-Bebe, ah, basically, be sure that people like, uh, who have contributed money over the contributing years are, uh, favored and so forth in general. As I said, there's a few, not much . . . as much as—I think—as 200 . . . available in the '74 campaign already"?

In the parlance of the White House, "200" meant $200,000; twice as much as the Hughes contribution. In fact, there may have been two funds, one held personally by Rose Mary Woods, of $100,000 (the Howard Hughes donation?); and the other of $200,000 to $300,000, kept in Rebozo's kindly care.

But there was still another scenario to explain what became of the billionaire's bribe. One of Rebozo's principal aides at his Key Biscayne Bank was Franklin S. DeBoer, a vice president and trust officer. He affirmed that at the time of the Hughes contribution, President Nixon had bought a $100,000 certificate of deposit. DeBoer was also reported to have boasted that he had been in charge of Nixon's "secret portfolio."

However, these statements were said to have been made after DeBoer had resigned in 1973 from the bank under pressure from the regulatory FDIC, on the grounds that he was not a suitable person to hold his position. The agency cited activities in which he had become engaged when an officer of National Home Products Corporation, and as a former partner in Baerwald and DeBoer, a brokerage firm whose license had been revoked in 1971. DeBoer himself had been debarred from acting as a broker-dealer in January 1972, after the SEC had accused him of violating federal securities laws. DeBoer consented to the SEC findings and penalties without admitting the charges. It was curious to find him a little later holding a position of trust in Rebozo's Florida banking monopoly.

The DeBoer affair recalls unpleasant memories of a yet earlier embarrassment involving Rebozo and his bank, back in 1968. In September that year, the important Wall Street brokerage firm of E. F. Hutton and Company, during a routine audit, discovered the loss of a big block of IBM stock certificates. Shortly afterward, in the first week of October, an FBI agent visited the Key Biscayne bank, and inquired about certain IBM shares that the bank had taken as security for a $195,000 loan to a certain Charles L. Lewis, of Atlanta, Georgia.

The shares referred to were 900 from a total of 5,500 IBM stock certificates stolen by mobsters operating from the Bahamas. Lewis was intermediary in a deal that had raised the $195,000 loan by pledging 600 of them as security for its face value, with the other 300 shares given to the bank as additional collateral, to guard against fluctuations in the share price of IBM on the stock exchange. Lewis was to turn $120,900 over to the mob, keeping the balance as his commission.

Rebozo allegedly called in the loan, and sold the IBM shares. As a result, he and the bank were named as defendants in a suit by E. F. Hutton, and by an insurance company which had covered the brokerage house. The sum involved was $284,880—the price Hutton said it had had to pay on the open market to replace the missing stock. A strange feature of the affair was that Rebozo apparently loaned the nearly $200,000 to Lewis without checking his credit. The bank was also said to have reassured itself about the "validity" of the IBM shares by a most peculiar means: a telephone call to the president's brother, Donald Nixon.

All in all, there are many blurred pages in the history of the banking career of Richard Nixon's good friend. How many other small banks engage in similar fuzzy deals, without emerging into the dazzling light of Senate investigations, nobody knows. And presumably nobody much cares, apart from the few thousand citizens, like those of Key Biscayne, who are served by each of them.

So far as the public was concerned, Bebe dropped right out of the news once the furor over the Watergate scandal subsided. For long months nothing more was heard of him, either bad or good, or of his bank, or his real estate business, or his other related activities in Key Biscayne. In its heyday, when the bank basked in the reflected glory of a chief shareholder and top officer who was the close friend and local neighbor of the president, it had been called the "biggest little bank in the United States." The biggest little bank got caught up in the biggest big poker game in the country. The bank—and Bebe Rebozo—were lucky to escape with their skins.

19. The Fortunate Fugitive

BANKS are places where we all keep money—including those of the human race who are crooks and con-men. The latter can kill two birds with one stone: using the banks to store the cash harvest that they reap from lesser mortals (lesser, that is, in worldly cunning) and also employing banks, bankers, and banking as combine harvesters for the reaping. What may well be the largest rip-off in modern times revolved around the skillful, crooked use of the banking tool. At the moment of writing, not one of the participants has been sentenced for his part in the caper, though one has at least appeared in court.

Early in 1976, the former head of the $2,300 million Investors Overseas Services (IOS) financial empire, Bernard Cornfeld, answered charges in Los Angeles. His alleged misdemeanor had nothing to do with the IOS collapse, but was concerned with illegally using electronic equipment to place telephone calls overseas without paying. Around the same time, a new indictment (the fifth) was brought by a federal grand jury against Robert L. Vesco. It accused him, together with six associates, of misappropriating more than $100 million of assets formerly managed by IOS. Vesco, however, was unlikely to appear in any court in the United States unless dragged there. He was holed up in a sumptuous hideaway in Costa Rica, the fattest financial fugitive in the world.

In fact, neither the founder and one-time undisputed boss of IOS, despite being accused of petty larceny, nor the impudent opportunist who had ousted Cornfeld from his imperial throne and despoiled what was left of its treasure, had anything to complain of monetarily. Cornfeld, the former Brooklyn social worker who couldn't read a balance sheet but had persuaded legions of investors from all over the world to pour money into his numerous funds, had survived a series of disasters —the IOS crash, a long period without trial in a Swiss prison, the final rip-off by Vesco—without ceasing to be rich. But on the face of it, even so smart a manipulator as Cornfeld had been comprehensively outsmarted at the last. Between him and Vesco there was one subtle but important difference. Cornfeld was something of a flawed genius at manipulating people, but Vesco was a master at manipulating banks. Banks, and his astute and allegedly unscrupulous use of them, were the key to the complex, tortuous process by which Robert L. Vesco ensconced himself as a fugitive in Costa Rica, ready to live in exiled opulence for the rest of his days.

Whether he could do so hinged in part on the political fortunes of the president of Costa Rica, Dr. José Figueres, who had befriended Vesco and his money, and repeatedly refused to extradite him to the United States. Vesco's father had worked for Chrysler as a Detroit assembly-line hand and foreman; the son rose high enough to become a co-defendant with two former Nixon cabinet members, John N. Mitchell and Maurice H. Stans, on charges of perjury and obstruction of justice, in connection with a $200,000 secret donation by Vesco to the ex-president's 1972 reelection campaign. Since Mitchell and Stans were acquitted of taking a bribe, Vesco presumably stood a fair chance of being cleared of giving one. But the enormous mass of evidence, including the various indictments and suits in which he features as the defendant, fully explains Vesco's reluctance to stand trial. Whatever the civil or criminal offenses of which Vesco is guilty or innocent, the last stage of the IOS saga, dominated by Vesco's exploitation of his contacts with banks and bankers, may stand as a textbook example of the blacker arts.

One bank and banker in particular served Vesco's purposes— Butlers Bank of Nassau in the Bahamas, and its head, Allan Butler. Both rested obscurely in their offshore tax haven until the Vesco connection threw them onto the world stage. The most amazing use to which Vesco put this unlikely ally was the way in which he manipulated Butler and his bank to bamboozle all and sundry into thinking that he, Robert Vesco, was acting as the agent for, and receiving the financial backing of, some of the world's most prestigious banks, including Bank of America and the Union Bank of Switzerland.

Allan Butler founded his bank with money put up by his wife, the second daughter and heiress of Sir Harry Oakes, a goldmining millionaire whose Nassau murder in mysterious circumstances in 1943 remains one of the great unsolved cases, like the fate of the *Marie Celeste*. The bank had already acted on behalf of International Controls Corporation, the New Jersey electronics conglomerate which Vesco had assembled and in which he held the controlling interest. Notably, the bank helped Vesco to stage a 1968 raid on the Electronic Specialty Company, a California fabricator of high-strength, high-temperature parts for the aerospace industry, which was ten times as big as International Controls.

Butler and his bank became even more useful to Vesco when he plotted to take over the remains of the IOS group, so much larger than

ICC even in its extremity that a lesser man than Vesco must have boggled slightly at the sheer arrogance of his scheme. At the pinnacle of its power and prestige, in 1969, the Cornfeld empire held a score or so of mutual funds and investment trusts, managing combined assets of some $2,300 million for close to a million investors from almost every country on the map. In addition, that same map was dotted with some 200 affiliates of IOS, the largest of them in banking, insurance, and real estate, providing auxiliary services to both the IOS funds and their clients, and in the process generating sizable additional booty.

This huge, unprecedented financial complex based on the investing of other peoples' money was always far shakier than it seemed— despite its touting of so-called people's capitalism, despite its creation of considerable personal wealth for the greedy salesmen who hawked IOS wares, despite the big names (James Roosevelt; Dr. Erich Mende; Sir Eric Wyndham White, former director general of the General Agreement on Tariffs and Trade) who were foolish enough to get sucked in, and despite dazzling public relations built around Cornfeld's personal flamboyance.

In truth, the operation was bedeviled with business incompetence; just as much of the money flowing into the funds had nothing to do with people's capitalism, but represented hot money fleeing from tax collectors in industrialized and Third World countries, and maybe money that was dirty as well as hot. However, a large percentage of all the individuals who entrusted their funds to Cornfeld (and who ultimately saw them disappear) were small investors, lured by the usual seduction of getting rich quick. Their disaster, and Vesco's opportunity, began when Cornfeld and Co. went for their own financial killing by offering shares in the parent company, IOS, Ltd., in September 1969. Up to that time, preferred shares had been available only to the gang, officially as an incentive and reward for performance, really as a means of feathering nests, aided by loans from the employer (themselves). The holders changed their preferred into the new common before the sale, and thus made themselves into the largest bundle of paper millionaires on the shores of Lake Geneva.

The public responded rapturously (or so it seemed); the $10 shares, of which 11 million were issued, were bid up to $33 before they even reached the market. But the great bear market of the end of the sixties on Wall Street was about to get under way. As shares generally retreated, and the value of the IOS funds declined, sour investors began to redeem their units on a massive scale. Leading banks in West Germany (whose nationals were said to make up about 53% of all IOS clients), which had long watched with suspicion and distaste the rise of the Geneva upstart, didn't have to give the slide much of a helping shove. In fact, the fund redemptions fed on themselves. Where, at its peak, the IOS group was pumping as much as $800 million a year into Wall Street, it was now pulling money out; and the massive IOS about-face must itself have weakened the market still further.

The stock of IOS, too, began to plummet, heading below the $10 issuing price—and with good reason. The profit forecasts were ludicrously optimistic, the cash outflow gigantic and uncontrolled. The IOS management company faced a liquidity crisis; the funds themselves were mainly faced by a crisis of confidence, which was even harder to cure. IOS could plainly not be saved without an infusion of fresh capital —but whose?

The Rothschilds, the U.S. investment bankers Loeb, Rhoades and Company, the British merchant bankers S. G. Warburg, a consortium of major European banks—all such reputable potential saviors, after looking the situation over, backed away. The Denver oil king John M. King, a suspect Cornfeld confederate, himself collapsed before he could step into the breach. By this time the panic-stricken IOS board members were at each other's throats. One faction was headed by the former international civil servant Eric Wyndham White, who after the setback had replaced Cornfeld as chairman of the board. A $5 million loan offer from Robert Vesco's International Controls Corporation was accepted over the fierce opposition of Cornfeld. You don't need hindsight to see that the opponents were right to fear Vesco. Even though he wasn't Greek, Vesco brought Greek gifts.

In truth, ICC did not even have $5 million; Vesco badly needed the IOS assets to support his own crumbling enterprise, which had been seriously undermined by the struggle to take over Electronic Specialty. In this ambiguous situation, the fortunate fugitive turned to a large and prestigious bank—or rather, to its name. The impression was that Vesco would get the money from the Bank of America, which had already made loans to ICC (so it had, for what that was worth). Furthermore, certain IOS board members were hoodwinked into believing that Vesco was actually acting as front man for America's largest bank, which wanted the IOS assets for itself but did not wish this to be known until the deal was completed (with good reason, given the unsavoriness of the IOS reputation and its current imbroglio). The bank denied the whole story, and does not appear to have helped Vesco in any way. In fact, after Vesco had scrambled together all the ICC resources he could find to deposit $5 million in the bank, the latter refused to let him withdraw the funds to make the proposed IOS loan, warning that if Vesco did so, he might violate his existing loan agreement with Bank of America.

But the ruse set up the IOS board for the kill. Vesco suddenly switched stories, admitting that BofA had turned him down, but adding that the money was forthcoming anyway from Butlers Bank of the

Bahamas. Sir Eric and his demoralized supporters in the battered boardroom gave in. They agreed to accept the ICC loan, on terms that gave Vesco the right to 4 million five-year warrants to purchase IOS common stock at a discount. Now, even the most jittery director must have seen that Butlers Bank was a very different animal from the Bank of America, being in no great shape itself. (Cornfeld's peculiar genius also consisted in finding some incredibly unstable birds to flock together with.) According to Robert A. Hutchison, whose *Vesco* is an authoritative history of the man and his coup, the takeover needed the help of a six-week tiding-over loan from Hale Brothers Associates, Inc.—a San Francisco investment company with which Vesco had close ties.

At the end of that crucial interval, ICC Investments, a new Bahamian subsidiary of International Controls formed for the purpose, received the loan from Butlers Bank, while in the same breath IOS itself deposited a like sum with Butler. The scenario was beautiful in its way. Vesco acquired control of IOS, Ltd., with its own money, and at the knockdown price of $5 million. Vesco consummated his triumph by appointing his nominees to the board; he held over his new acquisition the bludgeon of an onerous loan agreement by which, in effect, he could in future make IOS dance completely to his will.

First, however, Cornfeld's exit had to be engineered. Bernie was a member of the board and the largest stockholder in IOS, Ltd., with about 15 percent of the preferred shares still outstanding. To accomplish this second stage in his program, Vesco allegedly again made use of his pliant Butlers Bank ally (or victim, so the latter claimed) by the abuse of a prestigious, big name bank, this time the Union Bank of Switzerland. First, Cornfeld was eliminated by use of the loan agreement, which was violated when Cornfeld accepted (with Vesco's approval) a position as chairman of an IOS sales subsidiary without the written consent of International Controls. Vesco promptly called the loan, and presented Cornfeld with an ultimatum. Either he must repay the $5 million and buy back the 4 million ICC warrants, or sell his stock.

Cornfeld by this time was not only outmaneuvered but deeply disgruntled. According to him, the main reason why he decided not to fight was his belief that his interest was being acquired by the great Swiss bank. The same tactic used earlier with the Bank of America had spread the impression that the Swiss bankers wanted to keep the deal secret until all was signed, sealed, and delivered. The bank's supposed agent was a Zürich-based subsidiary, Bank Cantrade.

Both the subsidiary and its parent, however, were being used as a false front. Vesco had acquired from Bank Cantrade a subsidiary Panamanian company, Linkink Progressive Corporation SA; it was represented as still being part of the UBS family. With the aid of Linkink, Vesco bought out Cornfeld's stake through the agency of a numbered account in the branch of Manufacturers Trust in Frankfurt, West Germany; the account, it was broadly hinted, was in the name of UBS. Actually, it was owned by Butlers Bank. True to form, the Bahamian outfit had come up with the funds to buy Cornfeld's shares, not from its own resources (which were inadequate) but by means of another tiding-over or bridging loan, this time provided by the Arthur Lipper Corporation—a New York brokerage house which in the past had garnered a lot of IOS business.

Cornfeld claims that wool had been pulled liberally over his eyes. At any rate, he signed the necessary documents, handed over his shares, and withdrew from the immediate IOS scene. Vesco was now free and clear. The next exercise was to transfer the operations from the Swiss-French border, where IOS had become notorious and it was risky even to stay around. Vesco found out just how risky when he crossed into Switzerland at the end of November 1971, to testify in connection with a suit brought against him by a former IOS sales manager. The investigating Swiss judge had Vesco arrested on suspicion of improper conduct, fraud, and attempted embezzlement; the financier was released the next day, through the intervention of none other than John N. Mitchell, then U.S. attorney general. (No such high-level intervention was forthcoming for Bernie Cornfeld when he was arrested eighteen months later; he spent almost eleven months in a Geneva jail until bailed out—at the price of $1.5 million—by friends, including Tibor Rosenbaum of the local, later notorious, International Credit Bank.)

Far better to remove IOS from Europe, where the authorities were turning hostile, to the Bahamas, where regulations were much less strict. The islands were already a pet location for offshore financial operations, and there, most important of all, nobody so far had direct experience of Vesco and his methods. The move involved replacing the existing custodians of IOS cash and securities—respectively, Swiss Credit Bank and the Bank of New York—with others more amenable to Vesco's orders.

The cash assets were steered to the Overseas Development Bank in Luxembourg, which Vesco controlled. This was a tiny institution, with only eight employees and a capitalization of just $150,000. On the face of it, this violated an agreement which forbade the Swiss Credit Bank to turn over its responsibility to any institution with less than $5 million in capital. However, the necessary $5 million deposit had conveniently been placed in the Luxembourg bank—out of IOS funds. When the Bank of New York refused to remit to the same destination the proceeds of securities sold, Vesco simply appointed a new custodian —the small New Jersey bank used by International Controls, which did as it was told. Finally, having assembled all the cash in one place under his personal control, Vesco transferred it all to the Bahamas Commonwealth Bank, in Nassau.

This was much less impressive than it sounded—an empty or shell corporation, which Vesco had acquired from the ever-accommodating Butlers Bank, and which he controlled through a newly constituted entity, International Bancorp, Ltd., of the Bahamas. The latter in reality was a reconstitution of IOS's former banking interests. IOS, Ltd., was made the majority shareholder in International Bancorp, in return for turning over all the IOS banking interests in Europe and the Caribbean. With the creation of Bancorp just down the street, and with all available IOS cash safely stashed away in its subsidiary, Vesco had no more need for Butlers Bank. He abandoned it to fate. Shortly afterward the bank failed, and the Butlers, husband and wife, joined the already long list of claimants for restitution from and retribution for Robert Vesco.

But nobody could get at him, ensconced in his Costa Rican hideaway with a faithful band of retainers that included Donald Nixon, Jr., nephew of the ex-president. Just how much money Vesco had at his disposal was a matter for speculation. In the civil suit that the SEC brought against him and a number of close associates in 1973, the agency charged that some $224 million from the estimated $500 million or so in IOS assets that passed from the control of Cornfeld to Vesco were missing and unaccounted for. The indictment by the federal grand jury, based on the SEC investigations, at the beginning of 1976 reduced the sum to about $100 million.

Meantime the SEC, with the help of the authorities in Canada (where IOS, Ltd., had its corporate domicile), Luxembourg, the Netherlands Antilles, and elsewhere, had apparently been successful in freezing a large chunk of the fund assets, and in enforcing the liquidation of several of the related companies. Still, $100 million (or even some part of it) is a tidy rip-off. Let that be a lesson to all of us. Because a bank *calls* itself a bank, it doesn't mean that it is one. And because a man says a bank is behind him, it doesn't mean that it is. All it does mean is that we have been conditioned just like Pavlov's dogs. The word "bank," and the names of familiar banks in particular, lull even the shrewdest of men into a false sense of security—and that is the very confidence which the trickster needs and on which he thrives.

PART V

THE
EUROPEAN FARCES

20. The Twain Shall Meet

TRADITIONALLY the banks of America and those of Europe have been as far apart in style, and sometimes in substance, as they are geographically. Even before World War II, American banking had become popular—in the sense, that is, of popular democracy. Just as Western democracy was founded on the principle of one man, one vote, so the ideal of American banking was one man, at least one bank account.

Many Americans had more than one account, although few had as prodigious a number as the comedian W. C. Fields. Yet the proliferation of Fields's accounts, under a variety of unconvincing false names, reflected not love for the banks but profound distrust. Fields thought there was safety in numbers. Had he been born and grown rich in a later era, he would have sought still greater safety in a numbered account—in Switzerland, not America, where the bad odor incurred by banks in the days of rampant capitalism was only accentuated by the failures and foreclosures of the Depression.

After World War II, however, banks became prodigies of public relations in order to expunge the old image, in which bank robbers like Bonnie and Clyde could almost pose as heroes, and to substitute a new idea of banks and bankers that was consistent with new times. In fact, the times came to meet the banks more than halfway. From one angle, the banks were pressing loans in abundant variety to make their customers outspend their incomes. But from another viewpoint, the banks were only responding to the overtures and demands of a society hungry for goods and the good life.

It was, of course, their own money which the people of America were borrowing, paying out far more in interest on the loans than they collectively received on their deposits (that being the basis of all banking); but also paying out far more than they knew, in the majority of cases. The true rate of interest on loans with a reducing balance—as monthly repayments of the capital were made, but as interest was still charged on the total loan—came to a much higher figure than the face rate. And the banks were perfectly happy to proceed with this decep-

159

tion until the law forced them to tell the truth.

It was perhaps the least creditable and most prolonged monetary malpractice of the postwar boom, and the banks have plenty to be ashamed of. Customers who thought they were paying 5 percent on a personal loan for a year were actually paying twice as much. Sometimes the effective rates were 18, 20, even 25 percent—coming perilously near to the level of back-street moneylenders. But the extent of the iniquity was not matched by the proper degree of mass indignation: people probably didn't care.

The American citizen was first and foremost a consumer. In his (and her) eyes, the cost of borrowing money loomed far less large than the ready availability of money for every purpose, from the mortgage on the new split-level home to the holiday in Europe, stopping en route for this year's station wagon. For all these ends, money was available from the friendly neighborhood bank; and it is characteristic of the U.S. consumer society that only its banks claimed the quality of friendliness. Not that the American genus is especially friendly: bankers are bankers the whole world over. But some unsung public relations genius had cottoned onto the right message—the public was far less interested in the safety of money than its accessibility.

In Europe, the situation was reversed. The European can consume every bit as hungrily as the next group, but the safety of banks is the prime consideration, which is odd, considering that American bank failures were more common and more traumatic than Europe's in the thirties. A conservative banking public was matched by conservative bank practices. Their dyed-in-the-dark-gray-worsted traditions held that banking was not for the common people, but for the better part of the middle classes, the rich, and, above all, the businessmen. Banks were there to oil the wheels of industry, to finance and cosset the entrepreneur. Banks and business grew so close and cozy that it became the practice for the institutions to hold shares in their corporate clients —a habit that could (and sometimes did) become embarrassing.

This was a far less high, wide, and handsome lifestyle than that of the Americans. Despite the awkward fact that the latter were confined by law to only statewide, sometimes citywide, activity, the largest American banks grew to become the world's preeminent financial institutions, on any measure of size or riches. But mass banking was inimical to the European belief—still deeply entrenched in the middle of the twentieth century—that it was bad form, morals, and practice to encourage the common man to get into debt.

The European ideal of thrift used to hold that in some unspecified way it builds character, improves the soul, and produces self-discipline for a man to wait for his house, automobile, or refrigerator until he actually has the necessary cash. Ideal and reality began to diverge as soon as postwar prosperity came within shouting distance of the American standard of living. But the spiritual influence of that inbred aversion to the buy-now-pay-later philosophy still lingers on, as does the business-banking nexus.

As late as 1973, the results were astonishing, especially to American eyes. At the end of that year, the companies of West Germany collectively held shareholders' capital of DM 72,000 million, and owed their bondholders DM 29,000 million. Their debt to their bankers was a colossal DM 368,000 million—three and a half times as much as the other two categories put together. No wonder that the German Left at that point attacked the banks, alleging that they had the economy in a stranglehold.

The two disparate philosophies of banking could in theory have been maintained in isolation. But forces beyond the control of the bankers were working to bring East and West together, with unpleasant consequences for both. The first force was the internationalization of business, specifically, the growth and spread of the American multinationals. Just as, if there's a man in the moon, there must presumably be a moonwoman, so a multi-national manufacturer implies a multi-national banker.

The banks of America were not about to let the Europeans muscle into their racket by sweeping up the business of American firms entering the British or Continental markets. Despite the American enthusiasm for consumer banking, and despite the difference in the relationship of banks and business, corporate lending is as crucial to American banking prosperity as to European. The banks followed U.S. business; and they brought with them well-tuned, smoothly efficient techniques for corporate and individual customer alike.

The likes of the Bank of America, Chase Manhattan, Citicorp, and Bankers Trust were only the vanguard of the invasion. And the invaders were typically not the least modest about their talents. As they opened up in London, Paris, Frankfurt, Rome, and elsewhere, the Americans hinted that the local bankers had much to learn—in everything from consumer marketing to the principles of business lending—from the newcomers.

Conservative Europeans may at first have hoped that the competition would be killed by its own excesses. Every now and again some horror story would come out of the American consumer paradise; a credit card company bludgeoned by the coups of rascals who had stolen cards, a business client like Chrysler Corporation all but destroyed by its issues of commercial paper. However much the bankers of Frankfurt and Zürich thought, "I told you so," the day of judgment never came. The Europeans could not compete with the Americans by wishful thinking.

Inevitably, the competition bred imitation. Nothing cracks a good principle more permanently than a bad loss of customers. On the consumer front, installment lending, mortgage loans, even credit cards were added to the European armory. The transplant, although it did not change the basically conservative European approach, took well. West Germany's Deutsche Bank, for example, reported a deluge of demands from branch managers for their new and higher business targets, once they discovered how consumer lending could boost their turnover and profits. Just as the U.S. banks had always known, the consumer market was lucrative and to all intents and purposes infinite.

If the meeting of East and West had stopped at that point, nothing but good would have resulted. The Americans would have enlarged their empires, and the Europeans, responding to the new competition, would have learned some new tricks that, like most old business dogs, they needed. The Americans had something to learn, too. In corporate banking, even if they could hang onto their U.S. clientele on its migrations into Europe, they found it extremely hard to detach European companies from their existing connections. And in consumer banking, they stayed firmly stuck on square one.

This was partly because the British customer, for example, found the American idea of neighborly friendliness distinctly hostile. Citicorp had a plush branch off Berkeley Square in London; but plush customers didn't take it kindly when the bank, hungry for profit, informed them that unless they cared to increase their deposits at the branch, they were more than welcome to take their custom elsewhere. Nothing could have been better calculated to put off the English, whose normal correspondence with their bank managers is over the size of their debts, not their credits.

At any rate, Citicorp no longer has a branch off Berkeley Square —and the expected competition from American banks on the domestic front has not materialized. Where the Americans did prove effective was in the third market—neither U.S. domestic banking, nor European banking, but in between. This is the remarkable world of the Eurocurrencies: currencies held in Europe by owners who are not citizens of the country concerned. The Eurocurrencies are the rough monetary equivalent of stateless citizens, and by far the most abundant and important is the Eurodollar.

In the huge traffic that developed in borrowing and lending these footloose dollars, American banks were well to the fore. But as the Eurodollar billions multiplied, so it became more and more difficult to sustain two crucial positions: the parity of the dollar in terms of gold, first; and second, the more or less fixed relationship of other major currencies to the dollar. To put the point in its simplest form, there were too many dollars in the world, under any description. In the spring of 1973, the American currency cracked under an irresistible weight of payments deficit. President Nixon somehow contrived to give the impression that this was some kind of American victory—an economic Pearl Harbor in reverse. It wasn't. It was a defeat not just for the United States, but for international economic order.

With the linchpin of the dollar removed, currencies were set free to move about, or float, according to the tides of supply and demand. You can make out an excellent case for floating currencies as a theoretical economist. But in practice, for a banker or a bank's customer, floating rates are a liability. Under the old system everybody knew that currencies, except for rare and large reassessments, could move only by 2 percent each way. So the risks of losing money because of exchange rate adjustments were minimal—it was all, or nearly all, taken care of by the system.

A businessman making equipment for a power station, say, could quote for an overseas contract in reasonable confidence about what he would receive in the overseas currency. Under floating rates, the certainty disappeared even for quite short periods—a three-month export contract could be torpedoed by a fluctuation. The longer the period, the greater the uncertainty. If there had been no means of insuring against the risks, world trade would have dried up. But there was a way; so trade continued—and the banks took the results on their glass chins.

If you sign a contract today to make a delivery in three months' time for $1 million, you can sell the currency that will be received today, also for delivery in three months, but at the price currently being quoted for that delivery. Uncertainty is thus removed, but at a price. If your currency goes down against the dollar, your "insurance" will have cost you a fat profit: suppose the exchange rate is 1 for 1, and the dollar rises by 10 percent over the three months, that is a profit of more than 10 percent extra in your own currency for doing precisely nothing.

So the temptation, even for a businessman who knew nothing about foreign currencies, was to speculate, to take a view on how the exchange rates would behave in order to enhance his profit. All these transactions could only be executed through the banks. Part of their routine business, adding up to sums of incredible size, is to exchange daily the currencies required for normal, everyday foreign trade and investment transactions. Now they were also, from the spring of 1973 on, tempted to venture onto much more treacherous ground. Like their customers in the business world, they could take a view: if their view was correct, bank profits would be greatly enhanced by foreign currency profits. But what if their view proved to be wrong?

In fact, the long postwar decades of narrowly fluctuating exchange rates had left the banks inexperienced in helter-skelter currency transactions and totally unprepared for a hurly-burly for which, constitutionally, they had no real stomach. Speculative ventures are not the diet on which commercial bankers are reared. The rich food that they suddenly felt obliged to consume made many of the banks distinctly nauseated. What had been routine, relatively disciplined business suddenly became hazardous and uncontrollable, even when highly reputable clients were involved.

For one main example, a new dimension of hazard was introduced into the trade of handling the finances of multi-nationals—the richest commercial prizes in world banking. Any European bank that wanted to be worthy of its size needed a share of this trade. But these business giants, American or non-American, are forced to trade huge sums of different currencies on virtually a day-to-day basis as one affiliate deals with another, or as profits are transferred across the world. Investments and disbursements alike demand a complicated pattern of currency transactions—typically conducted via holding companies in Switzerland, Luxembourg, or some exotic offshore island in the Caribbean, where the multi-national money is free to come and go without let or hindrance.

The multi-nationals are inevitably open to attack as a result of these operations. If Trans-Global Enterprises is owed £20 million, for instance, yet takes a poor view of the prospects for British inflation, its treasurer would be sadly lacking in responsibility as well as competence if he did not sell the British currency ahead of its receipt. But to the uninitiated such transactions looked indistinguishable from sheer speculation. And many financial officers, juggling with multi-currency reserves, trying to preserve the overall value of assets, and seeking to compensate as the various currencies shifted in relation to each other, must indeed have borne an unhappy resemblance to the out-and-out currency speculator.

Who or what these speculators are is a matter that has never been satisfactorily determined. But there is nothing intrinsically unsavory in their activities. Currencies are commodities like any other, but with the advantage that the quantities are inexhaustible. If a speculator can obtain a large enough pile of chips, he only needs them, perhaps, for twenty-four hours in order to make a fortune by switching from a weak currency to a strong one: anticipating a massive foreign trade deficit in one country, say, or the fall of a government in another. These currency speculators, too, dealt through the banks; and the banks, even if they could tell the difference, did not bother to distinguish between speculative transactions and the genuine business variety. The commissions involved, after all, were equally attractive in either category.

European bank officers in the floating rate era could hardly fail to note the often fantastic short-term profits that were being earned, with virtually no effort, in this manner. It is not surprising that, once exposed, some bankers fell for the new and fascinating temptation: engaging in foreign exchange dealing, not as agents, but for their own sake, and working if need be through other banks in order to enhance their own profits. In a sense, they seemed the best equipped of all for the game. Nobody had better access to factual data and informed opinion on future trends in the world money markets. Nobody had more or better electronic data-processing equipment. Nobody had greater experience of trading in this field.

Unfortunately, information, computers, and past experience from the years of relatively stable exchange rates are no substitute for hunch and instinctive trading genius—attributes of which bankers are notoriously short. All the same, the great majority of institutions kept their exposure and their guesses within tolerable bounds. No news is good news in this sense, and only a few banks had to report failure in the foreign exchange markets. But the exceptions were on the grand, even the grotesque, scale. Still worse, the horrendous losses were failures not only of judgment but of simple management control.

Thus in Belgium, the Banque de Bruxelles, one of the country's largest, owned up to hugely embarrassing losses on foreign exchange dealings; the dealings were unauthorized and unrecorded. The Belgians have always prided themselves on the stringency of their control over financial institutions—a fact that in itself demonstrates how floating rates had driven a gaping hole through the banks' protective walls. The National Banking Commission reacted by imposing even tougher restrictions on currency dealings, but too late to save the Banque, which was merged into Banque Lambert for its sins.

In West Germany the two largest state banks, the Westdeutsche Landesbank-Girozentrale and the Hessische Landesbank-Girozentrale, both got into the same kind of hot water. If they came to no permanent harm, that was due to their state ownership rather than any commercial saving grace. Less fortunate was Bankhaus I. D. Herstatt: being a private bank, even though it was one of the largest and most prestigious in the country, Herstatt found nobody ready to throw a lifebelt in its direction.

In Italy the banking empire of Michele Sindona, self-styled financial wizard and one-time financial adviser to the Vatican, collapsed in ruins for much the same reason. Sindona's special achievement was to preside over the destruction, partly through foreign exchange fiascos, of institutions on both sides of the Atlantic: the Banca Privata Italiana at home and the Franklin National Bank in the United States. Another double deal was in Lugano, where the disastrous losses of Lloyds Bank International simultaneously tarnished the reputation of Swiss and British banking. The lessons of Lugano will doubtless be discussed by junior cashiers still unborn, as they ponder the damage that can be caused by a free-wheeling foreign exchange dealer and an insufficiently attentive branch manager.

Even the upright and austere Swiss Credit and Union Banks became caught in the toils. These and other falls from grace not only blackened banking as a whole, but left a long trail of debts and disputes. All foreign exchange deals, as the name implies, are swaps, mostly of lesser currencies for the American dollar. This is because of the predominance of the dollar internationally, itself a consequence of the size and wealth of the U.S. economy and of the massive outflow of dollars into the world's oceans of convertible currencies. If the dealer guesses wrong about the dollar (as the failed finance houses mostly did), he will owe a debt to another bank, the one with which he performed the swap—hence the chain reaction.

When the Herstatt bank collapsed in Germany, for example, a whole string of American banks—including such bluest of blue-chip names as Bank of America, Citibank, Manufacturers Hanover, and Morgan Guaranty—were left asking for money owed them on uncompleted foreign exchange deals. The British merchant bank Hill Samuel seemed for a while to be getting stuck on a transaction that had actually been completed when the Herstatt fell. The other way around, the U.S. National Bank of San Diego, when it came to grief, had debts outstanding to leading British and continental institutions.

The banks of America and Europe thus ended up in the same bed, and often found it mighty uncomfortable. The threat that the Europeans had perceived—that of "popular" banking—proved to have little substance. American banking reflected American society, it turned out, and could not easily be transferred to foreign soil. East and West met rather in the world of huge international transactions, where their interrelationship was not a matter of choice, and where the risks had suddenly been magnified, to an extent appreciated by neither side, because of the floating of currencies. Like the Mormons, the two sides were wedded both for the here and the hereafter. At times, for some of the banks, it must have seemed touch and go whether there would be a hereafter for either of the transatlantic parties.

21. The Basel Bubble

PRISON isn't a bad place to write a book. Time is in ample supply, there is plenty of opportunity to reflect, and distractions are minimal—ideal conditions for authorship. Such disparate characters as John Bunyan, Adolf Hitler, and the Birdman of Alcatraz have, in their different ways, profited from the literary life behind bars. They were joined in 1970 by an American banker, Paul E. Erdman, whose best-selling novel *The Billion Dollar Sure Thing* was written in a jail in Basel, Switzerland. Erdman spent ten months there from September 1970, awaiting trial on charges of disloyal management and falsification of documents while running a local bank belonging to the United California Bank.

Erdman drew on his intimate knowledge of banking for his book, a high-speed drama built around a threatened world financial crisis that arises when a prominent Swiss banker becomes privy to the secret plans of the U.S. government for a further devaluation of the dollar. The real-life drama that put Erdman behind bars fell far short of the scale of his fictional fantasy. But he did manage to preside over the loss of $80 million (using the 1976 rate of exchange) by his bank—a fair sum of money even for these times. More important, the collapse of Erdman's bank was the first sign, and should have been the first warning, that the international spread of banks and financial institutions had exceeded the legitimate ambitions and managerial competence of the bankers involved.

Erdman's bank lost its money through speculation in commodities, principally in silver and cocoa, with some fliers in foreign exchange thrown in. The specific blame fell on the specialists in charge of these operations—at any rate, a Swiss court sentenced the two main culprits and some other employees to imprisonment and fines. But the court pinned the prime responsibility on Erdman, the manager in charge of the whole operation, and (with the usual fierce justice that the Swiss reserve for financial offenders) condemned him to the much more severe penalty of nine years in prison. Although this would have given him time to have written many more novels, Erdman not unnaturally

167

preferred to pursue his literary career under more pleasant conditions. Instead of appearing with his colleagues for trial in Basel in October 1973, he forfeited the bail of $132,000 raised by family members and friends, and stayed free in England.

His autobiography would make a racy read under a title something like *How to Ruin a Bank and Stay in the Money*. The strain and pain were largely borne by the United California Bank, headquartered in Los Angeles, which compensated depositors and creditors in full. The mother concern made good the transgressions of its Swiss fiasco quite philosophically. By the time UCB had collected insurance, realized assets, and clawed back some income tax rebate, the Basel bank failure had cost the 1970 accounts a sum of $19.4 million, hardly catastrophic for a bank with some $5,000 million in assets. That, indeed, is a major part of the trouble—the big banks have so much money (our money) that they can afford and can cover grotesque errors of judgment and control that would slaughter lesser industries.

The crucial aspect of the Basel affair was not the sum of money lost, in fact, but the question of how the proud Los Angeles bank, one of the fifteen largest banks in the United States, the second largest on the West Coast (after Bank of America), and part of Western Bancorporation, the largest bank holding company in the country, got taken to the cleaners by a bunch of jumped-up clerks in a small bank in Switzerland. And the answer is that it got taken because of gross carelessness at every turn in the tale.

In the first place, the evidence turned up by the Swiss authorities during the eighteen months of pretrial investigation showed that the local bank was already in a hazardous financial position, and that its records had been falsified, when the United California Bank acquired a 58 percent interest in the spring of 1969. At the trial, the chief prosecutor declared that false entries had begun to disfigure the books in 1968. The accounts for that year indicated a profit of some $337,600, but the figures had been cooked to conceal a loss on commodities trading of around $2.2 million. The first quarter of 1969 again purported to show a profit of $363,000; in reality, the commodity loss had soared upward to some $10.4 million.

Yet throughout this whole period of dreadful and mounting gambling losses, the big California bank was calmly negotiating the terms for a takeover, and no doubt congratulating itself on its coup, which was effected at a moment when the Basel bank was technically bankrupt. The truth is that the Californians picked up their Swiss subsidiary almost casually, in the spirit of the era. At the end of the sixties, American banks were rushing to set up European operations in a highly competitive atmosphere. Having acquired the bank for millions more than it was worth (which was less than nothing), the bankers compounded their error by leaving it, more or less, to look after itself.

It hardly counts as an extenuating circumstance that the Basel bank was not really Swiss but American—the principal shareholders were as American as apple pie. The main one, Charles Salik, was a neighbor of UCB's, just down the freeway in San Diego; his chief partners were his father, David Salik, of San Antonio, Texas, and Dr. Maurice Rice, a physician of Santa Ana, California. UCB paid $4.58 million for their 58 percent of what was then known as the Salik Bank of Basel —one of the worst bargains of the age, as the California bank sought to prove after the crash. It sued the Saliks and Dr. Rice for $5.8 million in damages, plus additional sums "according to proof," claiming that at purchase time the bank's assets had been overstated by $2.9 million; maintaining that there had been a prior "fictitious" sale of $1.2 million of the bank's stock; and not failing to mention the $340,000 profit reported for 1968, when a loss of some $2.2 million had been overlooked. Nor had anybody told the buyers that they were at risk for over $5 million of commodity gambling on the bank's own account. The suit was settled out of court.

Before the grand disillusion, UCB had been only too pleased to do business with its friendly neighbors. A prime reason must have been that one of the assets in Basel was Paul Erdman, its American chief executive officer. He simply changed his title from president to vice chairman (the new chairman was Frank King, also chairman of UCB in Los Angeles and of Western Bancorporation). Erdman, still very much in charge, had been with the Salik Bank since it started in 1965; he had actually persuaded the Salik group to found a bank in Switzerland, and to make him its boss. The son of an American Lutheran minister high in his church's Canadian organization, Erdman graduated from Concordia College in St. Louis and did his postgraduate studies at the School of Foreign Affairs of Georgetown University, before moving on to a Ph.D. from the University of Basel.

At the European Coal and Steel Community, Erdman and a colleague wrote an attention-grabbing book about the European Community and the Third World; subsequently the Stanford Research Institute hired him as its European representative, and Erdman traveled all over Europe supervising research projects. His contact with the Saliks came about via Dr. Neil Jacoby, a director of the Institute, better known as the dean of the Business School of U.C.L.A. Charles Salik first hired Erdman to keep an eye on European companies for an investment company.

The idea for a Swiss bank in Basel, where Erdman's wife came from, was all his own. In 1965 the deal was set up with an initial capitalization of $600,000. The plan was to open a bank which, the original prospectus proposed, would act as a bridge "between conservative Swiss banking—characterized by extreme caution, stability, and a unique expertise concerning financial matters on a worldwide basis—and modern corporate and financial management techniques usually identified with the United States." Even at today's distance, the arrogance is breathtaking. Maybe it actually appealed to the management of UCB and Western Bancorporation, when they came to contemplate the takeover. They, too, seemed to fancy Erdman's fantasy of an institution that would combine the best of the United States and Switzerland. Assuming that they continued to read the prospectus, the Californians could have found still further revelations that would have served as warning signals to anybody more sophisticated than Li'l Abner.

"The Salik Bank has sought," the text continued, "to move beyond the usual areas of money management offered by many of the more traditional banks in Switzerland, and to provide 'total money management' by building its capabilities related to types of investment other than the usual stocks and bonds." Those other "capabilities" involved trading in foreign exchange, metals, and commodities—the very activities that eventually brought down UCB in Basel. At first, however, the basic business of handling clients' investments grew rapidly enough; the total portfolio managed rose from some $3.5 million at the end of 1966 to around $37 million by mid-1968. But the Salik Bank, probably by design, began to collect clients who were looking for above-average profits; gunslingers who needed to see some action.

To provide that action, the traders at the bank began to load their guns with increasingly chancy investments. Commodities are highly speculative at the best of times; not only clients' but also the bank's own money got plunged into the chosen situations. Moreover, the would-be wizards picked two of the most speculative games in town, silver and cocoa. No holds are barred in either commodity: in particular, there is no restriction on the amounts that can be staked, and the Salik Bank bet big. Its heavy trading in silver was profitable at first; but in the middle of 1968, when the price of silver inevitably began to go down, the bank and many of its clients lost money. Some of the latter threatened to accuse the bankers of careless management, and under that threat the management set out to recoup its losses by a new bout of inspired speculation, on both its clients' and its own account, this time in cocoa.

This treacherous crop also showed a profit for a while, until the end of 1968; but from then on the heavy losses surpassed even the silver fiasco. The losses were that much greater because the speculation was that much wilder: the bold spirits of the Salik, drunk on cocoa, seemed to be intent on creating a "corner" in the world cocoa market. But technically, control over so large a share of the total available supply of the commodity that you can dictate the price and the profits is impossible these days. Even in the tearaway twenties, when a caper of this kind was the dream of every financial buccaneer who sailed the Wall Street main, corners were rarely achieved. The more cocoa the Salik pirates bought, the more cocoa the shrewder men sold; the corner turned into a blind alley, with the bank committed to buying more and more cocoa when it already had huge losses on existing contracts.

Falsification of the bank's books thus became necessary to avoid revealing the gigantic extent of the losses to both clients and the bank's principals. The judge at their trial was probably right to say that neither Erdman nor the other defendants started out with intent to defraud; they were drawn deeper and deeper into tampering with the books to hide the mounting size of their speculative losses. Thus, United California Bank acquired its majority control of the bank in the spring of 1969 with immaculately bad timing. The new owners were at least sufficiently alert to tell Erdman and his staff to stop trading in commodities on the bank's own account, and to concentrate more on drumming up commercial business. However, UCB's bosses were not sharp enough to ensure that their instructions were actually obeyed.

The speculation went on regardless. Nine months after the takeover, losses on commodity trading had reached an estimated $30 million or so, concealed by a combination of cunning and deliberate carelessness. The book entries on silver and commodity dealings were described as "perfunctory"; there was no attempt even to balance the books at the end of the day to show the risks left outstanding and the amount at stake.

Erdman, whose own knowledge of the more exotic branches of banking, such as commodity trading, seems itself to have deserved the perfunctory label, appears to have given his boys their heads. And the boys, no doubt to spare his feelings, simply didn't record figures that they thought would prove too shocking. Dissimulation was aided by the weird fact that commodity trading was not run separately, being lumped in with foreign exchange and money operations. In the company's annual reports (meaningless, as it turned out), foreign exchange, foreign currency, and margin positions for commodities were combined in an overall figure.

In his book *Supermoney*, "Adam Smith," who, to his grief, lost a bundle in the Basel bank, reports that Erdman admitted to him that this practice was irregular: "We should not have combined the commodity, money market and foreign exchange departments. That made it too easy to cover by simply listing a time deposit from another bank. And if a department gives an order, the confirmation should go somewhere else, to be double-checked. Every position in the balance sheet should be verified, and it wasn't."

As he further explained, the bank was turning over as much as 5,000 million Swiss francs (just about $2,000 million) in foreign exchange and other transactions in any one day, and its own positions in foreign currencies might amount to a couple of billion daily. The figures for the commodity trading were smothered among these big digits, which easily concealed losses of a million here or there. Eventually, the losses became so enormous that an arm of the corpse stuck out from its improvised grave. Erdman's version is that when the bank's accountant queried a 25 million Swiss franc debit from a cocoa trade, in the summer of 1970, the chief executive was spurred to investigate the commodity trading department, whose head confessed (with notable lack of exaggeration) that things had "got out of control."

Erdman set out for Los Angeles with the bad news, which the top people at UCB apparently received with commendable equanimity, being more concerned with preserving their reputation by honoring the debts than with the financial setback. Outside auditors were called in to examine the bank's records—which neither the regular Swiss auditors nor the Swiss Banking Commission had seen any reason to challenge—and soon brought the buried losses to light. By the end of the summer, the damage had climbed to some $53.4 million, of which $31.4 million was the work of the demon commodity traders (at the dollar-franc exchange rate then prevailing). As a result, the institution was overtly quite bankrupt; that had been its technical position for some time. At the final close of business, it had assets of only $49 million or so to stack up against liabilities of over $81 million.

The list of offenses charged against Erdman and six of his colleagues included habitual fraud, continuous falsification of documents, acquiring notarization by falsification, publishing a false prospectus. One defendant died before he could be brought to trial; Erdman skipped bail; and the commodity trader, anticipating the worst, voluntarily spent the three-year pretrial interval in detention, calculating that the period would be deducted from his sentence.

The primrose path of the guilty men is easily discerned. They had taken risks in quest of above-average "performance," with the hope of attracting clients; but the species of client who favored such tactics could also turn savage if mistakes were made with his money. Massive mistakes were indeed made, the sensitive clients' money was lost, and in order to recoup the desperate situation, even bigger amounts of good cash were hurled after bad, with the further mistakes producing even bigger losses as the snowball rolled on toward the inevitable crash.

Harder to explain is the role of the United California Bank, which was guilty, at the very least, of naïveté in its approach toward business in a territory so far from base, and where, in many respects, conditions differed markedly from those at home. Instead of exercising more supervision than was considered proper in its own backyard—and more would have been both necessary and logical—the management had engaged in less. Its puzzling, casual approach dated from the very beginning of the association with the bank in Basel, when UCB Los Angeles failed to detect any evidence that the books had little connection with reality. The total lack of supervision is demonstrated by the astounding failure to check whether the order to cease trading in commodities with the bank's own funds was being obeyed.

Much of this offensive slackness resulted from pure trust in Paul Erdman. He made an apparently stunning impact on the management of his bank's future parent from the moment he first met members of the board in 1968. Chairman Frank King is described as treating Erdman like a son. The board made the retention of his services a precondition of the takeover, while at the same time barring the Salik group from retaining any further interest in the institution they had founded. Although Erdman failed his sponsors, at the same time showing a remarkable propensity to fall solidly on his own feet (provided, of course, that they never again touch down on Swiss soil), he confirmed his latent ability in more ways than one. Before disaster struck, he sold to the parent the $190,000 in capital stock of the bank that was in his wife's name. With talent and timing like that, author Erdman should really have made a better banker.

22. The Sindona Connection

How rich is the Vatican? Richer than any millionaire, or any bank? The answer to that question has been sought by many outsiders down the years, but the Vatican has given them no help. Every now and then some assiduous writer ventures into print, purporting to reveal all, but actually communicating very little besides fervid supposition and regenerated rumor about massive holdings and deposits in banks in Italy and abroad; of real estate investments in the major cities of the world; of fat stakes in capitalist businesses of every shape and size.

One man who undoubtedly has lifted at least two or three veils of silence is the financier Michele Sindona. The Sicilian-born entrepreneur was not only for many years a trusted adviser to the Holy See on its investments, but also a business partner (for example, in the ownership of banks in Italy and Switzerland). His close ties with the Church did Sindona no harm in his own financial machinations—and he in turn (or in recompense) was in no hurry to add to the harm he had already done when the machinations turned sour.

Sindona, in fact, started off by keeping mum about his irreligious role in religious affairs, a silence that was much to the Vatican's taste. For the Sindona connection became exceedingly embarrassing to the cardinals in Rome after the financier's once formidable international empire disintegrated, and he became yet another fugitive from financial justice—this time that of Sindona's native Italy. Sindona sought refuge in the United States from the charges of falsification of accounts and fraudulent bankruptcy which set the seal on an exotic career; a Milan court duly found him guilty of no fewer than twenty-five charges *in absentia*, sentencing the absentee to three and a half years in jail.

The Americans, too, had a keen interest in Sindona's past because of unfinished funny business in connection with the Franklin National Bank of Long Island, which collapsed while under Sindona's control. As for Sindona himself, he claimed to be broke, though living in extreme comfort in a Manhattan luxury hotel, supported (he said) by loans from friends, and passing some of his time giving lectures, for free, on the merits of the free enterprise system to students at Columbia, the University of California, and the Wharton Business School. He couldn't have been that broke, however. When the U.S. authorities finally took him into custody, after Italy sought his extradition, Sindona found $3 million of bail "in his own recognizance," plus $150,000 in cash or treasury bills, not to mention his wife's apartment at the Hotel Pierre. Since his alleged frauds totaled $222 million, the price of freedom naturally came high.

As a product and exploiter of capitalism, Michele Sindona had much to teach. He had traveled the rags to riches route (and $222 million is a fair amount of riches) in apparently exemplary style. Born in the small Sicilian community of Patti, near Messina, in 1920, he was repelled by the strictness of his own father, and adopted as father-figure the local Catholic bishop, who befriended him and encouraged him to become involved in Church activities. Sindona continued to develop the connection even after he enrolled as a law student in the University of Messina.

During the war, he was exempted from military service by being employed by a citrus grower and was thus in a position to reap the glorious opportunities provided by the landing of the Allied liberation forces in Sicily in 1943. Sindona branched out on his own, buying a truck and getting contracts to haul supplies for the occupation forces. The love affair with Americans and America thus begun blossomed at a later date in the publishing of Rome's English-language newspaper, the *Daily American*—an asset lost, along with all the rest, in the eventual crash.

After passing his bar examination, Sindona set up as a business consultant in Milan. He specialized in American clients, especially U.S. corporations wishing to establish Italian subsidiaries in the immediate postwar period. The deals he promoted, as it turned out, were not always satisfactory to his clients; but Sindona prospered, shrewdly taking payment in stock options when he could. As a result, at one time he sat on the board of some fifty corporations; he also began to acquire a personal fortune by speculating in real estate.

Before long, too, he became a banker. That was in 1959, when Sindona took over Milan's Banca Privata Finanziaria; it is said that the connection paid off here, in the shape of funds from the Vatican's Institute for Religious Works. Later, he bought a 51 percent interest in another bank, Banca Unione (in which the Vatican definitely held a 5 percent interest). Eventually the two merged to create a new institution, Banca Privata Italiana (with the Vatican pals holding 5–10 percent of the shares). Sindona's creation had assets of some $2 billion and provided a springboard for his later astounding leaps.

Ten years later, in 1969, Sindona took over the Vatican's one-third interest in Società Generale Immobiliare (SGI), the largest real estate and construction company in Italy, and possibly in the whole world, whose property all over the globe included President Nixon's nemesis, Watergate. This transaction is believed to have been executed through the good offices of Cardinal Guerri, manager of the Holy See's investment portfolio. Three years later on, in 1972, Sindona had acquired 44 percent of Edilcentro-Sviluppo, the fourth largest financial company in Italy, with its international ramifications including ownership of the Grand Hotel in Rome and the Hôtel Meurice in Paris. SGI and Edilcentro subsequently merged, and this side of the empire was strengthened still further by the takeover of the CIGA hotel chain, one of the largest in Italy.

Far from sated by this rich diet of deals, Sindona also acquired other enterprises—such as one of the largest currency brokers in Europe. His object (and ostensible achievement) was to create a large, complex, and flexible money machine, whose weight would be felt heavily in world finance. The final, conclusive masterstroke was to be the unification of the various components into a single instrument, which Sindona would then control through his personal, totally owned holding company, Fasco, AG, of Liechtenstein.

This mailbox company had been established in its cozy tax haven quite early in Sindona's career. Even without incorporating the vast assets represented by his holdings in Banca Privata and SGI-Edilcentro, Sindona already controlled a far-flung and exceptionally complicated structure. The liquidator appointed by the Italian government to sort out Sindona's affairs after the crash (and who seized hold of the Fasco mailbox) discovered a fantastic labyrinth of over fifty enterprises. The interlocking shareholdings and exotic names (such as Trocadero, Sabrina, Paloma, and Tuxana) stretched from Italy, Switzerland, Liechtenstein, and Luxembourg to the United States, the Bahamas, Panama, and Liberia.

At the peak of his career, when his personal fortune was estimated at somewhere between $450 and $500 million and he was the subject of adoring articles in the financial press, Sindona was poised to put the finishing touches to his complex empire-building in two simple stages. First, he would bring Banca Privata and SGI-Edilcentro under the control of still another of his enterprises, Finambro (whose only asset at the time was a small bank in Milan); then Finambro would come under the ever-ready control of Fasco. This operation would have made the Sicilian upstart master of a financial domain larger even than the Fiat fief of the Agnelli family.

The agent of Sindona's downfall was the other state headquartered in Rome—the Italian government. To absorb the two much larger operations, Sindona needed to increase the capital of Finambro from

$770,000 to $30 million, and then to $245 million. For that trick, he needed the approval of the Italian treasury—and the treasury refused, on the understandable grounds that it had no guarantee that the assets represented by the capital increase would remain in the country (the fears, in view of Sindona's Fasco plans, were well grounded).

Sindona's previous relations with the Italian government, and with the Italian Establishment as a whole, may well have foredoomed the whole project. A few years before the treasury's refusal in the spring of 1974, Sindona had stirred up a storm by his attempt to mastermind the first ever public takeover bid in Italy. At stake was the $200 million Bastogi, the country's largest holding company, whose proud possessions included an important block in Montedison, the chemical giant.

Sindona's buying up of Bastogi shares prompted the government to urge other Italian institutions to close ranks and block him. The governor of the Bank of Italy, Dr. Guido Carli, denounced the Bastogi maneuver, partly because Sindona's partners in the raid were foreign institutions like the Continental Illinois Bank and the London merchant bank Hambros (also supposed to have close ties to the Vatican). An asset as important as Bastogi was not to come even partially under foreign control. The Italian Establishment's opposition was motivated, it was said, by desire for revenge after Sindona's earlier success in spiriting sizable slices of the Italian economy away into foreign hands.

After his Bastogi debacle, Sindona turned his ample back on Europe to a degree and started carving out a new empire in North America. His cornerstone was 21 percent of the Franklin National Bank, acquired in July 1972. This effort boomeranged at the worst possible moment. Sindona, locked in conflict with the Italian authorities over his plan to increase Finambro's capital, was hit by reports from across the Atlantic that his American bank was teetering on the point of failure. Indeed, it was only shored up by massive assistance from the U.S. government. Depositors with Sindona's banks in Europe began to take understandable panic, and to withdraw their savings lest they run a similar risk to clients of the afflicted bank on Long Island.

Between June and August 1974, deposits at Banca Privata shrank pitifully from $1,300 million to around $570 million. To make matters worse, the run on the bank was accelerated by rumors that Sindona's Italian enterprises were also coughing badly, infected by losses in foreign exchange trading, by loans to other sick banks, and by dubious transactions within Sindona's global empire. The shares of the real estate affiliate, SGI, began to plummet on the Milan stock exchange amid fears that it, too, had caught influenza in foreign exchange trading. At this point, the Bank of Italy intervened, and took a close look at Banca Privata's books; careful scrutiny revealed that the bank was about $260 million down the drain. The Banco di Roma, which is state-

controlled, was instructed to revive the Banca Privata corpse with a
$100 million loan—but on terms that spelled out the writing on the wall
for Michele Sindona.

He was compelled to wave goodbye to 51 percent of Banca
Privata, and to half of his shares in SGI; later, as the real estate mess
worsened, the rest of SGI had to follow. Banco di Roma executives took
over the management, and Banca Privata was put into liquidation.
However, again on orders from the central bank, two other big state-
controlled banks joined with the Banco di Roma to guarantee payment
in full to all the depositors in the Sindona bank, with one very deliberate
exception: the proprietor himself and his associates.

The house-of-cards syndrome was now fully activated. The enforced bankruptcies of Sindona banks in both Italy and North America
led the Swiss authorities to close the Banque de Financement in Geneva, which Sindona controlled together with his Vatican confederates
(the Holy See reportedly held a 49 percent interest); and a small West
German bank, Bankhaus Wolff, in which Sindona had an interest, voluntarily surrendered its license. But the Sindona institutions were not the
only sufferers—when one financial empire develops pneumonia, others,
at the very least, are bound to catch a cold.

Thus, the Swiss Bank Corporation, one of its country's Big Three,
disclosed claims against SGI, the results of uncompleted foreign exchange transactions, which outside sources estimated at $35 million. In
lieu of payment, the Swiss grabbed hotels and other properties belonging to Sindona in useful places like the Champs Élysées and Monte
Carlo. Over in America, the First Boston Corporation admitted to creating a special reserve of $9.1 million, needed to provide for possible for-
eign exchange losses that its First National Bank of Boston subsidiary
had run up in dealings with the Sindona Banque de Financement. Most
embarrassing of all, the chairman of Britain's National Westminster
Bank, Sir John Prideaux, had to deny publicly that Natwest was sucked
into Sindona's maw: his institution "had no outstanding liabilities or
losses in relation to the Sindona group of banks or from foreign exchange operations undertaken by any of its units throughout the
world."

This unprecedented statement was enforced by Italian press reports that the papers turned up by the Sindona investigators included
an interesting letter in which he blamed the downfall of Banca Privata
on its role as agent in a super-colossal foreign exchange deal that had
come to pieces, leaving Natwest some $800 million on the wrong side.
According to this scenario, of which no evidence ever appeared, Sindona had chivalrously ruined himself to save the reputation of the
National Westminster. It was because of the latter's sorry plight, he

would claim later, that the Italian authorities had sent in the shock troops of the Banco di Roma.

As his fortunes slumped, the Italian financier expanded and embellished his role of injured innocent, chosen scapegoat, predestined martyr. Now it was the Italian Establishment that had deliberately encompassed his ruin, all because of Sindona's rugged refusal to conform. The plunge of SGI shares (none too mysterious in view of its troubles) on the Milan Bourse had been engineered by a "whispering campaign." Banca Privata had sunk only because Banco di Roma had reneged on a pledge to honor the Sindona creation's debts at the time of negotiating the $100 million loan.

The Bank of Italy and Governor Carli (who resigned his post in 1975) were not spared. For example, the charge that the Banca Unione books were cooked in 1970-71, Sindona claimed, had nothing to do with him—at the time he was a mere vice president with no responsibility for operations; the Bank of Italy, however, had approved the delinquent accounts, and the central bank and its top officer were thus implicated in any falsification. In June 1975, an Italian judge made the governor and three leading officers of the Banco di Roma appoint attorneys to defend themselves against certain charges preferred in connection with a suit brought by minority shareholders in Banca Privata. The latter alleged that Banco di Roma officials had covered up the problems of the Sindona bank so successfully that the outside innocents had not only failed to sell their shares, but had even bought more. Because of their legal responsibility for controlling the activities of all banks, the Bank of Italy and its governor were accused of mishandling the Banca Privata liquidation.

A gratified Sindona held that Carli and Company were responsible for "acts that damaged Italian banking prestige abroad." No pot has ever called a kettle black with greater impudence. But the financier made his verbal forays from a safe distance across the Atlantic. Back in Italy a number of his chief lieutenants had been indicted, and some arrested. To the charges against Sindona arising from his business operations, another had been added: that for three years or so Sindona had been making secret contributions, at over $1 million a month, to members of the Christian Democratic Party, which had ruled Italy uninterruptedly ever since the republic emerged at the end of World War II, and which broadly represents the views and interests of the Roman Catholic Church.

The Vatican, following its time-honored and canny custom, endured in the silence of the ages the blows to its fortunes and prestige inflicted by the Sindona connection. The Vatican had unquestionably lost material amounts of money from its association with the Sicilian, and probably also from his financial advice. It owned worthless shares in at least two of the failed Sindona banks, Banca Privata and Banque de Financement; in the latter case, the Holy See's interest was substantial. It was also said to have suffered heavy losses through dealings with the Franklin National Bank and the Wolff Bank.

The ecclesiastical apologists tended to minimize the damage. Outside, more objective sources set the erosion at some $300 million over five years—not counting the cost of cracked investment advice. Anyway, in the wake of the various Sindona debits, Monsignor Paul Marcinkus, an American Catholic bishop who had been Sindona's friend and confidant and had represented the Vatican in deals with him, was demoted and dispatched into obscurity. The blow to the image of the Holy See can never be assessed; maybe it is no part of a churchman's equipment to be financially shrewd. Still, that does not excuse blatant imprudence. The Church had trusted banker Sindona not wisely but too well.

As for the man himself, Sindona, like many other architects of the jerry-built financial structures of the sixties, survived the whole ordeal in none too bad shape, at least initially, and not just because of his continuing luxurious lifestyle. No one seemed to threaten him effectively with any kind of retribution for his financial collapse and its disastrous consequences. If the Italians were trying hard to extradite him, they were singularly unsuccessful over surprisingly many months. Many influential Italians had reason to fear what Sindona might say and do if cornered in his own country; he had already displayed an ominous capacity to fling mud, without much caring who was hit.

In America, he rode above the dark clouds which attended the last days of Franklin National, and which led his subordinates to court and conviction for irregularities; their chief stockholder at that point was unscathed while the investigations into his role continued. It almost seemed that, in spite of everything, Michele Sindona, failed financier and false friend of Mother Church, was enjoying something like the ancient privilege of benefit of clergy. But if somebody up there was protecting him, that protection appeared to have been withdrawn in the late summer of 1976 when the extradition proceedings at last got under way. The strange saga of Michele Sindona, failed global tycoon, might not after all be robbed of its deserved, possibly dynamite dénouement.

23. The Blotted Swiss Copybook

IN June 1977 the bankers of Switzerland, like so many penitents fresh from the confessional, promised to turn over a new leaf. Their past sins, though not actually admitted, were implied in what they pledged themselves *not* to do in the future. No longer would they take money from just anybody, but they would check scrupulously the credentials of all would-be clients to ensure that they were honest citizens; and the banks would shun any money tainted with even a suspicion of being capital that had been illegally exported or that was in flight from the tax collector.

This resolute code of good conduct, drawn up by the Swiss National Bank, the central bank, and subscribed to by the Swiss Bankers' Association, the trade association of the institutions, was not, alas, the result of a sudden flush of voluntary virtue. It was more or less forced on the banking brotherhood by the furor generated both inside and outside Switzerland by the Swiss Credit Bank debacle. This won the unenviable title of being the worst banking scandal in Europe since World War II—and it doesn't compare too badly with some of the prewar monsters.

The scandal was especially shocking since it emerged in 1977, when the calamities of the decade's earlier years were thought to be dead and buried. The noisome skeletons that came tumbling out of the Swiss Credit cupboard brought a new twist to big bank nefariousness. Some 2.17 billion Swiss francs (about $870 million) in the trust accounts of about 1,000 Italian clients of the bank's branch in Chiasso, just across the Swiss frontier, had been appallingly misapplied. The branch, instead of placing these assets on deposit with prime banks in the Euromarket, according to the standard instructions from headquarters in Zürich for "fiduciary" funds, allegedly channeled them to a Liechtenstein holding company, Texon Finanzanstalt.

The latter, controlled by the manager of the branch, one Ernst Kuhrmeier, and cronies, shuffled the billions on into 100 or so ill-found affiliates in the wine, food, restaurant, resort, plastics, and other industries. In due course these addled investments lost a large chunk of the assets. Credit Bank originally put the loss at some Sfr. 250 million (about $100 million), but outside sources estimated the figure to be far, far higher—and the National Bank later confirmed that the damage was huge.

Almost nothing could have jolted Swiss banking more severely. The tremor didn't demolish the structure—bank shares, and all Swiss shares, trembled for a spell, but then quickly recovered their equilibrium. It did seem that, whatever might befall the Credit Bank, the reputation of Swiss banking was firmly founded; but nevertheless, the industry was a whisker from disaster. How near the miss was is shown by the fact that in the after-the-fall period, there was even talk of abolishing Swiss bank secrecy and the numbered accounts that so closely guard that cherished privacy.

But, in the end, the battered authorities (who failed entirely to fulfill their own regulatory duties) limited themselves to stipulating that, in the future, secrecy should not be abused to shield malodorous people and practices. Swiss bankers deny that the purpose of accounts bearing only a number (and not, like regular accounts, also the name of the beneficial owner) is to protect the iniquitous. In fact, they never tire of stressing, somewhat sanctimoniously, the origin of numbered accounts in the thirties: to hide the identity of Jewish clients, who would have paid with their lives if the Gestapo had discovered they had funds in Switzerland.

In the intervening years, many outside Switzerland have had good reason to suspect that the device was put to considerably less worthy uses, such as concealing funds owing to foreign governments in taxes, hiding loot derived from gangster operations, and even protecting fortunes salted away by the Nazis. But there was another, even more pressing, reason why the politicians in Switzerland were suddenly so eager to erase any flaw that reflected on the image of Swiss banking even before the Credit Bank scandal exploded in their faces. That image had been unpleasantly tarnished by unfavorable publicity about earlier slips, all too patently showing, on the part of institutions that were unfortunately all too Swiss.

Moreover, not just small fry were involved. During the extraordinary period in 1973–74 when banking around the world went haywire, the biggest banks in Switzerland shared the adverse headlines. For example, the Union Bank of Switzerland had to admit to a loss of some $40 million on foreign exchange dealing. (The bank excused itself with the explanation that a big client had died suddenly, leaving his account in a highly exposed position—but, after all, who, if not the bank, had allowed him to perpetrate the indecent exposure?) The Swiss Bank Corporation was caught out twice—first, when it revealed big claims against the collapsed Sindona empire in Italy, arising from foreign exchange transactions unofficially estimated at around $35 million; and second, when some "dirty" lire, identified with kidnap ransom money paid by relatives of an unfortunate Italian girl (who was subsequently found dead), turned up at the bank's branch in Ponte Tresa, just over the Swiss border.

But the worst battering was reserved for the third member of the Swiss Big Three, the Credit Bank, even before Chiasso. Already in the autumn of 1975–76, the institution had attracted unfavorable publicity through two worrying incidents. In the first case, the U.S. Securities and Exchange Commission demanded that Credit Bank turn over some $250 million deposited at its New York branch; the watchdog agency claimed that the money represented the sale by certain American principals of unregistered securities illegally backed by gold; after considerable wrangling, the bank did transfer the funds to the custody of a New York court.

The second incident arose when the West German periodical *Der Spiegel* accused Credit Bank of masterminding the clandestine smuggling into Switzerland of vast sums in Spanish pesetas, money allegedly belonging to rich firms and individuals who had begun to take a poor view of the outlook for Spain (or for themselves in Spain), once General Franco was dead and buried. The bank's management ignored the criticism, as well it might. Smuggling pesetas, if it was a novelty (which was doubtful), would simply be a variation on a tedious theme. Everybody knew that money had for years been clandestinely siphoned to Swiss banks from other countries of Europe, from France, Germany, Great Britain, Italy—especially from Italy.

Which leads back to Credit Bank's near-disaster in Chiasso. Only Ernst Kuhrmeier, and the two branch management colleagues who were arrested with him after their misbehavior had been tardily discovered, could know how much (if any) of the Sfr 2.17 billion entrusted to their care had left Italy illegally. Up to the time the lucre made them personally filthy, the Chiasso bankers probably couldn't have cared less about its origins. *Their* responsibility began when they mishandled the funds by channeling them into the unauthorized investments which turned so sour. Credit Bank was left holding the depleted bag because the free-wheeling Kuhrmeier and his aides had allegedly pledged about Sfr. 1 billion (some $400 million) of the bank's money in guarantees to the depositors.

The head office committed itself to make good all claims. This it was able to do, out of its unpublished reserves, although the pain must have been horrible. At the same time, top management—in a move that was hardly a testimonial to its supervisory performance—disclaimed any knowledge of what had been going on. Yet doubt remained on this point. The two officers at Zürich headquarters who currently and formerly had been responsible for the Chiasso branch resigned, and with them went Dr. Felix W. Schulthess, Credit Bank's chairman, suffering possibly the worst disgrace ever inflicted on a prominent Swiss banker. The downfall of the principals apart, the convolutions of the affair—the unauthorized deals, the secret guarantees, the use of a Liechtenstein intermediary—only confirmed the suspicions of critics who charge that people put money in Swiss banks for dubious motives, mainly to hide it from the authorities in their own countries.

The Swiss bankers admit to this—they can hardly do otherwise; but they would say that the description applies to only a small section of their total clientele. It is an issue that can be debated endlessly without getting anywhere in particular. In any case, the bankers claim that the purpose of traditional bank secrecy has never been to serve the interests of criminals, even if at times the latter do take advantage of the protection. The banks point out, moreover, that if, in a criminal trial, a court orders the veil of secrecy to be torn away from a numbered account, the banks are obliged to comply, and are perfectly willing to do so. They cite the Zürich bank that provided the key evidence that led to the conviction for fraud of author Clifford Irving and his wife, Edith: the deposit of a check received from America for his fake biography of Howard Hughes.

As Swiss bankers explain it, the main aim of the account that bears no name, only a number, is to protect their client's right to privacy— a right guaranteed, incidentally, by the Swiss constitution. The stock illustration is of the famous Hollywood star, or the best-selling novelist, who has chosen Switzerland as his or her country of domicile for tax reasons—with the enthusiastic approval of the Swiss, who are content to take a reasonable slice of an expatriate's large income, rather than see the whole lot go somewhere else. How embarrassing for such beautiful people, the defense runs, if some teller in a local branch in the Alps tells all, revealing that the latest Hollywood super-diva or British pop idol has a seven-digit fortune stashed away in the bank; and how bad for the bank's business!

Anonymous digits thus conceal the identity of the beneficial owner from the eyes and mouths of the uncouth. The beneficial name will be known only to an elite coterie of impeccable discretion, bank officials who have been trained by a lifetime of experience to keep their counsel. But, even so, is the secrecy game really worth the candle? The banks vehemently and uncompromisingly declare that it is; they give the impression that, if their numbered accounts were to go, Swiss banking's very prosperity would vanish too. At times, indeed, the banks seem to protest too much, and so tend to arouse the very suspicions they seek to allay.

Other Swiss reason that whether, on balance, the numbered accounts themselves are good or bad, the glare of publicity that they attract has become more and more of a liability to the country. There is a quite widespread conviction abroad that the main purpose of numbered accounts is to attract the hottest of hot money; and there seems little doubt that Switzerland does attract more than its fair share of the same. Get rid of the accounts, and you would get rid of the suspicions —including those so persistently and naggingly nurtured by aggrieved internal revenue officers all round the world.

Undesirables would presumably have little use for a Swiss bank that could not guarantee to keep the identity of the depositor and the whereabouts of any ill-gotten gains a close secret. The impact of abolition, it is true, would be largely psychological; numbered accounts or no, Swiss banking personnel will not discuss their clients' business with just anybody. It is in that well-defined and maintained tradition that the true Swiss bank secrecy lies, as with all nationalities of banker.

The future reputation of Swiss banks and bankers, their success in continuing to attract hoards of overseas money, will overwhelmingly depend on the stability of the Swiss franc and on their own professional performance—not on any phenomenal ability as financial wizards. Unfortunately, in their professional role the bankers have shown disturbing signs of shortcomings, failures that should give more cause for concern than the fuss about numbered accounts. And, in recent years, some tension has arisen between political and banking circles in Switzerland; the criticism by the former of the latter in the matter of numbered accounts is only a symptom of this deeper unease.

The politicians seem to fear that the bankers may be getting too powerful for their own and the country's good. The mainspring of this preoccupation has been the impact on the Swiss economy of the vast and continuous inflow of "funk" money from abroad. The flood in the seventies increased the money supply and fueled the fires of inflation. At one point the rate of inflation surpassed double figures, something unheard of in modern Swiss experience, and promptly corrected with full Swiss vigor—though in a country where any hint of *dirigisme* is anathema, the authorities have little room in which to maneuver when taking remedial action.

But in 1973–74, when the boom began to froth over, the National Bank made the banking community one of the main targets of restrictive counter-measures, much to the dismay of the banks, which saw themselves cast in the role of scapegoat for the sins of a whole society. There was no open breach, of course; the contest was conducted more

in the spirit of peacetime maneuvers—at which the Swiss army is expert
—than in that of open warfare, of which the modern Swiss have no
experience at all.

The National Bank steered the banks under its supervision into
imposing a negative interest rate on new deposits by foreigners. At one
point in the autumn of 1974, people were paying seemingly ludicrous
rates of interest to have their money in Switzerland; the move was only
partially effective, because such people as put large sums of money into
Swiss banks will pay a very fat price for the safety of their capital.
However, this psychological attack was backed by a physical one, including such measures as requiring the banks to restrict credit, and to
deposit minimum reserves with the central bank.

Most far-reaching of all in its significance was the decision to abandon the traditional "gentlemen's agreement" approach, by which the
bankers had voluntarily accepted restrictions imposed on them in the
national interest. Instead, a harder line on regulation was substituted.
The National Bank assumed a new posture which, even·if far from
ferocious, involved a display of teeth; and which presaged an era of
sterner official surveillance of what until then had been a remarkably
unregulated Swiss banking business.

One area where the central bank indicated that its new bite was
likely to be more painful than its previous bark was in foreign exchange
dealing. As a first step, restrictions were imposed on forward sales to
foreigners of francs; the move had an instant, marked effect in curbing
this kind of transaction. There was even talk of licensing foreign exchange dealers, not only those employed by banks, but the many operating quite independently. These curious specialists are so numerous in
Switzerland that over 300 belong to their own association.

There was more radical talk still of creating a single foreign exchange market for the whole country; and, possibly, of imposing a tax
on foreign exchange transactions. The response of the banking fraternity to both notions was along "over-our-dead-bodies" lines. The banks
were equally repelled by suggestions that they should disclose their
hidden reserves—a concealment which, in the case of all enterprises in
Switzerland, banking or nonbanking, is as native as the *alpenhorn.*

But the Swiss banks should not have been surprised at the regulations being tightened. For the most part they probably recognized that,
in the final analysis, enforced discipline was the only effective curb on
tendencies to stray. Self-discipline had become frail in the face of temptation. The temptations to stray that titillated bankers during the era
of floating currencies, rampant inflation, and political and economic
instability were enormous; even Swiss banks of the utmost respectability were induced to swerve from the one true path.

It is, of course, necessary to distinguish between "Swiss banks" and "banks in Switzerland." Most of the grotesque scandals of the recent past have involved the latter; that is, banks doing business in the country, but which are, in fact, owned outside it—like the United California Bank subsidiary in Basel, the Sindona-controlled Banque de Financement in Geneva, the International Credit Bank, also of Geneva, the Lloyds Bank International branch in Lugano. But the massive aberrations with which these and other foreign-owned institutions were identified inevitably brought discredit upon the Swiss banking community that was their genial host—far too genial, some Swiss grumbled, until the Chiasso scandal removed any title to self-righteousness.

Other foreign banks, whose virtue was unsullied, suffered more than their Swiss counterparts from the consequences of tighter regulations and a more restrictive environment. Earlier on, during the Euro-dollar market boom, foreign banks rushed to set up Swiss affiliates, both to grab a share of the massive reservoir of capital on deposit in Switzerland, and to take advantage of the free and easy atmosphere. By the end of 1974, these invaders numbered just over 100, including branch offices, with total assets of some 27,700 million Swiss francs. They ranged all the way from banking subsidiaries set up by U.S. multinational corporations, such as Dow and Firestone, to the Wozchod Handelsbank of the Soviet Union.

But after the first flood, the pace slowed down to a trickle of two or three new entrants per year. One of the main reasons was the Swiss reaction to what they considered one-way hospitality; they started demanding a *quid pro quo* for their own banks abroad, which other governments, for the most part, were unwilling to concede. But what really applied the brakes to the foreign influx were the much tougher conditions that the Swiss Banking Commission imposed after the small minority of foreigners had lurched spectacularly off the track.

It would have been a comfort to the Swiss if they could have shown that only foreigners had been guilty of lapses in violating the code of conduct of which Swiss banking has boasted down the years. But it just didn't happen that way. True, Dr. Albert Matter, president of the Banking Commission, declared in an address to the Association of Foreign Banks, in June 1975, that foreign banks were relatively prominent among the seventy or so institutions that repeatedly presented the Commission with problems. But the locals cannot be spared the rod, especially after Credit Bank's fall from grace.

This was a massive native Swiss scandal, and something had to be done to show the world that the disgraceful spectacle, so damaging to the banks' carefully cultivated image of reliability and respectability, so devastating to the reputation of the national authorities, would not recur. The new code of conduct promulgated by the central bank, mild in itself, but ferocious compared with the previous gentle (indeed, fee-

ble) supervision exercised by Berne, required signatory banks to promise not to solicit funds from foreigners who might be even suspected of
sending them to Switzerland illegally; and to reject any funds about
whose eventual owners (the Mafia? terrorist kidnappers?) they enter-
tained suspicions.

The new regulations were to take effect for new depositors on July
1, 1977, and for existing customers a year later. Violations of the code
could be punished by fines of up to Sfr. 10 million (about $4 million),
and culpable officers could be removed from their posts. True, there
was no compulsion to sign; some of the smaller banks were expected to
decline, so as not to sacrifice their so-called suitcase trade in smuggled
currency. But the major banks would have to conform, after the disgrace of Credit Bank, and it is their reputations that count for most in
the outside world, their good name that attracts all that lovely money,
without which the Swiss would not, as now, be the richest citizens of
any industrialized country.

Furthermore, lapses by Swiss bankers tend to cause more conster-
nation than those of banks elsewhere, not so much because they sully
the image that these entrepreneurs seek to present to the world but
because, on the whole, the image is genuine. When it comes to banking,
to running a financial institution efficiently, successfully, and profitably,
the Swiss do it well, rather better than most; and their clients have
reason to be satisfied, including the great majority who are honest
citizens. That is why the Chiasso scandal is so shocking—and so dangerous for the Swiss, even the world, economy.

Not the biggest, nor the best known, nor by a long shot the most
publicity-conscious in world finance, the Swiss banks still hold a special
place in the international community. Time and again they have provided the eye of the hurricane, where people have been able to safeguard their all (or what was left of it) against the depredations of world
war, civil war, revolution, insurrection, or the equally devastating
consequences of economic and financial collapse, or runaway inflation.

If any of the big banks of Switzerland were ever to fail, any of the
really important banks, the impact upon world public opinion would be
out of all proportion to their size. It could, and probably would, touch
off an international financial slide. The fact that one of those banks could
allow a single branch to misapply $870 million of other people's money
was bad enough—so bad that the central bank hastily organized a guarantee (which the Credit Bank swore wasn't necessary) to assure the
world that the giant delinquent was secure. It had better be. Others
beside the Swiss must hope that the Swiss near-miss of the seventies
continues to prove to be as good as a mile.

24. The Floating Iceberg

THE individual's account at a branch rests for its security on the bank to which the branch belongs. The security of that bank, in turn, rests on the central banking system to which it belongs. The security of the central bank rests on the national financial system to which the central bank belongs. And the national system—winding up this structure in which every flea has a bigger flea on his back to protect him—fits into a world monetary structure, on which ultimately the smallest bank account in Peoria, or Pontefract, or Pontoise depends for its security.

The two, the individual's account and the world monetary system, could not be further apart in character or complexity. The simple questions like Who runs world money? have no answer. Various fingers, some political, some official, are in the pie. But the workings of international money are imperfectly understood even by those with a hand in its management. Moreover, their deliberations seldom emerge into the light of day, are never subject to debate or inquiry by outsiders, and often result in decisions which are never communicated to the outside world.

It is a secret government, none the less powerful for being largely unseen, none the more efficient for being unregulated and unsupervised. Indeed, anyone who based his economic judgments solely on the proposition that central bankers (these being the kingpins of the setup) are always wrong would have been not only right but exceedingly rich, as a result of the topsy-turvy developments of the postwar period.

The central bankers can, it is true, congratulate themselves on their part in sustaining worldwide prosperity, both before and during the commotions in the monetary system in the decades since World War II. But in reality their performance only looks good in comparison to what went before—the breakdown of a far more imperfect system in the thirties, a collapse that encouraged the rise of the dictatorships, weakened the resolve of the democracies, and doomed millions to years of depressed poverty, relieved only by further years of the holocaust of war.

When peace came, the victorious Allies, led by the United States, were determined to construct a new order in world monetary affairs that would safeguard international society against the failures of the thirties. The analogy was with the reconstruction of America's domestic finances under Franklin D. Roosevelt, whose Federal Reserve reforms lasted with ease into the seventies. Yet the theory and practical ideas used in the international context were those, not of an American, but of a Briton—the novel, indeed revolutionary, concepts of the late Lord Keynes.

His apotheosis was the agreement of the major industrialized nations, under the inspiration and leadership of the United States, to create a new order of monetary discipline. The Bretton Woods agreement was named after the obscure American community where the signatories foregathered in 1944. The basis of their concord was a commitment to maintain relatively fixed and stable rates of exchange between their respective currencies—to which end (among others) they established a new agency, the International Monetary Fund (IMF), in order to police the compact. Significantly, it was based in Washington, the capital of its spiritual and actual parent.

The IMF was given two main, specific directives. First was the task of enforcing the restrictions imposed on member countries when it came to altering their exchange rates (they could do so only under strict supervision and within narrow limits); second was the obligation to help any countries that might have temporary difficulties in their external payments by lending money from a fund to which all the participating countries contributed specified sums—the largest, naturally, coming from the supreme United States of America.

The monetary discipline also implied a measure of economic control, since the IMF was authorized, as a condition of its financial aid, to require the recipient nation to pursue those domestic and foreign economic policies that were considered necessary to restore good standing in world markets. The object of the whole exercise—an aim that came much closer to realization than any other in the postwar international field—was to enable the countries of the free world to cooperate in an orderly expansion of the world economy and world trade in a manner that would bring prosperity to all.

But the IMF only had real authority over countries in real distress. Otherwise, the responsibility for making Bretton Woods work rested fairly and squarely with the central bankers (and finance ministers) of the countries concerned. These were the dignitaries who wielded the power to control the money supply, regulate credit, and otherwise influence financial and economic developments. The banks in the respective countries danced to the tune played by their masters. But the latter, often unwittingly, themselves danced in response to forces that were only dimly perceived, or whose existence was even forthrightly denied.

Keynes, however, had done his work. His last great contribution to the world before his death, the agreement reached at Bretton Woods, operated effectively, probably more effectively than any other international agreement of similar significance, for the best part of a generation. It worked, in fact, for as long as the conditions prevailing at its birth, and influencing its creators, continued to exist. But all things change—and change is harder to detect when all is going well than when chaos has descended.

As long as international trade and investment were expanding (and both grew enormously), and as long as the currency reserves of the key countries were mounting (as most did), nobody had much cause to notice that the key to these highly desirable developments was becoming distorted in the lock. The motor of world trade was being lubricated primarily by an outflow of U.S. dollars. And the American economy was ultimately no more capable than any other of sustaining an uninterrupted drain on its financial reserves.

Other countries experienced similar problems in the golden decades, especially the unhappy possessor of the world's only alternative reserve currency—the pound sterling. The British clung to the role of sterling as the world's second most important currency far more resolutely than they tried to keep the remnants of the British Empire. But the results were as disastrous as, say, continued military occupation of India would have been or as the Suez invasion of 1956 actually was. Time and again, the United Kingdom's domestic economic interests were sacrificed on the altar of the pound.

Yet the great United States of America was not expected, like the British, to clamp down on domestic growth and force up interest rates to curb a large and threatening balance of payments deficit. The outflow of dollars was plainly benefiting the rest of the world—a kind of foreign aid program that did not have to be voted by Congress. So the Americans, to general applause, simply refused to abide by the rules of monetary conduct that they had laid down for the rest of the world.

At this point it is necessary to backtrack in time in order to recapture the psychological climate that made it so difficult for the world's bankers to adjust to change. When the Keynesian system was set up, nobody imagined that the Americans would ever be on the receiving end of monetary punishment. Not only had the United States emerged from the war with a virtual corner on the free world's gold and foreign exchange reserves, but the besetting problem of the era was the American tendency to rake in more and more—the famous "dollar gap."

The gap was closed first by foreign aid and military spending abroad, then by an outflow of private investment as American firms built up their investments outside national frontiers, until (in the way of all conventional economic truths since time began) the gap was reversed. There was still a dollar gap—the other way around. Now America's gold was pouring into the treasuries of Western Europe and Japan, and nothing that successive U.S. administrations tried in order to stem the flow seemed able to solve the problem.

The reason was that the Americans stopped far short of the severe economic restraints that lesser nations had to impose to cure their balance of payments diseases. The first American retreat from responsibility, though it aroused no great concern at the time, was highly significant. One of the clauses of Bretton Woods allowed the signatory countries to exchange a surplus currency for gold, which was regarded by most central banks as an insurance against fatal deteriorations in the value of paper currency. But there was only one major source of the delectable metal—the United States.

As the Americans willingly shelled out gold in exchange for the dollars accumulating abroad, the hoard in the possession of the United States (mostly then held in the Federal Reserve Bank in New York, and not in the fabled Fort Knox) dwindled from some $30,000 million to $10,000 million by 1969. This twenty-three-year drain was hardly arrested by the last act of the Eisenhower administration, a ban on the freedom of the American citizen to hold gold. From that moment on, the world had changed. Step by step, the Americans came nearer and nearer to the brink—until in 1971 they stepped right over, led by President Richard ("I don't give a shit about the lira") Nixon.

The president announced that the United States would now refuse to surrender gold for the dollars tendered by other countries. Although this was an act of necessity rather than policy (if the aforesaid creditors had presented only a portion of their claims, the U.S. reserves would have been wiped out), the Nixonian stroke removed the main prop from the Bretton Woods system. This had been valued in terms of the dollar and through the dollar to gold.

Because the dollar was literally as good as gold, in that it could be converted to gold at any time, the dangers in the expansion of world reserves by dollar outflows had been minimal. But keeping the dollar as virtuous as gold demanded disciplines that the Americans were simply not prepared to accept, either before or after the Nixon *démarche*. In fact, rather than accept the discipline of gold, the Americans set out systematically to downgrade the monetary status of the metal. If the dollar couldn't be as good as gold, then they would make gold as bad as the dollar.

The trouble with this strategy was that it left the Bretton Woods system with no currency base at all. The pound by 1971, despite all the posturings of British politicians and the sacrifices of their voters, was a shadow even of its former feeble self. None of the other European currencies had a wide enough circulation or broad enough economic base to fill the gap. Gold would actually have done nicely. But its reuse as the key element in world reserves would have left the United States, already denuded of its reserves, at a disadvantage in relation to the French and the Germans—and that would never do.

As for the other countries, their economic diplomacy against the United States, ever since General de Gaulle left the scene, reflects all the courage you would expect from governments which depend heavily on American military protection and finance, and which, in any event, are hostage to the great amounts of dollars accumulated in their own treasuries over the deficit years. Sometimes protesting, usually not, the Europeans and Japanese have trailed along in the American wake.

The second blow at Bretton Woods was struck by America's unilateral devaluation of the dollar (by around 40 percent in the case of the Swiss franc and D-mark) and by the announcement that henceforward the dollar would float—that is, its exchange rate would be determined by the market and not, as under the shattered rules of the International Monetary Fund, be kept within narrowly prescribed limits. A number of European countries, distressed by the uncertainties of the new floating world, created a mini-mini Bretton Woods among themselves, the "snake in the tunnel," so called because it restricted the currencies involved to wriggling within only a confined space in relation to each other. But this would have been no substitute for the dollar, even if it had worked (it couldn't, because one currency, the D-mark, was persistently too strong and another, the lira, too weak).

The crucial importance of these events passed most citizens by, even though their own finances were about to feel the impact disastrously. The world was brimming with dollars—currency which the bankers of the West were only too happy to mobilize, earning interest and huge commissions in return. These dollars were outside any kind of world monetary regulation or any national control. Under a floating regime, they became of uncertain value as well. In the conditions of the early seventies, when governments were stimulating economic expansion after the shock of student and worker rebellions, the burning of the Bretton Woods agreement was like throwing a match into a gas tank.

The tanks could hardly have been fuller. American dollars deposited in European banks (or branches of American banks) accounted for the vast bulk of the new "Eurocurrencies." The Eurodollars, originally supplied by the American deficits and then further enlarged by the activities of American corporations in Europe, amounted in mid-1974 to the dimensions of a tidal wave. At that point, the peak of the phenomenon, the banks of Europe had outstanding loans in the new "currency" valued at some $200,000 million, to which could be added another

$160,000 million or so representing transactions between these same institutions. The startling statistics show, not just the overwhelming size of this money mountain, but the eagerness with which the banks exploited the wealth within.

The attractions were manifold. Prime among them was the fact that dollars in Europe were not subject to any restrictions that the American authorities might impose at home. External constraints—like the interest equalization tax that the Americans imposed in one of their vain efforts to dam the dollar deficits—could also be circumvented. American dollars that flowed out to Europe could be borrowed back by American corporations to purchase European assets. Investments denominated in the new currency, moreover, could be made tax-free, anonymous, and freely transferable—all great advantages to the world of money and moneyed men.

Since there were no reserve requirements with Eurodollars (such as the domestic rules stipulating that for every loan there must exist a given proportion of cash deposits or assets), the banks could expand their lending at will. Nor were deposits any problem; if a bank ran low, it could always borrow from another bank. Strange initials, of which even the most sophisticated bank customer knew nothing, suddenly became of great importance—for example, LIBO, meaning the London interbank offered rate.

The City of London, blessed with a convenient location and considerable expertise, became the hub of the Eurodollar traffic and the natural Mecca for all banks anxious for a share of the action. And the action was led, most aggressively, by American institutions, some of which had never seen the world beyond the Midwest before opening their branch on or near Lombard Street as they pursued the millions of traveling dollars. In 1972–73 alone, at the height of the stampede, some sixty U.S. banks hung out their shingles in the City; not just giants from the New York megalopolis, but banks from North Carolina, Texas, Ohio, Michigan, Pennsylvania. The invasion took on something of the aspect of keeping up with the Rockefellers.

Other nations joined in, not in the dozens but in twos and threes: Japan, Germany, even Communist Europe. The very avidity of this dollar rush eventually proved self-defeating. As the gold prospectors of earlier eras had found, there wasn't enough treasure for all. Even the Eurodollar mountain had its limits, especially when the usual unforeseen developments intervened to mar a picture of eternal financial bliss. As competition for the loan business increased, profit margins inevitably suffered. At the same time the quality of lending weakened, as the institutions in general looked for increased volume to offset the lower returns, and as the smaller and less regarded entrants scrabbled around (sometimes ignorantly) in search of the crumbs from the rich banks' tables.

Syndicates were formed in which a major international bank (the usual leader) would contract for a loan running into hundreds of millions, if not billions, and then split it with other banks, including the small fry. Sometimes a hundred or more participants were involved. This spread the risks and spread the jam too; but it resulted in some motley assortments and strange bedfellows. The net effect was to weaken further a structure that had never had the benefit of planning or serious thought in the first place.

In those early days, however, the borrowers were almost exclusively exclusive: the governments of industrialized countries, blue-chip multi-national corporations, and the like. But as the scramble for deals grew more intense, standards lapsed. By the mid-seventies the biggest debtor was the government of Italy, whose $9 billion of outstanding loans were not only a major burden on the back of the Euromarkets, but had provided the wherewithal for the country to continue its rake's progress toward virtual bankruptcy and political crisis.

In too much fullness of time, very belatedly, some of the richer countries took steps to restrain the ballooning of Eurodebts within their banking structures. The developing countries of the Third World showed no such anxiety. By 1973 the indebtedness of clients in Asia, Africa, and Latin America also exceeded $9 billion Eurodollars, much of which must have rested on shaky security. Add to these piles the debts that the industrialized nations, rushing back in, raised to pay their oil bills after the energy emergency of 1973, and the degree of political exposure becomes frightening. For instance, in the first half of 1974 alone, the United Kingdom took some $5 billion, more than its total of such borrowings over the previous four years—and over half in the form of a single loan.

By such means the world monetary system and the stability of the banks themselves were weakened alike. Many European banks, moreover, were taking on commercial business that was far more dubious than their political lending. Eurodollars were highly active in financing the great boom in tanker construction, which became one of the postwar world's biggest busts, as after the oil crunch super-tankers were laid up even before being completed. The money also found its way into the most vulnerable sector of the American economy—the real estate investment trusts whose days were being numbered even as the Eurodollars arrived.

The rashness, ignorance, and greed of banking men played a part in undermining world money. But the bankers can be excused on one ground. The conditions for collapse were created by two linked decisions, taken over the years by the American authorities and endorsed by their European equivalents: to allow an unprecedented increase in the volume of dollars held abroad to continue long after the necessity for that outflow had passed; and to weaken and finally destroy the link between the dollar and gold as the consequences of the dollar outflow came home to roost. The banks were overextended by their lending, and overexposed by the new risks of trading in currencies whose value could change, not by 2 percent in either direction but by great leaps and bounds.

The banks, and our bank accounts with them, had come to resemble the passengers on the *Titanic*, speeding all unawares toward a perfectly visible iceberg. Like that doomed liner, the financial community only scraped its side on the hazard. But a jagged hole was torn below the waterline, and only some desperate repair work prevented total disaster. For manning the pumps so successfully, the world's bankers do deserve credit; they would deserve far more if the rescue operation had not been necessary in the first place.

The financial *Titanic* struck the iceberg in June 1974, when the West German bank I. D. Herstatt collapsed. The immediate cause was foreign exchange dealing, but the event alerted the whole banking nexus to the terrible dangers of the new money world: one deprived of the core of reliability built into the Bretton Woods system, the steady and utterly trustworthy dollar. As reports of other banks in serious difficulties circulated (some of them confirmed, others kept under wraps by various forms of official concealment), the financiers cut back on their commitments, tightened their internal controls, even abandoned the Lombard Street offices opened with such fanfare only so recently.

The security ratings of both banks and borrowers came under much greater scrutiny, although some banks and financial institutions that had technically gone bankrupt were preserved, at tremendous cost to the taxidermists, in order to prevent a circular collapse of confidence. These massive domestic "lifeboat" operations were matched internationally by belated initiatives to develop supervision of world banking business. Regulations everywhere were tightened up. Just as the sinking of the *Titanic* made the Atlantic crossing safer for later passengers, so the sinking of the Herstatt made the crosscurrents of world money more navigable for subsequent voyagers.

In 1975, lending on the Euromarket even recovered to the 1973 level. But this remarkable recuperation did not mean that the danger had done more than recede. Messy situations, as in the property and tanker loan fields, remained to be cleared up. There was an enormous pileup of obligations—notably the loans extended in the lifeboat operations—which might or might not ever be met. The huge politically risky loans, especially to developing countries which had sometimes already been unable to meet interest payments, still hung over the banks. Above all, nothing had been done to repair the wreck of Bretton Woods, the event from which all subsequent damage flowed.

In the past, currency crises had been fairly frequent, but they were confined to one or two weak currencies (notably the overvalued pound) or else speculation had been confined primarily to the private gold market, a relatively safe receptacle for footloose money. Now all currency crises were general, because all paper currencies were linked only to each other. Small wonder that as the dust began to settle, some bankers began to long for the fixed exchange rates that had once seemed so irritatingly inflexible. All human life can be viewed as a struggle between the forces of anarchy and order. Money, it turned out, was too important to be left to anarchists.

PART VI

THE JUGGLING ACTS

25. Trouble in Paradise

THE staff and even the managers of midget branches of mammoth banks must often bewail their lot. There they are, tucked away in a remote backwater; nobody knows about them, nobody cares about them, and so far as head office is concerned, they exist only as names and numbers to be rigidly controlled by an all-powerful paperwork system. Nothing can end this state of far from splendid isolation and impotence—or so their distant masters must have thought in more innocent days. Now the latter know exactly how these mere extras on the banking scene can leap into the limelight, usurp starring roles, and bring the head office galloping to the spot.

Two extras—the foreign exchange dealer and the branch manager of Lloyds Bank International in Lugano, Switzerland—hold the all-time record in this respect. Their branch only had a total staff of sixteen, minding their own (and supposedly the bank's) business in the sedate, semi-tropical resort which basks on Lake Lugano. Its closeness to the Italian border adds money-trafficking to the citizens' natural and prosperous business in tourism. Nonetheless, the inhabitants are totally unused to being thrust into the stage center of world finance, as they suddenly were in August 1974.

Top officials of Lloyds Bank International (LBI) then descended on the Lugano branch at all speed to halt foreign exchange transactions, which at that point had poured some $54 million of LBI's money down the drain. The authorities of Canton Ticino, in which Lugano is the largest community, spelled out the story the next October, when foreign exchange dealer Marc Colombo (twenty-nine years old) and his manager, Egidio Mombelli (age forty-one), came to trial. These appalling losses, the court established, had been caused by the "disloyal administration" of both men, who had also violated Swiss banking regulations. Disloyalty and violation were treated with mercy. Respective sentences of eighteen months and six months in prison were suspended for these first offenders, and their fines were only the equivalent of £365 apiece. Colombo was also bound over for four, and Mombelli for two years; their brief financial stardom was at an end.

Lloyds Bank International was far more the injured party than the Canton of Ticino. Dropping $54 million is no small slip of the hand, even for the international offshoot of a British bank with the size, resources, and prestige of Lloyds. The bank duly paid off the creditors without a murmur—no other course was feasible under the circumstances. The depositors lost nothing; only the Lloyds' shareholders had cause to grumble, since the profits were truncated accordingly (by an estimated $25 million at least, allowing for insurance and tax relief).

If the bankers could only have had their way, the affair might have been muffled up; with the offenders dismissed and the price paid amid the deathly hush which other banks, trapped in very similar fixes, had managed to contrive. But the Ticino authorities were upset by the malodorous publicity raised by bad behavior by a small minority of the banks in their midst (where they are not universally welcome, since the visiting banks pay most taxes in Zürich, Geneva, London, Paris, Rome, New York, etc.). They decided to make an example or two— which was tough on Lloyds Bank International.

The whole dizzy merry-go-round, as unfolded during the four days of the trial, turned upon a series of bad guesses by the *cambista* (the local word for a foreign exchange dealer). Marc Colombo won his notoriety in a critical and dangerous time for his fraternity—the period that followed the Yom Kippur war of autumn 1973, which was dominated by the subsequent conflict over oil supplies and prices between the Arab sheikhs and the industrial countries of the West. The major currencies of the world were fluctuating erratically against one another.

The pound sterling, the U.S. dollar, and the Swiss franc had been set free to float with the partial intention of discouraging currency speculation. The reverse, of course, happened. Since it was extremely difficult to predict what pounds, for example, would be worth in terms of dollars or Swiss francs in a year's time, or even the day after tomorrow, the simplest commercial money transactions became speculative. The disarray in the world economy caused by the oil embargo hugely increased the uncertainty and the speculative element. Dealing in foreign exchange, especially so-called forward transactions (in which one currency is bought or sold for another, but for delivery at some future date when the relative values will depend on that day's market) was rather like dancing the Charleston on a tightrope. Colombo, unfortunately for himself and Lloyds, missed his footing; had his career not been stopped, he could have broken the bank's neck.

As the *cambista* told the court in Lugano, until November 1973 he was dancing along quite neatly, and showing a profit on his books. Then, with the energy crisis at peak intensity, he made his first monumental miscalculation. He sold forward, for delivery in three months' time, $34 million in U.S. money in exchange for Swiss francs. His fond belief was that the dollar would fall in relation to the European currency; Colombo, or rather the bank, would then profit from the difference between the exchange rate at the time of the transaction and that on the date of delivery, and the Lugano extras would be starring heroes in the eyes of their overlords.

But the dollar refused to oblige. In January, before the contract ran out, the American currency strengthened. Accordingly, an anxious Colombo decided that he had better cut his losses and cover himself by buying forthwith an equivalent amount of American dollars, in case the latter went higher still. This produced a loss on the deal of 7 million Swiss francs—not bad for starters. Colombo did not report this little matter to his superiors, he said, because of professional pride; he also felt that a few million francs, though a large sum for Lugano and a fortune for a twenty-nine-year-old dealer, was indeed a little matter for a bank with the overall financial weight of Lloyds.

To extricate himself, Colombo decided to go into reverse. This time he would buy for forward delivery $100 million, half with Swiss francs and half with German marks, gambling that the dollar rise would continue. But he proved wrong again. By the time this transaction matured in March, the dollar was on the way down and his losses had piled up to Sfr. 50 million—seven times the original damage.

By now Colombo knew that, if he revealed the true state of affairs, he would be promptly and furiously fired. One last gamble was called for. This time the sum involved was $550 million, and Colombo, who doesn't seem to have had much courage in his convictions, changed his bet again. Now the dollar was to go on falling. But again the U.S. currency behaved contrariwise, and the paper loss stood at some Sfr. 222 million, or about $54 million, when Lloyds officials from London—tipped off, of all things, by a competitor bank—hurried out to investigate.

Caught red-handed with the evidence, Colombo made no attempt to conceal his operations. He was unrepentant and mysteriously unshaken in professional self-confidence; indeed, he criticized the bank for intervening, claiming that, left to his own brilliant devices, he could still have salvaged the wreck. His defense lawyer even produced figures, "independently audited," to prove that if Colombo had merely held to his position of August 1974, by the end of February 1975 his books would have shown a profit of Sfr. 61 million; LBI must have shuddered at the thought.

The branch manager stuck obstinately to his story that he had not the slightest knowledge of Colombo's pranks; that he did not himself personally supervise the operations of his subordinate, nor had he delegated any of the other fourteen people at the branch to do so. The presiding judge confided that Mombelli had made a "disastrous" impression upon the court as a bank manager, a role for which he seemed singularly ill-adapted. Mombelli's main line of defense was that he was overworked, and hadn't a moment to study and apply the regulations in LBI's book of rules for the guidance of all its managers. If the Lugano duo had played by those rules like any English gentleman, complained one English bank director, Colombo would effectively have been kept on his tightrope.

This "famous book of rules," as it was called repeatedly, and sarcastically, by judge, counsel, defendants, and others in the court, is a symbol which starkly defines a basic difference of attitude between British and Swiss bankers. If the LBI overlords had understood the difference earlier, they might have saved themselves much pain. Swiss banks—at any rate, in the Ticino—have no such books of rules and regulations.

In fact, one defense lawyer described such banking bibles as an "Anglo-Saxon mania," remarking that in Britain and the United States, companies employ whole teams of managers to draft rules, "just as a copy of every letter has to be sent to about twenty-five people, and on a flight between England and America, they spend all their time on the telephone" (a neat trick, but one sees what he meant). The defendants, Mombelli and Colombo, claimed that if the head office drew up rules, the head office should enforce them. LBI's managers, on the other hand, presumed as true Britons that rules were mandatory on the underlings to whom they were issued, and that this would apply to the denizens of the Lugano branch.

This fatal misapprehension does not excuse the failure to exercise enough supervision to ensure that the *cambista* and manager were following their orders. The Zürich branch (the main arm of LBI in Switzerland) was the supervising intermediary between London and Lugano, and its manager in Zürich resigned when Colombo's escapade came to light. However, he was not charged with any wrongdoing, either by LBI or the Swiss authorities. And his role still does not remove the responsibility from LBI itself.

How could so small a branch office, with its mere sixteen employees, have become involved in foreign exchange deals running into the hundreds of millions? In the normal course of events, a branch of Lugano's size was unlikely to transact much business, or cause much in the way of headaches. But Lloyds of Lugano had been allowed to deal in more foreign exchange than either of the two considerably larger branches, in Zürich and Geneva, which are internationally important banking centers. The total volume of Colombo's transactions between November 1973 and August 1974 came to an unbelievable £4,850 million (of course, all this aggregate fortune was never outstanding at any one moment) or $8,245 million at the 1977 rate of exchange.

How could that monumental kind of money have passed through the hands of a comparatively young *cambista* at a small branch in a resort community? The key to the whole fantastic affair is the fact that Lugano, small and remote from the world centers of finance, is a financial center in its own right and one of a peculiar nature. It plays host to no fewer than forty-odd banks (at a momentary count; newcomers are always popping in). Banking employs between 3,500 and 4,000 people in Lugano, which contains branches of Citibank, Banque de Paris et des Pays Bas, and Banco di Roma, as well as the unfortunate LBI.

They are not in Lugano for the weather or for the local business, which could, for that matter, be handled with ease by much smaller branches of the major Swiss banks than the latter actually operate in Lugano. This formidable financial presence has nothing to do with the Luganesi at all, nor even with the Swiss as a whole. All is for the convenience of the Italians whose country begins about twenty miles away, across from the frontier town of Chiasso. It is *their* money, Italian lire, exported both legally and illegally into Switzerland, that generates the big business done by Lugano's bevy of banks; money looking for the fast action that a brash wheeler-dealer like Marc Colombo was prepared to initiate, and a careless manager like Egidio Mombelli was prepared to condone, if only by negligence.

When good Italians die, you might say, they go to Lugano. The Swiss resort, with its limpid lake, its palm trees and semi-tropical flowers, and its generous quota of sunshine even in midwinter, offers Italians all the attractions and comforts of home plus the bonus of Swiss order, discipline, and security—blessings upon which they can no longer count in their own disturbed and discordant society. A Milanese, for instance, cannot help contrasting the calm of Lugano with his own environment, disfigured by strikes and demonstrations by the trade unions, clashes between factions of the political Left and Right, bank robberies with the holding (and shooting) of hostages, and the kidnappings of prominent businessmen, the children of the wealthy, and, in one outrageous case, a sixteen-month-old baby. Small wonder if the accessible Italian-speaking Swiss community tempts the imagination of a Milanese with visions of an earthly paradise.

A few of the luckier and wealthier Italians actually achieve the transition in their lifetimes. A multitude of others, for one reason or another (including the strict Swiss rules governing the admission to residence of foreigners), are frustrated, and settle for the next best thing. They send their money to Lugano instead of themselves. The impregnability and anonymity of a Lugano bank account have attracted astronomical sums of lire across the border from Italy to Switzerland on

regular milk-runs. According to sources among the Swiss, to whom
currency smuggling is only an amusing peccadillo, in the period between 1960 and 1974 some 9,500 billion lire (that is, about $10.7 billion)
had been whisked between the two countries, most of it ending up in
banks in and around Lugano; some 1,000 billion lire (about $1.1 billion)
made the trip during 1974 alone.

Some of this money leaves Italy legally. Chiasso (which, comparatively speaking, is even more overbanked than Lugano) is without question the principal north-south transit point for merchandise moving up
and down the European continent by the St. Gotthard rail and road
artery. The traffic has greatly increased since the creation of the Common Market, and this traffic alone generates vast foreign exchange
dealing, in which the Italian lira has a prominent role. The Italians
naturally (even by nature) take advantage of such legitimate business
to fiddle money into Switzerland, by overstating the value of imports
and understating that of exports on their invoices.

This is very likely only the short end of the business, outdistanced
considerably by the millions in funk money that Italians send every year
to Switzerland, some of it legally, but the bulk by clandestine methods
that violate foreign exchange regulations and cheat the tax collector.
Some smugglers take the risk of passage themselves, while others employ expert couriers, who demand a high cut for their pains. Italian
border guards are much more vigilant than they used to be, and now
and then they reap a rich haul of checks, securities, or hard cash. But
most of the moolah gets through, and arrives safely in Lugano—ready
to be put to work.

In normal times the Italo-Swiss money would earn its keep invested in shares on Wall Street, or built into the local real estate which
has solidly, but unaesthetically, gobbled up the pastures and vineyards
that for centuries graced the shores of Lake Lugano. Many Italians do
not even furnish, let alone occupy, their flats and villas; just owning the
land and the property is like gold in the vault. But during the early
seventies Wall Street plunged, and the Swiss authorities restricted the
purchase of real estate by foreigners, in an effort to curb a super-heated
construction boom.

About that time the floating currencies swam into view: here was
a wonderful, new speculative game to be played, not unlike the gambling to which the Italians are passionately addicted and in which they
sink small fortunes in the casino of Campione (the Italian enclave just
across the lake from Lugano). Besides, in the case of foreign exchange,
the short-term rewards can be fabulous; provided, that is, that you guess
right about the movement of the U.S. dollar *vis-à-vis* the Swiss franc,
or the other way around; and provided that you have the means and
the nerve to play with high stakes.

How Colombo and Mombelli came to be handling such enormous sums of money in relation to the minute size of their branch is thus explained by the strange nature of banking in Lugano, which in turn explains, no doubt, why LBI opened a branch there in the first place. Anyway, foreign exchange dealing is a perfectly legal, essential activity for an international bank. Part of the trouble was probably that, in Lugano, LBI hired badly. It arrived rather late on the scene, in 1970, when the best of the far from abundant local talent had doubtless been sewn up by well-established rivals. The talent that Lloyds needed was highly specific: locals with the right contacts, specialist experience in banking, and a knowledge of British banking practices. The scarcity attracted high rewards; Colombo and Mombelli were hired at what most British bank employees—and many Americans—would consider fancy salaries of respectively $17,000 and over $30,000 a year.

But the recklessness of the one and negligence of the other only plunged Lloyds Bank International into the mire because of the bank's own failings. It seems to have adopted a somewhat casual attitude toward its comparatively minor subsidiary—in exactly the place where it could least afford to relax its vigilance. Just to deal in foreign exchange in an environment like Lugano's, with its notorious Italian connection, was to take undue risk. It was mandatory to monitor closely and continually what was done in the bank's name. Very few businesses lose $54 million at one go; hardly any lose that much through mistakes, not of top management but of one small branch. It is not a record of which Lloyds Bank can be proud.

26. The Fall of the House of Herstatt

IN June 1974, the West German banking community was rocked to its foundations, and the German people—to whom saving is something of a religion and bankers nearer to God than most mortals—were filled with dread by shocking news. The authorities had forcibly closed Bankhaus I. D. Herstatt, one of the country's leading and most respected private banks. As the shock waves from this psychological storm resounded through the economy, not only the banking community but the nation's insurance industry endured agonized moments; for the largest shareholder in Herstatt, Dr. Hans Gerling, happened also to head one of the greatest insurance empires in the land.

The repercussions by no means halted at the border; they, too, broke like tidal waves on many foreign shores. Herstatt's shutters were crashed down with such haste, in the middle of a trading day, that banks in the United States, Great Britain, and elsewhere were left with huge sums owing on foreign exchange deals which they feared, in their first dazed shock, they might never be able to collect. Their resentment, and that of the many German creditors, including a host of small savers, was understandably intensified by reports that the central bankers in the Bundesbank, who ordered the peremptory closure, knew well in advance that something was rotten in the state of Herstatt, but did nothing until far too late in the doomed bank's day.

What exactly happened on June 26, 1974? According to Tom Clausen, president of California's Bank of America, which had some $5 million at risk, "It was like putting a hundred-dollar bill on the teller's counter and asking for five twenty-dollar bills—and the phone rings. The teller answers the phone, then hangs up, and closes the window saying, 'I'm sorry, we're closing the window.'" The analogy is exact, except that instead of just $100 the amounts stuck behind the teller's closed window ran into many hundreds of millions.

The liquidator appointed to wind up Herstatt, an expert from the Deutsche Bank, the country's giant, went through the books and found that he was obliged to report to a scarcely crediting world that I. D. Herstatt had current liabilities amounting to some 2,189 million Deutsche marks (about £365 million, or $840 million, at the going rate of exchange); unfortunately, it could only muster assets of some DM 984 million (£165 million, or $380 million). The books were thus 55 percent short of balancing—a little matter of $460 million. About half the deficit represented losses incurred on dealing in foreign exchange forward (that is, for future settlement). The bank had signed contracts for currency that it had not disposed of to an appalling total of $9.5 billion. Another 30 percent or so of the deficit consisted of claims for damages by customers in both foreign exchange and precious metals.

Nonbank creditors were owed more than half the DM 2,189 million total; prominent among those victims was the city of Cologne, where I. D. Herstatt had its headquarters. But the roster of banks caught short by the sudden closure really made the headlines in the world's press; an understandable reaction, given that the aggrieved bankers were banging on the door for DM 484 million (some £80 million, or $189 million).

Prominent among those in sackcloth and ashes was the British merchant bank Hill Samuel, which was faced with a potential loss of some $21.5 million. Beside that, even Bank of America (with its $5 million) and Citibank ($10 million) were almost insignificant—certainly in relation to the financial strength of the institutions concerned. Manufacturers Hanover was in worse trouble, to the tune of some $12.5 million, while Morgan Guaranty was owed around $500,000 more. The First National Bank of Chicago was also suffering. But the Seattle-First National Bank rang up the biggest claim quoted, some $22.5 million; the citizens of Seattle should never have wandered so far from Washington State.

The Chase Manhattan, although free from any direct liability, was immersed up to its ears by having acted as Herstatt's New York clearing agent. In this unlucky role, the bank had to divulge that twenty-four institutions, American and others, had descended on Chase Manhattan Plaza as claimants or potential claimants against the West German bank's account in New York. Some quickly moved to obtain attachment orders for funds said to total around a very hot billion.

The way the Herstatt was closed was enough to upset anybody— but especially an American. The Bundesbank stepped in to halt business at 3:30 in the afternoon, West German time (it didn't officially inform the management of its action, apparently, until 4:15). Because of the time differences, that was still only 10:30 in the morning in New York and three hours earlier in California. The American banks that were trading D-marks or other European currencies for dollars (or vice versa) in Frankfurt or Düsseldorf had no reason to doubt that there was ample time for the deals to be completed that day.

But as the U.S. bankers were sipping their mid-morning or breakfast coffee, they suddenly received the astounding news that there would be no deals, not that day, possibly ever. Morgan Guaranty, the big New York bank, according to the suit it subsequently filed, delivered the D-mark equivalent of $13 million to its correspondent in West Germany to buy dollars at ten o'clock in the New York morning. But before the U.S. currency could be handed over, the Herstatt tellers, under orders, closed the windows.

As Bankhaus I. D. Herstatt was a privately owned bank, the mountainous claims of disgruntled customers were against individuals. In the first instance, that meant the sixty-year-old general partner, Dr. Ivan David Herstatt, who had founded the bank (by reviving an earlier institution) some twenty years earlier. Dr. Herstatt attempted to present his liability largely as a moral one; there was no doubt about the moral blame, especially as in a rash moment two months before the crash of the bank bearing his name and initials, he had enthused publicly over its "excellent results." The doctor waxed especially eloquent over the foreign exchange and gold trading, whose profits, he declared, had offset losses in other departments.

Verbal burdens are one thing, money burdens quite another. Financially, the weight fell far more heavily on the shoulders of Dr. Hans Gerling, who had bought some 81 percent of the shares in I. D. Herstatt; the remaining fifth was split about evenly between Dr. Herstatt and the prominent West German financier and industrialist Dr. Herbert Quandt. The unhappy Gerling was not only compromised as its principal shareholder; he was far better known as owner of the Gerling Insurance Company, both inside and outside Germany. The sensational crisis at Herstatt created all kinds of rumors about the condition of the insurance empire, and even of the insurance industry in general.

Who had struck the Herstatt down? How far was Gerling himself responsible? Some eighteen months after the Herstatt had been drummed out of business, a Frankfurt court ruled that the insurance tycoon was personally liable for the losses sustained by creditors—and so was the bank's former financial director. This contradicted an earlier ruling in a Cologne court which had absolved Gerling from responsibility, and from the charge that he had neglected his duties as the chairman of the bank's supervisory board. As for Gerling, himself, he told a sorry tale of woe and wickedness. A special report prepared for the liquidator claimed that the Herstatt irregularities included the opening of a special account to hide profits and losses on foreign exchange dealings away from the official accounts. Somebody, too, it was alleged, had dealt in foreign exchange at arbitrary prices, bearing no relation to the market, with "important international banks." That being so, said Gerling, his subordinates were to blame.

The same official report made still more hair-raising charges. The bank's computer had apparently been tampered with, so that confirmation of foreign exchange deals in the "billions of dollars" could be printed out but not recorded on the books. The foreign exchange department had also fed the central bookkeeping department with false information to conceal the horrendous extent of the losses. In an interview with the popular newspaper *Bild,* Dr. Gerling went even further; large sums had been embezzled, he complained, from Herstatt and himself—simply shipped across the border into Switzerland into numbered accounts owned by Herstatt employees.

The creditors, not surprisingly, charged that if such monetary mayhem had been committed, Gerling, as boss, carried the ultimate blame. Recriminations and counter-recriminations bounced back and forth like tennis balls during the autumn of 1974, until the West German government, perturbed by the bad publicity, stopped the games. No less a personage than Chancellor Helmut Schmidt threatened to launch an official investigation. That was enough. In the last days of 1974, a settlement was agreed to by the thousand and more creditors.

The private creditors of Herstatt got 65 percent of their claims; foreign bank creditors and public authorities, 55 percent; and West German institutional creditors, 45 percent. The necessary funds came from the DM 984 million in assets that Herstatt still carried on the books when it collapsed. The rest, about DM 270 million, was raised out of a settlement fund, to which Dr. Gerling (thus paying a pretty price for his responsibility, or lack of it) agreed to contribute DM 200 million.

Whatever his sins of omission or commission, or both, the financier was compelled to pay still more for his blighted association with Bankhaus Herstatt—no less than surrender of control over his insurance empire. Its future, anyway, was something less than certain because of the disquiet aroused by the Herstatt scandal. The fears were only allayed when Dr. Gerling, under compulsion, sold 51 percent to a consortium of leading West German firms (with 25.9 percent); and to the Zürich Insurance Company (25.1 percent), one of the world's top rankers.

Somehow or other the big, stodgy Establishment institutions always seem to end up holding the choicest morsels when a carcass has been dismembered. The members of the consortium included such blue-chip companies as Bayer, BASF, Krupp, Siemens, Bosch, Daimler-Benz, Klöckner, and Mannesman. The West German public's anxiety about the insurance industry was thus soothed, and the Swiss presence in the business was neatly strengthened. The new Zürich stake in Gerling fortified the insurance group's already imposing presence via big companies in Frankfurt and Cologne.

The new interest cost the Swiss DM 50 million; a similar amount from the rescue consortium gave Gerling half of the DM 200 million he needed; the other DM 100 million was lent by a consortium of banks. So eventually the creditors began to collect. Among the first, as a rare matter of fact, were the smaller clients; 33,000 with deposits of less than DM 20,000 were repaid in full out of a "fire-fighting" fund hastily raised by the banking community. In 1975 the foreign banks began to get their dues, helped by the freeing of the assets that the Chase Manhattan had held in New York. West German creditors had to wait longer—not unreasonably in the circumstances—but they, too, in the end would get their allotted portion. The best was thus made of a very bad, a pitifully botched, job. But the Fall of the House of Herstatt is not a nine months' wonder. The memory of the disaster will linger on, not only in banking circles but also among the German general public, and in the courts. In August 1976 eight former executives, led by Herstatt and his one-time chief foreign exchange dealer, were arrested by the police after more than two years of investigation. Stable doors that were being shut had burst open again—and it would be a long time before anybody could forget that the horse had bolted. The executives were released on bail.

The Americans, hurt in their pride as in their pocket by being caught off-base when the West German authorities shut down Herstatt, were determined not to be trapped again. The major New York banks introduced a system by which any institution for any reason could demand reversal of a domestic or international inter-bank clearing transaction on the day after funds had been transferred; this pleased the foreign banks not one bit. The U.S. authorities were of the same mind. The very day after the Herstatt Bank trap was sprung, the Treasury Department drafted regulations under which U.S. banks with positions in any foreign currency over $1 million would have to report dealings weekly and monthly. The West German authorities were hard on the American heels with similar stable-locking exercises. The finance ministry, cooperating with the banks, hastily started building defenses to ensure that another Herstatt-type scandal could never occur.

Currency speculation was curbed; controls over credit tightened; the banking law changed to permit a temporary payments moratorium for any institution getting into financial difficulties; and the powers of the supervisory authorities extended to include the power to replace bank managers. A deposit insurance scheme for commercial banks, also covering nonbank depositors and extending to foreigners, was proposed, to which the German banks would be urged to make voluntary contributions. Meanwhile, an involuntary levy was imposed on the entire banking community to enlarge the fire-fighting fund to the point where it could protect deposits up to half a million DM. Furthermore the national bank, the Bundesbank, and the commercial banks—with the state clearing, savings, and cooperative banks—banded together to create a liquidity consortium, with an initial billion-mark reserve to bail out banks in trouble. The size and scope of the remedial measures were impressive, from one angle; looked at from the other end, however, the extent of the reforms showed how devastatingly weak had been the protection of the German banking system against its sinners, and of the public against the sins.

When the Herstatt disaster first hit, in fact, near-panic was reported among the population—the overwhelming majority of Germans have some savings stashed away in some kind of a bank, somewhere. The president of the Bundesbank, Dr. Karl Klasen, felt it necessary to offer official reassurance that the Herstatt crash did not mean "another 1931," with banks falling flat over one another's faces. He proved to be right; and other similar debacles failed to prove that the domino theory worked in world banking (though many feared that they would). The West Germans went on depositing more money than ever with the banks. After all, what option do they—or we—have?

But many aspects of the Herstatt affair remain cause for concern, especially the feature that was unique even among the numerous bank failures or near-failures around the same date: the terrible timing. It was not merely bad judgment, and bad manners, to pull out the rug from beneath customers who included some of the world's biggest banks as the West German authorities had done; it was also culpably rotten central banking.

This was not the view solely of disgruntled clients. In September 1975, a court in Frankfurt ruled that the German central bank must pay at least DM 10 million recompense to Hill Samuel, plus costs and other damages claimed by the British merchant bank. The court upheld Hill Samuel's charge that the Bundesbank had not exercised due care in its procedure. Funnily enough, the aggrieved British bankers—who did not have the same time zone problem as the Americans—attacked the Bundesbank on exactly opposite grounds to those advanced by their counterparts in the United States. They accused the Bundesbank of acting too slowly and too late. The court agreed. By two o'clock West German time on the fatal afternoon of June 26, the central bank knew that Herstatt was down the drain to the extent of some DM 620 million; yet the word was not given until ninety minutes later, by which time the situation had grown much worse. In that vital interval, several additional hundreds of millions flowed down that same drain.

The court also rebuked the Bundesbank for not fulfilling a legal duty to warn banks doing business with Herstatt of the impending closure. Examination of the Herstatt's books revealed that losses on foreign exchange transactions totaling some DM 100 million were already evident a full sixteen days before the central bank took any action. It was further alleged, in a mounting dossier of damaging testimony, that four days before the debacle Dr. Gerling had himself reported a deteriorating situation to the Bundesbank.

Even the central bank's defense did not help its cause. Before taking the irrevocable step of closure, the Bundesbankers reportedly argued that they tried to stage a rescue operation. This desperate last-ditch maneuver involved calling in three leading commercial banks to provide aid; the aim, presumably, was to engineer a takeover or merger. The revelation only raised a new critical storm, on the grounds that this placed the three solicited banks in a far more privileged position than the other clients who for four days more went on doing business with Herstatt in far from blissful ignorance of the impending disaster.

The Bundesbank, naturally, contested this interpretation of events by the Frankfurt court all along the line. But outside the courtroom, equally disquieting stories were circulating. For example, the *Financial Times* of London reported that the Bundesbank had reason to know that Herstatt was involved in foreign exchange trading excesses in 1973, when the Banking Supervisory Board investigated the matter; however, "the auditors somehow gave the bank a clean sheet in their audit of the 1973 results." A written question in Parliament was answered by the West German finance minister to the effect that as early as March 1972, the Bundesbank had received hints from Swiss banks about very heavy forward foreign exchange transactions by Herstatt; that by mid-1973, the subject was being discussed in banking circles in Cologne and Düsseldorf; and that at a February 1974 meeting in Basel other central bank governors specifically raised the matter with Bundesbank President Klasen.

In the teeth of his own evidence, the minister blandly maintained that both the central bank and the Banking Supervisory Board had "used every opportunity available to them" to prevent Bankhaus I. D. Herstatt from becoming insolvent. This was impossible to accept. The conduct of the West German authorities throughout the whole affair was as inconsistent as it was ineffective. The sluggish reaction to hints that horrors were in store, and the brusque coup when it became all too clear that the horrors must come into the open, alike pointed to a fatal weakness—one that the Bundesbank possessed along with other central banks. Its civil servants, it appeared, simply lacked adequate understanding of how commercial banking worked and of what risks and actions were and were not acceptable. It had acted rather like a police-man who allows a mugging to proceed under his eyes and then not only kills the assailant but shoots the victim in the leg. Given that they had this incoherent degree of protection, the West Germans were lucky to get away with no worse than the Herstatt tragedy.

27. The Israeli Capers

DURING the desperate days of the 1929 crash, so folklore holds, passers-by on Wall Street went in peril of their lives as failed financiers fell from the upper floors of adjacent skyscrapers. Other times, other customs. Half a century on, financial tycoons who come to grief (and the latter-day tally is lengthy) rarely choose the dramatic, simple, and final solution to their problems. Either nerves are stronger in our time, or consciences weaker, or ruin less absolute—or all three.

Yet in the summer of 1975, William E. Robinson, an Israeli financier and industrialist, did leap from the balcony of his daughter's sixteenth-floor flat in Tel Aviv. He chose this tragic exit from a crisis that followed the enforced closure by the Swiss banking authorities of the institution bearing his name. He was the principal shareholder in the Bank Robinson AG, with branches in Basel and Geneva; it was subsequently put into liquidation to safeguard the interests of creditors. The Swiss manager was arrested on suspicion of fraud by the affronted Swiss, never slow to slap handcuffs on those suspected of blasphemy against the nation's most sacred totem—money.

What aroused the Swiss Banking Commission was the suspicion that Bank Robinson had incurred certain liabilities that were not to be found anywhere on the balance sheet. Whether this was the fault of William Robinson (a former director of the Jewish Transport Agency), or of his son Michael David, who ran the bank until shortly before his father's death, was not immediately clear. At any rate, it was the elder Robinson who jumped—and in circumstances that, compared to other Israeli scandals of the epoch, seemed so mild as to suggest that William Robinson took the blow to his conscience too hard.

The Israeli connection does not, however, carry the moral of this tangled tale. The appalling adventures to be described show how easy it is for unscrupulous men to start or get control of a bank; how rapidly an apparently healthy asset position can be built up; how little control there is over deposits made by rich corporations, or over their use once banked; how weak the regulatory oversight of the authorities proves to be in practice; and how fortunate bank customers are that more bankers do not abuse their freedoms to the same extent as the freebooters of the shadowy world of privately controlled banks.

The cloud over the Robinson setup, with declared assets of some £6 million when the bank's operations were forcibly suspended, was no bigger than a man's hand; the darker thunderheads overhung two much more prominent Israelis and their financial empires. Tibor Rosenbaum headed Geneva's International Credit Bank (ICB); and Joshua Bension led the Israel-British Bank (IBB), of Tel Aviv. When these two crashed, in the summer and autumn of 1974, the noise rang around the world, for the implications were not only financial but also political.

Larger banks in many countries were left with doubtful debts; but that was only part of the damage. The two principals were prominent in the State of Israel and international Jewish circles. When they were accused of converting to their own use (by illegal transfer into Liechtenstein bank accounts) money entrusted to them as ostensible champions of the Jewish cause, the scandal made an odious impression on both Israelis and Israel's well-wishers.

Rosenbaum was not only the principal shareholder in ICB; he was also treasurer of the World Jewish Congress and a director of the Israel Corporation, a prestige-laden outfit which sprang from the so-called Millionaires' Conference of wealthy Jewish leaders—including Baron Edmond de Rothschild, Sir Siegmund Warburg, Sir Charles Clore, and Sir Isaac Wolfson. Set up following the Six Day War of 1967, the Corporation was designed to promote Israel's industrial development. Rosenbaum did not join the board until a later reorganization in 1971–72, and then, it is said, over the strong opposition of a few foresighted directors and shareholders.

Rosenbaum was a controversial figure even before his bank collapsed. He had earned respect and prestige by rescuing fellow Jews from his native Hungary during the Nazi years. And he had served the State of Israel well in financing big oil deals and secret arms transactions. On the other hand his bank, founded by Rosenbaum in Geneva in 1959, had a reputation for taking money from anyone, anywhere, and investing it in risky high-yield ventures.

A *Life* magazine article in 1967 included ICB in a list of banking home-from-homes for Mafia funds that were skimmed from gambling casinos in the United States and the Bahamas, then recycled to "legitimate" businesses owned by the mob back home. Some of ICB's "hot" money was believed to have been laundered through Bernie Cornfeld's IOS mutual fund operation, a Geneva neighbor with which ICB had close links. Rosenbaum and his bank provided part of the $1.5 million bail that finally sprung Cornfeld from the Geneva jail where he spent eleven months in 1973–74, and the Israeli banker was actually credited with first suggesting to Cornfeld the masterly idea of launching international investment funds based in Europe but dealing in dollars.

Rosenbaum's family connections, too, have had an unhappy time of late. His brother-in-law is one William Stern, an overambitious American who ran Britain's Nation Life Insurance into the ground and had the dubious distinction of achieving the biggest crash of all London's property developers (his insurance group was owed £1 million, incidentally, by Rosenbaum's Geneva bank). Although his base was in the Swiss city, Rosenbaum maintained close ties with influential Israelis, closest of all with Michael Tzur, a boyhood friend who at the time of the crash was managing director of the Israel Corporation, and had formerly run the Israeli Ministry of Commerce and Industry. The two cronies fell together.

Then there was the Williams mess, another in-law situation. In-law No. 1 is Joshua Bension, brother-in-law of No. 2, Harry Landy, a former vice president of the prestigious Board of Deputies of British Jews. Both married daughters of one of the money world's little-known Mr. Bigs. The late Walter Nathan Williams, the tycoon in question, died in 1971 in possession of a large and diversified financial empire based on banking, insurance, and property. The Williams wealth lay mainly in the United Kingdom, but was controlled from headquarters in Tel Aviv. The key Williams interests in the subsequent saga were the Israel-British Bank (IBB, for short) in Tel Aviv itself; its British subsidiary, Israel-British Bank (London); a couple of insurance companies; and a property company, publicly quoted, in which both IBB (London) and the two insurance firms were shareholders.

On the founder's death, the sons-in-law grabbed control, Bension at the Israeli end, Landy at the British one. Their dominion lasted a mere two years, cut short by the disintegration signaled in July 1974. The parent IBB was forced into receivership and shortly afterward liquidation, with outstanding obligations of no mean sum—about $43 million. The Bank of Israel, the country's central bank, took over when it found out that a liquidity problem, attributed at the time mainly to foreign exchange speculation, had ruined the sons-in-law's prime asset. The central bank pledged itself to reimburse depositors in Israel, but repudiated any responsibility for the creditors of IBB (London). That was legally a British institution, and the Israeli argument was that the Bank of England should carry the baby.

None too overjoyed at the privilege, the British central bank promptly closed down IBB (London), where some £50 million of other people's money was on deposit (this was the first time, incidentally, that a fully authorized bank in the United Kingdom had ever been allowed to fail). The British IBB was short by some $88 million against the claims of depositors, including no fewer than eighty clearing banks—among their number some of the leaders in both Britain and the United States (including names that were to become regulars in these lists of misfortune, such as the Chase Manhattan in New York and the Crown Agents in London).

One disaster in an Israeli-controlled international bank would have been more than enough. But the woes of Tibor Rosenbaum's ICB were also surfacing fast. In November 1974, ICB applied to the Swiss authorities for a one-year payments moratorium; its outstanding liabilities were put at around £55 million. Six months later, the Swiss authorities caught Rosenbaum at Geneva Airport on his way to Paris and swiftly incarcerated him (he was later released on £825,000 bail) along with a close associate. The charge of mismanagement of ICB was brought by Baron Edmond de Rothschild on behalf of the Israel Corporation; Rosenbaum's boyhood friend, Michael Tzur, had apparently made a $2 million deposit in the Corporation's name with ICB, at Rosenbaum's instructions, when the bank was manifestly in no position to repay the money.

Altogether some $23 million was deposited with ICB in the name of the Corporation, without the by-your-leave of the board authorization. Tzur, stripped of his jobs (managing director of the Israel Corporation, board chairman of the Zim shipping line), was sentenced in 1975 to fifteen years in jail for fraud, bribery, and illicit money deals. But where did the $23 million go?

The obvious question produced a totally unexpected and disgraceful charge: some $8.6 million which legally belonged to the Israel Corporation, and another $11.5 million of Zim's, wandered into a Liechtenstein company controlled by Tibor Rosenbaum. From there the money's alleged destination was the purchase of a hunting estate near Ostia, the port of Rome. The book value of this bauble was written up from $6 million to $90 million within seven years—even though the building permits needed for its planned development were never granted by the Italian authorities. Quite apart from this ingenious deal, ICB itself was charged with making expensive, speculative long-term real estate investments, though most of its deposits were short-term, despite repeated (and plainly useless) warnings by the Swiss authorities to mind its manners.

In the case of IBB, the bezzle (or the sum embezzled) was bigger: an alleged $43 million. Joshua Bension was tried and convicted in Tel Aviv District Court, accused in addition of plunging IBB Israel some $30 million into the red by speculating in commodity and other futures. As for the $43 million, all but $2 million had been transferred to banks in Switzerland, on the way to two Liechtenstein companies both controlled by the parent Williams group.

Bension recorded these transactions on the books as normal deposits by IBB with the Swiss banks used as intermediaries. This apparently aroused no suspicions in the minds of either the auditors or the bank examiners—though the latter did query the fact that out of the $43 million, no less than $35 million was shown to be deposited with a single bank; and, in a peculiarly feeble display of prudence, advised a broader spreading of the risk. Bension was also accused of keeping secretly in his home the records of the instructions to the Swiss banks to shuffle the funds on to Liechtenstein.

The Liechtenstein capers led indirectly to the downfall of IBB (London) as well. Its problems, according to Arthur Cheek, the official receiver appointed to wind up its affairs, largely arose from payments made from 1969 onward at the Tel Aviv parent's behest into various bank accounts in different parts of the world that were debited to those dreaded Liechtenstein companies. By the time IBB (London) was forced to close, it was owed some $35 million by the two Liechtenstein operations.

Of the combined amount of $35 million, some $8 million was recovered (partly by closing at a profit the foreign exchange positions of the London affiliate). But much to Cheek's disgust, a total of £32 million proved "totally irrecoverable" after Harry Landy, and a co-director in London, Arthur White, had done their bit: "In the opinion of the official Receiver the failure is mainly attributable to the conduct of Landy and White, in that they permitted the company to advance sums in excess of £30 million to overseas companies without making proper inquiry as to the use of the funds, or adequate arrangements as to security and repayment."

The damage done by these collapses was not confined to the pecuniary pain—though that was sharp enough. The creditors of Tibor Rosenbaum approved a settlement in March 1976 which gave small creditors compensation in full up to 5,000 Swiss francs; those with larger claims got only 17 percent of their demands against the bank. Most of Rosenbaum's personal assets in Israel were transferred to the Swiss liquidators by the Israeli official receiver. (The Israel Corporation, which earlier had asked for the assets to be blocked, gave in on the point.) The assets included two large textile concerns, Ata and Lodzia, and Rosenbaum's share in a chain of duty-free shops. The Israel Corporation, for its pains, received his shares in the Corporation—and his flat in Jerusalem.

But even full material restitution would never have compensated for the public relations damage done in the eyes of the world by these two Israeli banks with their oddly similar initials. There was an obvious temptation to see the ICB/IBB cases as something specifically to do with Israel, with the decay of the idealism on which the State had been founded, and with its supercession by a baser realism. The unfairness of this verdict is equally obvious—even the Garden of Eden had its serpent, and the sins of Rosenbaum and Bension had parallels in every other banking community. In a jittery era, jittery and greedy men were bound to seek to squirrel money away in places like cozy mailbox companies in Liechtenstein. The greediest were also certain to ignore little matters like exchange control regulations (of particular importance to a beleaguered economy like Israel's) and even, in the worst cases, conveniently to forget that the money wasn't actually their own.

But the dust of the misdeeds of the crisis years has inevitably rubbed off on the nation from which the miscreants originated. The ICB and IBB scandals involved too many important national personalities, including former government officials. The embroilment of the Israel Corporation was too close to home, because of the semi-official status of an institution in which the state and the national labor organization both had stakes. And the disgrace of men who were regarded as leaders of the Israeli cause in the international arena was bound to be damaging to that cause itself.

Finally, the end of two affairs, from which singularly few emerged with any kind of credit, left some mighty institutions mightily miffed. The Bank of England and the British Foreign Office were displeased by the abrupt and callous landing of the IBB (London) pieces on Britain's doorstep, when the complicity of the Tel Aviv parent in the disintegration was glaringly obvious. The big American banks, stuck with doubtful deposits in London, put pressure on congressmen, who in turn put pressure on the Ford administration—the notion being that a "no repayment, no arms" tactic, or a similar piece of strong-arming of the Israelis, might get the banks off the hook.

Indeed, when all the damage is totted up, the Israeli authorities, though they cannot be excused for the regulatory laxity which helped the disasters to arise in the first place, could be forgiven for wishing that the unhappy example of the late William E. Robinson had been followed by the more conspicuous offenders among his banking colleagues. No doubt some affronted Israelis wouldn't have minded giving the law-breaking in-laws a helping push.

28. The Hessische Landslide

THE link, so bitterly demonstrated in the thirties, between political and financial stability still exists and was tested anew by the crashes of the seventies. The feckless Israeli bankers generated political repercussions far beyond the borders of their own state. The fall of Tibor Rosenbaum's International Credit Bank even touched off a political crisis in West Germany; at one point the imbroglio could have threatened the coalition in Bonn between the Social Democratic and Free Democratic parties. The unfortunate connection is that one of the principal shareholders in ICB, with 36.4 percent of the blighted bank, was the Hessische Landesbank-Girozentrale. This is the state bank of Hesse, the German region that includes the main nerve center of the country's banking system, the city of Frankfurt.

Still worse, the prime minister of Hesse, Albert Osswald, headed the Landesbank, and his Social Democrats were the majority partners in coalition with the Free Democrats—paralleling the situation in Bonn. Piling misfortune on misfortune, when ICB got into difficulties in late 1974, Osswald was fighting an election. His party had enjoyed an absolute majority in the Hesse Parliament ever since democracy had been restored to Germany postwar. But not after 1974—the opposition Christian Democrats seized on the ICB scandal as an unexpected, highly exploitable issue. Osswald squeaked home, but lost his absolute majority en route; from then on he depended upon the grace and favor of the Free Democrats to stay in power.

Had Osswald been beaten, or the Free Democrats transferred their aid and comfort to the opposition, the consequences would have reached national level. It almost happened. When the ICB scandal broke, Herbert Karry, the Hesse economics minister and federal treasurer of the Free Democrats, was alongside Osswald on the Landesbank board. Karry promptly removed himself, charging that others in the know had deliberately kept him in ignorance of developments at ICB —and the inference was that the knowing included Osswald.

A serious split between the Social Democrats and Free Democrats in so important a state as Hesse would have had ominous implications for the national coalition in Bonn. However, the rift with Karry and his colleagues was patched up when the prime minister survived the election. Only a curiosity of Hesse politics had landed Osswald in his fix in the first place. Alone out of the provinces into which West Germany is divided, Hesse made the prime minister *ex officio* chairman of the state bank. Each of the Länder has its own bank, which advises the state on, and helps to finance, development projects and which also acts as a clearing bank, and to some extent as a wholesale bank for the state's savings institutions.

The two functions are closely interrelated, since the Landesbanks are responsible for investing the deposits of the savings banks, which they channel mainly into state infrastructure projects—housing, roads, schools, hospitals, and the like. Consequently the savings banks are equal partners with the state in ownership of the Landesbanks. The one in Hesse (known as Helaba for short) is second only in size to the Westdeutsche Landesbank-Girozentrale, which serves the industrial hub of the Rhineland. (The latter also got a stern press whipping around the same time as Helaba when it reported a loss of some $45 million on 1973 foreign exchange foolery.)

Helaba's fall from grace was particularly embarrassing because, shortly before the tribulation caused by its unfortunate liaison with Dr. Rosenbaum, the management had taken prominent ads in Hesse to trumpet its proud achievements to the voters. The state bank, so the copywriters enthused, was financing one-fifth of all the state's investments; one-third of all bank assets were in municipal loans; and during the twenty-five years since 1950, it had financed 600,000 houses. One out of every six employed Hessians was a customer of its building society subsidiary; and Helaba also cleared the 1.7 million accounts of the fifty-six savings banks in the state. A commendable catalogue—but conspicuously incomplete.

Certain other types of activity in which Helaba had become involved more recently were unaccountably overlooked. The state banks in West Germany, for no very good reason, are allowed to compete with regular banks in the latter's normal rackets. They can join in new issues business, both domestic and foreign; they can set up foreign branches. They can diversify—Helaba has an investment banking affiliate, which explains how it became embroiled with the ill-famed ICB.

In 1972, the Landesbank was blessed with a new chief executive, Dr. Wilhelm Hankel, a protégé of Dr. Karl Schiller, West Germany's former renowned economics minister. Hankel, who was reputed to be a brilliant academic, launched Helaba on a new era of expansion and diversification. Easily the most far-reaching of these bold swoops into the unknown was the 36.4 percent participation in Tibor Rosenbaum's

Swiss outfit, an investment made for several reasons, one being that Hankel regarded the Geneva bank as a "suitable foreign base for foreign transactions." He is also said to have regarded Rosenbaum with favor as a "Jewish patriot"—like a good many of West Germany's postwar Socialist politicians, Hankel is pro-Israeli. In making the judgment, Hankel overlooked other less savory characteristics of both the banker and his bank, such as ICB's reputation for excessive risk-taking, and alleged connections with dubious clients—drawbacks that should have been evident from even a cursory investigation.

In fact, as we have recorded, ICB proved no more reliable as a foreign base than its chief shareholder did as a patriot. Both errors of judgment cost Helaba and its chief executive dearly. As soon as ICB collapsed, indeed, Helaba took the rare but somewhat redundant step of returning its stake to Rosenbaum, on the grounds that his past actions "did not correspond to usual practices in the international banking business." Its renunciation could not save Helaba from the consequences of ICB's debacle; several of the latter's larger creditors filed suit against the Landesbank, claiming that its management could be held responsible financially for some of the Swiss bank's losses. They argued that Helaba officials should have checked ICB's bad books, and spotted its bad risks.

Hankel's misfortunes were not confined to the Rosenbaum connection. Earlier in 1974, he had to resign when other policy mistakes came loudly home to roost. Both the parent and its investment banking subsidiary (where Hankel had upped the Helaba stake from 25 to 79 percent) had come ingloriously unstuck in the property market, as addled investments in large building projects (located in Frankfurt and Munich) turned thoroughly sour.

The subsidiary institution Investitions and Handelsbank (IHB) became so precariously balanced that a DM 280 million lifeline had to be extended by three minority shareholders, the Westdeutsche and Norddeutsche Landesbanks, and the Bank für Gemeinwirtschaft (which is unique in being owned by the trade union movement). Eventually, in early 1976, a permanent rescue operation for IHB was worked out, which included buying out the aggregate 4 percent holding of small shareholders. A sadder, wiser, and smaller institution, IHB would henceforward confine itself to the safer world of joint transactions and syndicate business.

As for its mother, Helaba, its assets had been written down by some DM 800 million in 1973—before it got into *real* trouble. When near-disaster hit, with the news of the ICB collapse in Geneva, the savings banks of the state of Hesse (not to mention their depositors) were plunged into a state of shock. They had to be rescued by the West German Savings Bank and Giro Association, which guaranteed interest-free loans of DM 30 million a year for five years to help keep Helaba afloat.

The fact that since Helaba is ultimately backed by the state of Hesse it cannot go under is a mixed blessing for the citizens—and the politicians. Its problems have hung around to haunt Osswald and his administration for many a long day. Early in 1976, the bank was back at the State House with its hand out yet again. The begging was done by the second man to fill the obviously hag-ridden post vacated by Hankel. The first successor, a former president of the Hesse Central Bank, actually came out of retirement to try to sort out Helaba but suffered a heart attack shortly thereafter.

His successor had to report that the Landesbank's writeoffs for 1975 would total between DM 400 and 500 million. After using up all its own available resources, the bank would still face a yawning gap of around DM 200 million, which only the state could bridge. The grand total of Helaba writeoffs for 1973 to 1975 inclusive had soared to some DM 2,200 million—not bad for three years' work. Among the bank's latter woes were a DM 100 million contribution toward the reorganization of part of the Gloeggler textile group, which had collapsed in 1975. Further calamities had been suffered by the bank's property investments. Helaba had originally counted on divesting itself of problem properties within two years; the faulty estimate had to be doubled— hence the request for another DM 200 million handout on top of the DM 600 million in cash and DM 850 million in guarantees for which the bank had already stuck its backers.

Naturally, the state was assured that all this money was needed to repair old damage, and that no new follies had been committed under the new administration. Perhaps this was some small comfort; but there was also some positive assurance that the ghastliness of the mid-seventies would never again be repeated. This assurance was not left to the politicians: the principal actors on the banking side, scared out of their previously inadequate wits by the experience, did not intend to repeat it.

The Hesse savings banks, before passing on to Helaba the interest-free loan from their national parent association, and providing other financial aids, published a five-point program of reform. The savings banks as a group, and the state of Hesse as the other principal shareholder, should each put up DM 200 million in fresh capital; the executive board should be strengthened with three financial experts; the bank's constitution should be changed to reduce the political influence and improve the management control; the bank's policy should become more "realistic," especially in the vital areas of credit and property investment; and firm direction should be exercised in future over the IHB investment bank.

The politicians, having fully shared the traumas, scarcely needed the blows from this blunt instrument to know that radical changes were essential. After the election, Prime Minister Osswald promulgated a new constitution for the bank, which bore an unsurprisingly neat resemblance to the savings banks' manifesto. No longer would the prime minister of the state be *ex officio* (and so vulnerably) the chairman of the board of the state bank. Osswald did not even wait for the new constitution to be legal, but resigned the hot seat like a shot. The supervisory board which he left, and the executive board beneath it, were not only wholly reorganized but also supplemented by a new "guarantors committee," half nominated by the Hesse government (one of them *ex officio* the prime minister) and the other half by the Savings Banks Association. With this extra watchdog bristling over the operations of Helaba and its subsidiaries, a repetition of the dismal autumn of 1974 has probably been ruled out. Which leaves one crucial question: Who left the bank so open to disaster in the first place?

Chastened and (it was to be hoped) contrite, the Hessische Landesbank-Girozentrale set about the task of refurbishing its public image—an uphill job. In the eyes of the public, and especially the men and women of Hesse who had entrusted their savings to one of the state's savings banks, the publicity surrounding Helaba's errors (above all its flirtation with Tibor Rosenbaum) was as disturbing as it was disagreeable. What were their banks doing, getting mixed up with an outfit that kept such bad company?

It cannot be proper for an institution partly owned and controlled by government to solicit business in competition with commercial banks, and at the taxpayers' expense—especially that much expense. Taking part in public financing is legitimate enough, but playing the full commercial game is something else again. Nor should a publicly owned institution ever have been exposed to the enormous open-ended risks of foreign exchange dealing—a criticism which the Westdeutsche Landesbank's horrors rubbed home.

How much the undue political influence over the Hesse bank contributed to the disaster is hard to establish. Totally nonpolitical banks, after all, succeeded in making just as thorough a mess. Helaba's troubles would have been less had greater competence and attention been applied at the top—prime ministers, even state prime ministers, are busy people, and the time they can spend running banks is strictly limited. But the prime failure lay in entrusting actual operations to officials who lacked the necessary caliber and experience in banking, a specialized profession not lightly left to amateurs.

For the politicians as well, the change embodied in the drafting of a new constitution for the bank seemed likely to prove a blessing, and by no means in disguise. For, if there was one lesson that the frustrated hopes and the blighted ambitions of the Hessische Landesbank-Girozentrale had to teach, it was surely that banking and politics don't mix. You have only to ask Prime Minister Albert Osswald of the West German State of Hesse—or rather ex-Prime Minister Osswald. In 1976, an hour after the polls had closed for that year's election, he resigned, citing the Hessische scandal. And in 1977, the electors of Hesse threw out his party, which had governed that state uninterruptedly for over a quarter of a century. Everybody in Hesse knew why.

29. Horsing Around

ONCE upon a time, in that same charming community of Lugano—before the Lloyds Bank International disturbance already described—there was a little Swiss bank. It can serve as a demonstration of how, across the world, the word "bank" did not mean what the world had been conditioned to expect. Everybody accepted that this particular bank was Swiss. It had a typically Swiss name, Bank Vallugano. Its board of directors was studded with respectable local burghers, lawyers, businessmen, and merchants. The publicity with which it wooed local deposits stressed all the time that it was "a genuine Ticinese institution."

The people of Lugano, like the burghers of Hamelin purchasing the services of the Pied Piper, hurried to entrust their savings to the Vallugano Bank. The little bank grew bigger and bigger. And it really seemed as if everyone was going to live happily ever after. But then, one less fine day, the burghers of Lugano learned that the Vallugano Bank was not a Swiss bank after all. Instead, it was owned by an Italian, who had been systematically robbing them of their money through an account at the bank opened, of all things, in the name of a racehorse.

What pained the victims was not only the injury, nor the insult thus added to it, but a well-grounded suspicion that the local directorate —their neighbors and, in many cases, friends—had known all along that the bank was controlled by an Italian; and that, after his frauds had been discovered, those respectable citizens kept quiet while the thief went on accepting deposits from the public. The villain, the Vallugano's principal shareholder, was Giovanni Pasquale, age sixty-eight, from Bologna. The other Italian in the case, Egidio Mazzola (age forty-three), was the bank manager. The seven members of the board of directors were all Swiss save one. In December 1975, the Lugano criminal court found them all guilty of offenses ranging from major fraud (Pasquale), to complicity in this fraud (Mazzola), and minor fraud and violations of Swiss banking regulations (the rest of the defendants).

The actual offenses dated all the way back to 1971 and earlier. The wheels of justice ground slowly because the chief defendant, Pasquale (in a display of shyness typical of the bank criminals and neo-criminals of the epoch), could not be coaxed back over the Swiss border to stand trial. His reluctance must have been fortified after the court sentenced him to seven and a half years in prison. Mazzola got two and a half years; the minor defendants escaped with suspended sentences or fines.

Pasquale's absence was explained, according to his doctors, by a heart condition which forced him to shuttle back and forth from luxury villa to luxury clinic; at any rate, the court accepted the evidence of the medical certificates, and Pasquale, to the regret of all others concerned, missed the tragicomedy—which at times approached pure pantomime —of the three weeks of hearings. The "Aleppo" account was the center-piece of the trial, this being the account at the Bank Vallugano which the owner opened for a racehorse in his stable; and which, according to the testimony, at different times appeared under seventeen different headings on the books.

The generous horse-lover did not escape retribution altogether. Apart from the divine variety (his periods in the hospital included an operation on the urinary tract), there was human punishment—Pasquale spent the whole of 1972 in jail in Italy before being released on bail. The Italian authorities had their own charges of fraud against Pasquale, in connection with the failure of an Italian company he controlled, Finanziamenti Diversi Bologna (FIDIBO); its liabilities amounted to some 11,800 million lire, including 5,000 million owing to the Vallugano. According to the Italians, Pasquale juggled funds between his Italian and Swiss institutions, both for legitimate purposes (he invested in property, produced films, and published books) and also, allegedly, for dubious activities such as smuggling butter and financing arms for the Palestine Liberation Organization.

Pasquale was not accused of actually delivering arms to Arab terrorists, but of lending $1 million for this purpose to the Italian publishing millionaire, Giangiacomo Feltrinelli—an eccentric, killed when a charge of dynamite exploded while he was attaching it to an electric power pylon outside Milan. (The arms that Feltrinelli bought and shipped to the guerrillas were intercepted by the ever-alert Israeli secret service.) The money that Pasquale readily supplied to the rich terrorist was presumably laundered through the Bank Vallugano. In Lugano itself, of course, nobody knew any more about this skulduggery than they did about Pasquale. He concealed his Vallugano connection by operating through nominees on the board. If their word was to be believed, even some of his fellow directors were not aware of their benefactor's shadier activities as swindler, smuggler, and financier of terrorist movements.

They knew him only—so they claimed—as a successful Italian

businessman, prominent public figure, and leading sportsman. Apart from his racehorses, he was at the summit of the world of soccer (which in Italy rivals the Roman Catholic Church as a state religion), president both of the League of Professional Clubs and the Italian Association Football Federation. His passion for the racetrack, however, provided the main entertainment for spectators at the Vallugano trial. The bank account in the name of a horse by means of which Pasquale perpetrated his frauds was opened in 1966, two years after the Vallugano was founded, and shortly after Pasquale acquired his controlling interest. The horse Aleppo quickly became a debtor of the bank; as the years passed, the improvident quadruped went deeper and deeper into the red as its owner financed his legitimate and illegitimate wheeling and dealing by this cunning means.

To conceal the mounting tally of debt, at the end of every month when the figures had to be reported to the Swiss banking authorities, the bank engaged in what is known in the trade as "window-dressing." Even respectable banks use this technique to ensure that they put the best possible face on their balance sheets. The Vallugano's operation differed in heinous motive and massive scale, in relation to the bank's size. Checks in transit from other banks were deposited to the credit of the horse. The Aleppo account was immediately debited again at the beginning of the following month. The real nature of the transactions was further disguised by recording them as ultra-short-term deals, on which the Vallugano was supposed to be earning ultra-high interest and commissions.

At one point, manager Mazzola kept in a desk drawer a savings book issued by the Commercial Bank of Italy, showing a credit of some 5 million Swiss francs. This was supposedly a guarantee of the Aleppo account, to be flashed in front of auditors or anyone else whose suspicions might be aroused. When the passbook had served its purpose, it traveled back to Pasquale in Bologna. With the nature of the Aleppo account thus artfully concealed, the transactions were systematically understated. For example, at the end of 1968, the loans outstanding were tabulated at some Sfr. 2.7 million; but an investigation of the books before the trial showed the truth to run at around Sfr. 13 million. By the time the Vallugano closed down for keeps, on May 13, 1971, the diversion to Pasquale's pockets had reached Sfr. 35 million.

Maintaining a deception of these heroic dimensions required fast footwork, and at one point in 1969 even the nimble Pasquale was caught on the wrong foot. *In extremis,* he pulled off a coup which, although it staved off disaster at the time, set Nemesis in motion. It was named at the trial as Operation Butter. This fat caper enabled Pasquale to pay some 60 million French francs into the Aleppo account at a moment when it was devastatingly overdrawn; as a result, at the end of 1969 he was able to window-dress the account to show a credit balance of around Sfr. 500,000.

The French francs flung so opportunely into the breach represented collateral pledged to a French marketing agency in connection with imports of butter into Switzerland. For a time, Pasquale had covered his tracks with the butter. But in spring 1970, when the auditors were checking the Vallugano's books, they were at first puzzled, and then horrified, by the discovery of large sums guaranteed to the French agency that had never entered into the regular accounts. It took months to uncover the complicated conspiracy. But once the financier's mechanism was revealed, the days of both the Bank Vallugano and its chief shareholder were numbered.

Pasquale's fellow directors joined the auditors in demanding an explanation, and in urging him to find a remedy for the bank's dangerous situation. Pasquale made promises again and again, but he probably could not have kept them, even if he had wanted to. In its final despair, the board itself reported the facts to the local authorities, and begged for a six-month moratorium on payments to depositors. This was granted; and on May 14, 1971, the Vallugano closed for business for the last time. (It was subsequently taken over by another local bank.)

The crash of the Vallugano caused a large and unpleasant sensation in Lugano and the neighborhood. Its depositors were mostly locals, some of them people acquainted with and trusting in the Swiss directors who lent Pasquale's operation the respectability of their names and reputations. Many of the depositors were typical small savers, but others had quite considerable sums at stake. The directors deserved the resentment of their neighbors and friends. They must have known that the "genuine Ticinese institution" was, in reality, about as Swiss as Spaghetti Bolognese. How had they not known about, or at least suspected, the nature of the Aleppo account? How could it have been used without their knowledge? If they were truly ignorant, they ought not to have been. In fact, in the course of the trial witness after witness disclosed that his board colleagues were worried about the size of the Aleppo overdraft, and repeatedly called upon Pasquale to reduce it. They could not have had less success if they had asked the horse.

The prosecution produced letters and internal memoranda on the subject, dating back at least to the summer of 1969, when one director warned Pasquale of the dangers of a run on the bank if any whisper of the Aleppo scandal should spread around the community. One memorandum positively affirmed that "the bank's policy is not healthy, and puts in danger the small deposits of many of our clients." Similar qualms were expressed time and again. In July 1969, at a board meeting in Milan, so much pressure was put on Pasquale that he promised to reduce his large deficit and to substitute Swiss collateral for Italian collateral against his borrowings. The fact that loans against their deposits were being made on Italian collateral was also hidden, of course, from the depositors, who would have been horrified had they known.

Nastiest of all, even after they had discovered the sordid truth about the Aleppo account and the rest of the mess, some of the directors still allowed the public to continue making deposits for at least five months more. Two of them, with greater scruples, resigned from the board at the moment of truth, unwilling any longer to be Pasquale's accomplices. They got the mildest punishment—fines of Sfr. 5,000 each for violations of banking regulations. The other five got short suspended prison sentences, for minor fraud; and specifically for continuing to accept deposits from the date fixed by the court as the point beyond which it could no longer be accepted that these directors knew nothing about Pasquale's misdeeds.

The luckless depositors had thus been conned into putting their money into a bank whose chief shareholder abused his position first to borrow huge sums without adequate security; and then, when in danger of exposure, to alter the books and conceal the fraud with the aid of a compliant manager. It was small consolation to the bilked customers that they would not be left entirely bare. In 1972, the liquidator appointed by the authorities paid some money back to the 1,000 or so smaller depositors; a miserable return of between 30 and 40 percent of their funds.

The five directors of the Bank Vallugano adjudged guilty of fraud were ordered by the court to put up Sfr. 500,000 (the liquidator had sought Sfr. 3 million) for distribution among defrauded depositors. A civil case for full restitution was to follow the criminal trial. But even that could not compensate the Luganesi and others for their anguish and stress. Everybody in the community seemed to have some relative or friend harmed by the collapse of the Vallugano.

Other banks in the Ticino that were known or suspected to be under foreign (especially Italian) control encountered that sinking feeling in popular esteem. Everybody knew that many Italian citizens with plush-lined purses thought it not enough to deposit funds safely in a bank in Switzerland. To exploit that privileged haven to the full, far better retain total control over the loot. Swiss bankers might prove overscrupulous in their interpretation of the rules; further, they might restrict the free-and-easy disposition of the funds on which a free-wheeling speculator of the Pasquale breed depended—and Pasquale was certainly not alone in his financial tastes.

Not that the Swiss authorities showed themselves to be unduly restrictive in the Vallugano affair. That bank was an Italian pirate ship flying under false Swiss colors; why hadn't the regulators rumbled the deceit? And what about the firm that audited the bank's books?

At the trial it came to light that, almost from the founding of the Vallugano in 1964, both regulators and auditors intervened repeatedly to complain of irregularities which involved at least a bending of the rules governing banks and savings institutions. The Vallugano's management was rapped more than once for the unsatisfactory conduct of its credit operations, and for a lack of proper vigilance in general. Moreover, in their 1967 report on the bank's financial statement, the auditors had already identified the infamous Aleppo account by name.

In 1968 and 1969, again the same worries were expressed. For some years before the crash the financial experts must have known that the Aleppo account was dangerously enough exposed to threaten the stability of the bank as a whole. Nothing was done by the auditors to warn the depositors of the extreme risk which, in all innocence, they were running. The banking commissioners are guilty on the same count. The auditors had fussed about the shortcomings of the credit department, and other disquieting symptoms; the commissioners had warned the bank's management, and Pasquale in particular, about the deficit on the Aleppo account. But the interests of the little people were allowed to go by default—and default is what they went by.

It was not until 1969 that the Swiss government itself, in fact, enacted legislation requiring the disclosure of foreign ownership of banking and similar institutions. By the time that the stable door had been bolted, the horse Aleppo was off and running. But the story shows yet again that the powers that be, inside and outside banks, are more interested in bankers than they are in bankees—the masses whose money keeps the bankers in business, and gives the financiers, honest and otherwise, the terrible illusion that the money is truly theirs.

EPILOGUE

30. The Nick of Time

THE dog that didn't bark in the night perplexed Sherlock Holmes. But the most curious minor incident of the prolonged banking crisis of the seventies was that of the dog that did bark—and then promptly apologized, with much embarrassment, for making such an unseemly din. In August 1976, the Federal Reserve Board in Washington turned down an application by Bankers Trust New York Corporation, proprietor of the nation's seventh largest bank, which wanted to buy a little upstate bank. The Fed gave as its public reason the continuing "financial difficulties" (its very words) of the great bank.

Within moments of the statement, the wrath of Wall Street began to fall on the Fed's shoulders. On the same day the Fed gave forth another, self-evidently contradictory statement, lauding Bankers Trust as "a sound institution with responsible management." From one angle, the confusion perfectly illustrates the central dilemma of bank regulators: they are supposed to do everything to keep bankers on the straight and narrow path of banking rectitude, while simultaneously doing nothing to scare the living daylights out of bank customers. This awkward straddle can be maintained while the banks are in fact behaving themselves; it becomes acutely uncomfortable for everybody (not least the customers) when financial impropriety abounds.

The dilemma so neatly demonstrated by the Case of the Barking Dog explains a great deal of what went wrong in bank regulation in the sixties and thereafter. But the two opposed statements about Bankers Trust also point up a pregnant truth about the large banks. Many of them were assuredly in financial difficulties in the wake of the disasters, overstocked with bad loans, and too close to their safety margins to have any justification for new ventures and old dreams of empire. But it was also true that the banks were sound and their managers responsible. The whole tragedy of the crisis was that the soundness and responsibility with which banks, by and large, went about their day-to-day business were negated by strange and total lapses of judgment. These failures were more understandable in fields where the banks were relatively

237

green (such as speculation in foreign exchange) than in traditional areas like lending to large commercial and municipal customers.

Part of the reason, indeed, is that the banks have become too close to such clients in too many respects. President Eisenhower worried in his valedictory speech about the impact of "the military-industrial complex" on American society (as well he might, given what was about to happen in Vietnam). He could as justifiably have worried about the financial-industrial-political complex. The cozy links between politicians and banks at national and local levels, and the interlocking relationships of the great banks and large corporations, are long-lasting features of American society. They became insidiously dangerous in the sixties when the banks were virulently infected by the ideas of their business customers.

The virus attacked and immobilized one of the checks and balances in the system. The old strict rules of banking prudence were a curb on the borrowing and thus the excesses of politicians and corporate chieftains alike. In turn, political sensitivity to the dangers of financial power was a check on the ambition of the bankers. But when the politicians gave way to pressure from the banks for more freedom of action, the path was cleared for these basically "sound and responsible" managements to behave with the unsoundness and irresponsibility that nonbanking businessmen often exhibit when they are pressing too hard for dynamic expansion and high profits in their own, well-known fields —and still more frequently when they push into strange areas.

The American infection was transferred to Europe in the bodies of the American banks. It was primarily because of their invasion that the first stirrings of the entrepreneurial itch among Europe's bankers became exacerbated into a real lust to show that they, too, could be as aggressive, as marketing-minded, as dynamically managed as anybody else. And so they attacked, marketed, and managed themselves into writeoffs and dead ends to a degree that had never previously featured in their worst dreams. It wasn't a case of clowns longing to play Hamlet but of a bunch of Hamlets playing the clown.

The criticism applies not just to bankers but to banking authorities; the latter were too close to those they were supposed to regulate, and too anxious not to rock a leaky boat. But when the intensity of the crisis had passed without bringing down the economic civilization of the West, both sides, the regulators and the regulated, were quick to don the trappings of a new sobriety—of which the amazing strictures on Bankers Trust were one clear example. From failing even to rap the knuckles of knaves and fools, the Fed was now hitting everything in sight with a blunt instrument.

As for the bankers, they moved in a changed world. John Thackray noted in *Management Today* the reaction of a small manufacturer in

Denver who reported that where the banks once eagerly lent on a 3 to 4 assets to liabilities ratio if they liked the look of a company, they now required a 3 to 2 picture before they would consider a loan. All the way from New York, the great Manufacturers Hanover had once sought out this man's firm and made it a $2 million loan. "Bankers traveled from all over the country to come to talk to us." After the sea-change, they came no more; and Manny Hanny in 1976 turned down a loan request from the Denverite.

The caginess is hardly surprising, considering U.S. provisions for loan losses totaled nearly $5 billion in 1974 and 1975 combined—an amount that certainly grossly understated the true liabilities. The bankers also widened the crucial gap between the interest rates they paid and charged, doing everything in their power to boost the profits on which ultimate recovery depended.

Banks in other countries, according to their differing national situations, reacted in much the same safety-first way. As for the new ventures that were once so enticing, they glittered less attractively, and even those that did shine sufficiently (as the Bankers Trust found) were more likely than not to get the official thumbs-down. In the world of regulation, restriction had taken over from permissiveness. The Fed in 1974 and 1975 turned down no fewer than eighty-five applications to form new holding companies or to make further nonbanking moves. Half of the refusals were on the grounds that the plans were unsafe, since they would not add materially to the proposers' strength.

The Fed had also pledged itself to bail out any institution that might get into difficulties. In West Germany, reflecting the same necessity, a liquidity bank known as a "bank of banks" was established, first on an *ad hoc* basis to clear up the Herstatt mess, and then on a permanent basis. The crisis also spurred measures for central bank cooperation on an international scale. "Fire-fighting funds" were established to prevent a flare-up in the banking community in one country from spreading into a general conflagration. The world's most highly industrialized countries, through the Organization for Economic Cooperation and Development, founded a $25 billion Financial Support Fund for the purpose; it would work closely with the Bank for International Settlements in Basel, the club of the central bankers.

Under the latter club's own program, the membership collectively undertook to help out commercial banks in any country in any crisis by acting as lender of last resort. However, the guarantee was conditional; it depended upon fulfilling certain conditions designed to prevent crises occurring. Among the stipulations were stricter reporting procedures for banks, particularly for forward currency transactions; a clampdown on "insider" trading by foreign exchange dealers on their own account; and the closure of loopholes by which banks could get around the monetary restrictions imposed by their national governments.

The multi-national approaches have been backed up by the measures of individual governments to close loopholes and prevent abuses. The West Germans introduced new, tighter regulations governing the issuing of bank licenses (no more, for example, would be granted to "one-man banks") and imposing limits on lending. A credit insurance scheme for the protection of depositors was expanded.

In Britain, the Bank of England introduced stricter reporting procedures, and the rules governing secondary banks were tightened. As a leading international financial center, the City of London took the initiative in laying down rules for the consortia of banks from several countries; their pivot was the written guarantee of support ("letters of comfort," they came to be called) for each consortium member on the part of its parent. The City was also the focal point of efforts to introduce some order and discipline into the sometimes wild and woolly Eurocurrency market.

The Americans sent inspectors over to Britain to "police" the scores of U.S. institutions that had set up subsidiaries there. At home, intervention was often bluntly direct. Not only had the Fed more than once thrown out proposed acquisitions outside banking, but most of the stable doors were already shut. Enthusiasm for diversification had waned among the U.S. banks as they became increasingly disillusioned by their experience and minuscule profits in such areas as mortgage banking, consumer finance, and leasing.

The mood in America favored revision of the banking laws, not only to ensure tighter supervision of the banks themselves but also to monitor the agencies that regulated them. The resignation of the head of one of those agencies, James Smith, comptroller of the currency, under a cloud, could only increase the pressure. The fact that the regulators themselves needed more regulation was no surprise, considering that the agencies were financed by the very same banks that they were supposed to discipline.

A serious attempt was made to end the anomaly by which U.S. banks had three separate disciplinarians—the comptroller, the Federal Reserve Board, and the Federal Deposit Insurance Corporation; and to telescope these into a single organization, or, at the worst, two. Another obvious and advocated reform was to have the presidents of the twelve Federal Reserve Banks—the arbiters of national financial policy, along with the Federal Reserve Board—appointed by the president of the United States and confirmed by the Senate, instead of being chosen by the boards of directors.

But the banking reform, when brought forth into the light of day, was what the *Wall Street Journal* called "only a pale shadow of the bold overhaul plan" originally sponsored by Democratic members of the

House Banking Committee. The powerful bankers' lobby in Washington had worked with its usual skill and command. Herein lay the seeds of possible trouble and danger in the future. Bankers in the United States had run out of control because financial developments on the global scale, themselves predominantly determined by U.S. foreign economic policy, had provided temptations that the banks were no more likely to resist than they proved able to shun the opportunities for lavish lending offered by the gimcrack corporations of the sixties.

The root of the evil was the collapse of the link between the dollar and gold, the chain that held the Bretton Woods monetary structure together. It was taken apart piece by piece: by the ban, for a long while, on the holding of gold by American citizens; by the two-tier gold system, with one price for the commercial market and another for purposes of international exchange; by the introduction of special drawing rights, not based on gold; by the ending of dollar convertibility into gold. A monotonous series of platitudinous international conferences dealt not with the real problem, which was the constantly mounting excess of dollars floating about the world, but with ways of preventing that excess from having its natural effects.

The refusal of the Americans to recognize that the continuous monetary crises were an American problem was of a piece with the resistance of the bankers' fraternity to attempts at reform. The status quo was too comfortable for vested interests—never mind how many disasters were created on the side. For the bankers to put their house in order, they would have had to accept closer regulation and greater restriction. For the United States to stabilize the dollar, it would have had to accept limitations on economic policy at home and abroad. It was simply impossible to fight the most expensive war (dollar for dollar) in history, to finance huge social programs at home, to orchestrate a global investment drive by U.S. business, to help sustain the economies of less developed countries all over the map—all at one and the same time. Even for the greatest economic and financial power the world had ever known, resources were not inexhaustible.

The converse of American overspending was the buildup of claims against American resources, especially the claims of those other nations that had taken in and husbanded what the Americans had handed out. If the dollar had remained as good as gold, no problem would have arisen. But the oversupply of dollars guaranteed that the goodness would deteriorate. The world financial system was never intended to cope with a buildup of volatile balances in one currency of uncertain value, backed by nothing more than the word of its government. The surplus dollars did not stay out of sight; they mostly found their way into banks, the principal channel of distribution of the money supply. The banks, naturally enough, lent the paper money they acquired, and with no reluctance at all—since every loan in theory creates a profit.

The excess of funds at their disposal allowed the banks to generate excessive amounts of credit, of which the obverse was the towering debt erected right across Western society by governments, business enterprises, and individuals alike. Alongside the skyscraper debts were high-rise buildings of speculation. As 1929 should have proved, speculation lives off excessive credit; and the two combined produce an economic atmosphere with a dangerously intoxicating content. When the big bankers themselves succumbed to the desire to share in the hyperperformance which they saw all around them, unreasonable risks began to appear not just sound but inspired.

Does the resistance of the U.S. banking lobby to banking reform, as designed by Congress, constitute another unreasonable risk? The bill may not have been ideal, and some of the changes engineered by the bankers may have been justifiable. But after the traumas of the recent past, the guilty (and many were very guilty of sins of both omission and commission) cannot afford to let anybody suspect that they are against reform on principle, or that they exercise enough power to thwart the workings of the Great Democracy.

The power of the major U.S. banks, and of the famous families that control them—the Rockefellers and the Mellons, and their lesser brethren, and their many allies in the elite—was once naked and unashamed. Today, partly because of the ferocious and justified reaction that this power provoked, the influence of the bankers is heavily clothed in discretion, hidden by coyness. Some have tried to lift the garments of secrecy. They suggest that the leading U.S. banks cooperate to an extent that amounts to collusion, bound together by secret agreements, interlocking directorates, and other manifestations of undercover power. In a long study of multi-national corporations, Richard Bennett and Ronald Muller noted that four out of the top five companies in the United States in terms of assets were global banks; and that by 1970, the top fifty banks had 48 percent of all the assets in commercial banking.

A subcommittee of the U.S. Congress (headed by no friend of the banks, the late Congressman Wright Patman) found that in 1967, the top 49 banks held a 5 percent or greater share in 147, or nearly one-third, of the top 500 industrial companies in the United States; and 17 of the top 50 transportation and merchandising companies. Bennett and Muller, using the research of others, allege that large banks have pooled their resources to enhance their mutual power, notably in the case of the Rockefeller-Morgan group: ". . . the coordinated financial operations of the descendants and beneficiaries of John D. Rockefeller and J. P. Morgan. . . . The power base of the Rockefeller-Morgan group is made up of five of the country's largest banks—Chase Manhattan, of which David Rockefeller is chairman; First National City Bank; Manufacturers Hanover Trust; Chemical Bank of New York; Morgan Guaranty Trust." During the years 1962 to 1966, according to the Patman subcommittee, these banks dramatically increased their holdings of each other's stock.

There is no question that some such banking super-power does exist, although there is a considerable question mark over how great the power is or how it is used. The five cited banks do indeed crop up time and again in association, as the heads of underwriting syndicates responsible for major financial operations throughout the U.S. and all over the world. They have bobbed up time and again in this book, in the unfavorable light of botched-up situations, of misplaced loans to the ill-fated real estate investment trusts, of misguided support to mismanaged corporations such as Lockheed and the Penn Central; of overindulgent lending to beleaguered municipalities, such as New York City, and struggling overseas economies.

Time and again, the same big banks have thus been in the forefront of the roster of victims (or culprits, according to the point of view). Concentration of banking power is not unique to the United States, of course. It is repeated in other countries; in West Germany, two or three leading institutions, such as the Deutsche Bank, the Dresdner Bank, the Commerzbank, have a hammerlock on the economy, both directly and because of their huge holdings of company shares. These shareholdings have begun to trouble left-wing politicians, and today the big German banks have constantly to justify their positions and influence.

Even in Switzerland, where the banks are the country's leading industry (in a sense, even its greatest exporters), the eminently conservative politicians have begun to worry whether the banks have come to exercise too much power. In Britain, the more radical wing of the Labour Party has been committed to the nationalization of the largest banks—which, thanks to the concentrating mergers of the last few years, means a mere four giant institutions. Everywhere, banks are on the defensive, asked to demonstrate that they exercise a degree of responsibility commensurate with their power.

Yet there is something curious, paradoxical, about this great and worldwide power. Power implies the ability to control events. But the disasters described in this book show emphatically that the banks had no control over events that damaged them severely—unless, that is, you believe that bankers deliberately inflicted injury on themselves. The cases of the Franklin National, the Herstatt, the United California Bank in Basel, and the rest, admittedly, were not the work of the leading bankers, although they were heavily involved in the messes. But the failings of these failed banks were the faults of their elders and betters, writ large on too small a canvas.

A little humility would not be amiss. Yet it is difficult to develop humility in towering headquarters skyscrapers, with their plazas and malls, suggestive of the strongholds of robber barons designed to over-awe the populace in former times. In comparatively modern times, bankers were indeed robber barons; but their successors today are in no position to dragoon or harass the populace. The ultimate cost of soliciting the millions of the masses is that no bank is in reality more solid than the confidence reposed in it by its humblest depositor. Banks hardly operate even with their shareholders' money, but overwhelm-ingly with that belonging to others. That money is not committed to a bank's care like an investment in business, which might be lost. On the contrary, the central, essential belief is that the money will be pre-served intact until it is required by its owner.

Naturally, there will be accidents en route, the theory of banking being no more sophisticated than the old principle of safety in numbers. The losses on bad loans will be absorbed by the great ocean of profits on sound lending. But the unpalatable truth of the seventies is that this theory did not work. The losses failed to pile up to the status of catastro-phe, not because the banks had the resources (in the shape of the depositors' money) to withstand the shock, but because government, which had learned the lessons of the thirties more thoroughly than the banks, provided the inexhaustible backing of its ability to create money. The supreme irony is that the private enterprise bankers, who hate above all else the government's cavalier way with the nation's wealth, were saved by the very profligacy they despise.

The new sobriety is welcome as far as it goes—which is as far as the context of a post-recession climate demands. The real test will come, not when bankers are still hard at work repairing the damage to balance sheets, but when a new wave of economic euphoria sweeps the West—if it does. In the last wave, bankers stuck neither to their lasts nor their principles. In so doing, they not only endangered their own finances but totally misunderstood what their customers (and their cli-ents, the borrowers) wanted from their banks.

We don't have any interest in seeing our banks become dynamic. We don't care a bit if they are marketing-oriented, aggressively seeking new deposits and new loan business. All we want is that they should look properly and prudently after the business they have—our business. We want total security and reasonable service: no innovation, no initiative can possibly outweigh those two crucial needs. It is the essence of our demand that banks be fuddy-duddy, cautious, unadventurous, uninspir-ing, conservative, dyed-in-the-wool, deliberate, and dull—all the things that modern bankers have hated to be called.

In their chastened mood, fuddy-duddily is exactly how bankers have been behaving, and how the regulators have demanded that they should behave. To that extent, everybody has benefited. The answer to the key question posed by this book—Can you trust your bank?—is probably, Yes, more than you could five years ago. If the question is rephrased—Can you trust your banker?—the answer is No. There is still quite a good chance that he will invest the bank's money foolishly, exercise inadequate control over subordinate operations, provide no control over large delinquent corporate clients, and in consequence of such faults incur large and horrific writeoffs.

In such incidents, too, the banking authorities will almost certainly lag abysmally behind events. But it will not matter—because in the end, the state (any state) will take any action in its power to ensure that the system that is the pivot of our world continues to revolve, so that the economies of the West can turn with it.

Before we, or the bankers, take comfort from that fact, however, the full implications of what happened, and how and why the damage was contained, need to be considered.

The ultimate verdict starts with the observation that in the past decade the world's bankers, great and small, made a series of gratuitous blunders which might have destroyed deposits just as thoroughly as the runs on the banks that were halted by FDR. The misdemeanors were so gross that the fact that our bank balances survived (if only to be ravaged by inflation) was in a bizarre way convincing testimony to the inherent financial strength of the capitalist system. What we learned was that, if you can't trust your bank, you can trust your government more. Which doesn't say too much for the bankers.

INDEX